SELECT POEMS

John M. Bennett

With an Introduction by
Ivan Argüelles

2016

LBP

POETRY
Hotel
Press

SELECT POEMS

For C. Mehrl Bennett, who saw most of this happen

Published by Poetry Hotel Press
and Luna Bisonte Prods in 2016

ISBN: 978-1-938521-25-6

Poetry Hotel Press
P.O. Box 347063, San Francisco, CA 94134-7063
www.poetryhotelpress.com

Luna Bisonte Prods
137 Leland Ave., Columbus, OH 43214-7505
http://www.lulu.co/lunabisonteprods

Front cover art, *que en la lluvia se despierta*, by John M. Bennett
Back cover photo by C. Mehrl Bennett
Ivan Argüelles' introduction edited by Jack Foley
Cover and book design by Clara Hsu

PREFACE
John M. Bennett

Yikes! So much stuff to go through! A "selected poems" seems especially awkward to me in two ways: one, I think of and construct my work as large swaths, not individual "poems", of a groping toward something I can't exactly define; and, two, the sheer amount of work I have produced, not all of it much good, makes the job of selecting a few fragments daunting. What you have here is a tiny tip of a very large iceberg: I have selected pieces from some 77 of over 400 monograph titles. I have also limited the selection to textual works, and some black-and-white works of visual poetry. What is not here is the wide variety of visual poetry, performance scores, audio and video works, conceptual and artist's books, and the huge universe of collaborations I have done with other artists and writers in all genres. Each of these would require a separate volume. This selection also does not include juvenalia, but does include a few pieces of what might be called post-adolescentia.

The process of selecting for this book has reminded me that I have written in so many different ways that it is hard for me to wrap my mind around what I have done. Or was it "me" who did all that? What is "me"? "When" is "me"? Unanswerable questions, for sure, but this anthology is a short step toward understanding these metaphysics, and Ivan Argüelles' article, included here and for which I am very grateful, is a much longer step.

Why do I write? It's an annoying question, in large part because I don't really know the answer. I need to write, it's how I best think, and how I feel I exist; it's a process which is an end in itself. I'm not interested in creating the "perfect poem", but of course that is exactly what I am constantly trying to do. The problem is that what might be "perfection" (a metaphysical concept if there ever was one), changes with every word I write. No, with every *letter* I write. So it's totally different from the start to the end of a poem, of a stanza, of a line, and thus a perfect poem cannot really exist.

Why do I write so much? It's not because I am interested in "poetry". Maybe it's because I need to write language in ways that approach something I can't explain. Noth-ing else I do comes closer. If I don't do it, my mind goes dead and I feel awful. I feel invisible, as if *I'm not there, or here.*

Note: Many of the selections compiled here were scanned from the original publications. Thus the different fonts, sizes, minor defects, and the like.

May 2015

Table of Contents

v PREFACE, by John M. Bennett
viii JOHN M. BENNETT, INNOVATIVE, EXPERIMENTAL AND UNIQUE by IVAN ARGÜELLES
24 Found Objects, New Rivers Press, 1973.
27 White Screen, New Rivers Press, 1976.
29 Do Not Cough: Select Labels, Luna Bisonte Prods,1976.
34 Meat Watch, Fireweed Press, 1977.
36 Nips Poems, Luna Bisonte Prods, 1980.
38 Puking Horse, Luna Bisonte Prods, 1980.
41 Burning Dog, Luna Bisonte Prods, 1983.
45 Blender, Ghost Dance Press, 1983.
47 Ant Path, Proper Tales Press, 1984.
50 No Boy, Laughing Bear Press, 1985.
53 Spitting Ddreams, [1981-1986], Blue Lion Books, 2009.
58 Cascade, Luna Bisonte Prods, 1987.
59 The The Poems, Curvd H&Z, 1987.
62 Stones in the Lake, Luna Bisonte Prods, 1987.
63 Swelling, Runaway Spoon Press, 1988.
64 Regression, Luna Bisonte Prods, 1988.
66 Span, Runaway Spoon Press, 1990.
69 Was Ah, Burning Press, 1991.
73 Reversion: Piles of That, [1990-1991], Luna Bisonte Prods, 1994.
94 Bleached, BGS Press. 1992.
95 Know Other, [1992], Luna Bisonte Prods, 1998.
105 Blind on the Temple, Luna Bisonte Prods, 1993.
106 Blanksmanship, Luna Bisonte Prods, 1994.
112 Just Feet, Texture Press, 1994.
114 Fish, Man, Control, Room, Semiquasi Press, 1995.
116 Spinal Speech, Runaway Spoon Press, 1995.
120 Eddy, Luna Bisonte Prods, 1995.
122 Ridged, Poeta, Juxta Press, 1996.
127 Cul Lit, Potes & Poets Press, 1997.
129 The Seasons, Spectacular Diseases, 1997.
130 Mailer Leaves Ham, Pantograph Press, 1999.
141 rOlling COMBers, Potes & Poets Press, 2001.
152 Ditch Cloth, Xtant Books, 2001.
153 The Peel, Anabasis Press, 2004.
156 Glue, xPress(ed), 2005.
160 Instruction Book, Luna Bisonte Prods, 2006.

my tongue I thought ,on a shelf

JOHN M. BENNETT, INNOVATIVE, EXPERIMENTAL AND UNIQUE
by Ivan Argüelles

Tristan Tzara: "DADA remains within the framework of European weaknesses, it's still shit, but from now on we want to shit in different colors so as to adorn the zoo of art with all the flags of all the consulates."

A critic once said of *Lost and Found Times* (John M. Bennett's seminal underground press mag, 1975-2005): "*Insults...the past 3,000 years of literature.*" One could apply that criticism to the whole of Bennett's dazzlingly varied and maddening output. One could even ask with some justification: Is this *poetry*? Where to begin analyzing let alone writing about this baffling and certainly most "avant-garde" of all artists/poets living and working in the U.S.A. today? I recommend checking out his short video (one of many he has created) called "Olvido del surr," in which he reads with Luis Bravo; one gets both the intended oral quality of the poem (which sounds like some eerie Meso-American Indian ritual chant) as well as its visual and typographical effects. For, above all, Bennett's "poetry" is more like a meta-poetry that requires all the visual and aural senses to appreciate it. His experimentations over the years have encompassed particularly the expanding world of visual poetry (vispo), an extension of what used to be referred to as "concrete poetry" (particularly successful in Brazil). The structure of the poem on the page gradually becomes a work of art, divorced from its mere semantic sense (or lack thereof) as it seems to appear to the reader. Bennett employs numerous techniques, not the least of which is his own "polyglottery," frequently moving in and out of English, Spanish, Portuguese, French or some Mesoamerican language. In the above mentioned video, "Olvido del surr," all these "techniques" are brought to bear.

To invent John M. Bennett one has to invest in a fascination with words. As an infant he preferred books—and his first writing was before he could "write," when he would take little pieces of paper and do "picture" words on them, things that were more word-like than picture-like: a boat a house a cat, whatever, like what you might see in a Mixtec codex. He recalls chanting words over and over (to the annoyance of his parents) and when he heard a new one—*cloud cloud cloud cloud cloud mailbox mailbox mailbox mailbox*—would go on and on. (Many of Bennett's maddeningly obsessive "poems" continue this practice.) In 1949 and 1951, on the ship to and from Japan, he wrote such little notes, by then including alphabetic words, wrapping them up in boxes and/or bottles, and throwing them overboard. He still does that and still keeps up the chanting. So in a sense he's always been writing poetry, though he didn't know it was "poetry" until much later—in the 6th or 7th grade? And at that point he started haunting bookstores and libraries, reading whatever came his way so that his "influences" may be something innate in him. He lived in a house full of books, being fascinated by the typewriters and writing/drawing tools there at home. He says he never took a typing course, never a drawing class—except briefly as a child in Japan - and never studied "writing"—only literature.

Bennett lived in Japan from 1949 to1951, where his father, an anthropologist, was doing acculturation studies for the occupation authority. These few years made a very strong impression on him in various ways: his sense of aesthetics developed there. Japanese writing and art resonated with him in a big way. (He remembers seeing *Ra-shomon*, a new film at the time, in a Japanese theatre, and understanding it, even though his Japanese was very sketchy.) With his parents he visited temples, museums, rural towns, fishing villages, etc., all of which was formative. He had his first culture shock on returning to the US, which in some ways still feels like an alien place to him. Bennett's fascination with inventive typographies may go back to impressions of Japanese calligraphy, and many of his pieces which "feel" minimalistic may have unconscious roots in Japanese haiku or Zen koan. As for the culture shock he felt, this also may be reflected in the multilingual, continental and Latin American tendencies his work has taken from the onset, hence disassociating it from an American bias.

As for the authors he read that impressed him and that had resonance of some kind, these vary at different times, though naturally with some of them the resonance was more long lasting and is still present. The list includes Keats and Shelly, the Elizabethans—Shakespeare and George Herbert, and maybe Donne; and especially: Whitman, Lorca, Machado, Jiménez, Neruda, Vallejo, Parra, Huidobro, Huidobro, Huidobro, Argüelles, Baudelaire, Rimbaud, Verlaine, Manual Acuña, Mallarmé, and lately going back and rediscovering people like the two Heredias, Valéry, Lezama Lima (as novelist), Góngora, Sor Juana, Burroughs, Dickinson. This is just a sampling, it misses many—principally the many poets, his contemporaries, whom he values greatly and who "get his juices flowing." "Influence" for Bennett is a tricky word in that he does not feel influenced so much as being in the presence of all these voices that are part of an atmosphere he breathes—in an odd way for him it is almost as if he is writing in them, rather than that they are a part of his voice. Bennett says that obviously much of what he does, or any poet or artist worth their salt, is completely unique, but at the same time it's also a collaboration with all these other voices. They collaborate with him or he with them, which is not the same thing as an "influence." In fact Bennett's actual collaborations with other contemporaries are many (e.g. *Chac Prostibulario*, in collaboration with Ivan Argüelles), and more recently he has taken to combining parts of poems from contemporaries and well-established poets to form new poems. He has also become fond of using "faux quotes" ascribed to other poets living or dead, or fictional.

Bennett's education includes attending high school at a lab school at Ohio State University (though he graduated from a big public school in St. Louis, another culture shock!); BA cum laude at Washington University, St. Louis, double major in Spanish and English, 1964; MA in Spanish language and literatures from Wash U, 1966; Certificate of

Competence (really a 2nd MA) in Latin American studies from Wash U, 1966; PhD in Latin American literatures, UCLA, 1970. He was an assistant professor in the Romance Languages Dept. (Spanish section) at Ohio State University, 1969-1976, teaching mostly Latin American literature and some Spanish literature.

Bennett has worked in the OSU Libraries since 1976, at first in the Latin American Studies Library, then in Rare Books and MSS Library, where he started the Avant Writing Collection. In this manner he wove connections between his work and his art. There had always been a connection there: he studied Spanish because of the literature, which meant something to him as a poet, and because he felt that in English there would be a conflict between his art and his professional work. When he was still in high school, he discovered that what he wanted to do was "*to change the language.*" With that arrogant goal in mind the bland and somewhat repressive nature of English departments would cause him big problems. Not only did he find the literatures in Spanish more interesting, but the culture in the Spanish departments was much more open to the new, and things were really happening there. Because of his PhD in Spanish/Latin American literature, he has a scholar's familiarity with such diverse authors as the 20th century Chilean poet Vicente Huidobro and the great *Siglo de Oro* poet Luis de Góngora. Equipped with these professional skills it was no accident he came to be the curator of the "Avant Writing Collection," "The William S. Burroughs Collection," and "The Cervantes Collection" at the OSU Libraries. At this point one might say his artistic and professional careers intersect in a manner that again displays the intellectual depth and variation which are at the core of Bennett's artistic forays, multiple and many directed.

The death of Charles Olson in 1970 and the ascendancy of the Iowa Writers' Workshop in the late 60's mark the end of a period when poetry was still a spontaneous creative activity by "poets" as such, best exemplified at the time by such movements as the Beats and the New York School (Allen Ginsberg, Frank O'Hara, etc.). The workshop influence was pervasive and not necessarily healthy as it demanded more and more that a "poet" be defined by his or her earning an MFA. The poetry was self–defined as "well crafted" verse and more often than not was based on an "ego" narrating some critical event in its life. The system became ingrown and self-perpetuating, each qualified MFA holder was entrusted with teaching positions and setting up more workshops around the country. At the same time the post-modernist L=A=N=G=U=A=G=E school received a great deal of attention as the next big thing in poetry, but in fact the practi-tioners of this movement were also by and large "academics" who in turn isolated this movement in its own ivory tower. As an unconscious (perhaps not so unconscious) reaction to the "academicizing" of poetry there arose like a fungus a plethora of small presses and little magazines dedicated to publishing writers who did not fit the MFA profile required of "poets." In fact this was the arena where real experimentation in poetry continued and thrived. Not that all of this output was good, much was ephemeral, but the experimentation was heady and fertile.

It was in this atmosphere that John M. Bennett got a start with something called The Frustration Press; he did chapbooks of his own work, mostly using a ditto machine, "the fading blue spirit ink." Then he started Luna Bisonte Prods as a front for various dadaesque, surrealesque, fluxusesque and mailart activities. *Lost and Found Times* began as "mailart publications," and mailart was an element of the magazine throughout its run. *LAFT*, which went on to become one of the most influential of the small poetry mags throughout the 70's and 80's, was characterized by original zany dada surrealism pitched efforts with a strong visual typographic orientation. Its appearance was unique, always with a sort of blurred or out of focus graphic representation of some kind. It is to Bennett's credit that through his press he fomented the work of many upcoming experimentalists on the poetry scene, and he continues to do so. As Bennett puts it, he continued to publish *LAFT* in "order to publish great stuff people kept sending me that couldn't be published anywhere else but that NEEDED to be published. That was the underlying general editorial motive." The Avant Writing Collection at OSU is based on the same underlying idea/practice.

With respect to Bennett's start as a poet in the 70's, he felt he did NOT fit into any of it–what he was doing didn't jive with any of the publishers of that time, with the exception of C.W. Truesdale, who published two books of his in the early 70's (*Found Objects* and *White Screen*). But much of the reason he started Frustration Press and then Luna Bisonte Prods was to publish stuff that no one else would, of his own, and then also of others who gradually came out of the woodwork, who equally couldn't be published. It seems that a lot of poets who are now fairly well known in the "avant-garde" scenes were first published in *Lost & Found Times*, a fact of which he is quite proud.

There are so many aspects to Bennett's "poetry" that in a sense the term *poetry* does not adequately cover the whole of Bennett's creative endeavor and output. Under the impetus or guise of poetry he has done so many different kinds of things that keep evolving into new things that it is difficult to make something of the whole work step-by-step. Through the late 20th century he often reached a point where he decided to make a "big leap" forward into something very different. He would get himself worked up to do it and then take a plunge into the unknown without any idea as to what he was about to do. The results were generally satisfying in the long run. He still does this, though less dramatically, perhaps, and there's more of an evolutive process. Much of what he has always done through these changes is to incorporate aspects, often minor ones, of previous styles into the new one, expanding on them so that they became a major aspect of the new style/approach: a mix and match, so to speak, layering various "schticks" to create something "new." And indeed when one looks at the range of his "works" in some sort of chronological order these efforts at shifting styles, mixing and matching, etc, intensify to the point where something utterly new results, such as in many later texts which are sometimes totally visual (*Sacaron navajas*), or emphatically visual with some vestiges of poetical "text" interspersed (*Las Cabezas Mayas*).

Language for Bennett is inextricable from consciousness, and thus very hard to talk about because of not being able, really, to get outside of it. Unlike the so-called L=A=N=G=U=A=G=E poets, for whom language is an abstract postmodernist speech act of objectification divorced from any intent of lyrical expression or narrative, in short an anti-poetry, Bennett's language is more of a metalanguage, a conscious employment of words to metamorphose themselves in weird, disjunctive combinations that may baffle or annoy the reader. As William Burroughs says in *The Ticket That Exploded*: "Would there be any time if we didn't say anything?" So for Bennett language is *much more* than a "linear construct to...describe events and emotions." Events and emotions occur *in* language (as well as elsewhere). Bennett employs language to say it *all*, that is, to recreate the entire world, but in as few words as possible. His poetry is almost of necessity a minimalist approach to incorporating the *whole*. For Bennett "a poem is a kind of singularity in the center of a black hole, matter in an impossibly dense mass, including time." The many gimmicks and wordplay he employs constantly in his poems are to this end: to say as many things as possible *all at once*. Almost unique in contemporary poetry is Bennett's use of multiple languages; e.g. English, Spanish, French, Nahuatl, etc., all of which swarm in his "head or heads." Bennett's concept of language is that every word is related to every other word ever made, in every language, present, past or future. In Bennett's words: "another way of describing what I do is that I work in that zone of resonance of all those other words/languages... the technique of 'transduction' is one way of doing that: instead of *translating* a word I use another word that sounds like it or in some other way resonates with it." Bennett's use and concept of language compares with James Joyce's *Finnegans Wake*. Further, Bennett says what he has found "through my own work and through working with patients as a poetry therapist, is that each of the functions of language—speaking, thinking, writing, translating, reading, learning new languages, etc. —involves a separate mental process, and each of those processes must be learned and practiced separately. There is some overlap, but in general each works on its own. Part of what I try to do is to combine those processes into a single process."

Clearly for any attempt at comprehending what Bennett's poetry is about, his views on language and languages are at the core. Once it's understood what these views are, the apparent nonsense and chaos of the "poems," as such, while not taking on any more meaning than they had before, become comprehensible as a system to express his own particular *Weltanschauung* through language. But Bennett's work did not arise from a vacuum; it has its antecedents or roots in various earlier movements and poets. One could begin by citing Mallarmé's "*Un coup de dés*" with its visual outlay on the page. But perhaps the principle historical movement by which Bennett's work could be identified is Dadaism, with its emphasis on the absurd, its deliberate syntactic breakup and its typographical display on the page. Two obvious antecedents from the Dada-ist era are the Chilean Vicente Huidobro, whose masterpiece *Altazor* is marked by a mounting wordplay, frequently reduced to nonsense syllables, and Guillaume Apollinaire, whose

Calligrammes may be the first book published in the 20th century which is comprised wholly of visual poetry and remains among the most brilliant examples of that genre.

One may well ask what differentiates Bennett's poetry, which seems so implicitly based on language as such, from the L=A=N=G=U=A=G=E school of poetry. For one thing L=A=N=G=U=A=G=E poetry is rooted in the academy, and its practitioners are a well soldered group, insular and exclusive, that adheres to strictly postmodernist theories of literary deconstruction. Theirs has become a socially entrenched style that presents itself as in some way definitive. While there have been some interesting writings to come out of it, there is a serious dogmatism about it, not dissimilar to the surrealistic dogmatism of Breton, that makes it feel like a peculiar attempt to apply "politically correct" ideas to a style that seems irrelevant to those ideas. Bennett's poetry is wholly outside the academy, and like so much of the very best poetry written since 1970, is apparently *sub rosa*, barely visible to the mainstream publishing houses that profess to promote "poetry" such as Wesleyan or Pitt. Bennett's poetry is truly "experimental," and again like so many others of the best poets of his generation, he has had to rely on fiercely independent small presses that do not live by the grants-and-foundations-mill of the Poets & Writers establishment. L=A=N=G=U=A=G=E poetry as such began it seems as an experiment against the "canon" of poetry, but almost immediately became a genre co-opted by the academy. It's safe to say that Bennett's work, as well as that of other experimentalists or innovators in poetry since 1970, has been flat out rejected by the jealously-guarded main stream poetry world that thrives on Iowa Workshop graduates to perpetuate itself. For Bennett language is organic, palpable, multidimensional, swarming and breathing, and not a deconstructed postmodernist theory.

The visual aspect of Bennett's work cannot be emphasized enough, as it is again language exploited for its appearance on the page. This visual aspect has always been important to him: to visualize the text as it appears on the page, as a random or not so random design, as it were. Perhaps the first major explicitly visual work beyond textual poetry was some collage poetry he did in the early 70's. A selection of these pieces was published by C. W. Truesdale in a book-in-a-box called *Found Objects*, and others in *White Screen*, and in a number of Luna Bisonte Prods chapbooks. From that practice, and from handwriting he began doing calligraphic work, his own calligraphy (never having studied the formal kind) which he still does. In fact, Bennett's idiosyncratic calligraphy (a zany sort of scrawl all but illegible at times) is one of the earmarks that sets a Bennett poem off from anybody else's. The drawing developed out of the calligraphy. He says his drawings are basically writing, hieroglyphs as it were. One of the best examples of that kind of thing is *Las Cabezas Mayas*. Like the sound and oral work he does, this technique is just another way, not so different, of achieving some of the aspects of language and linguistic expression which characterize Bennett's prolix and often complex body of work. An extension of what he calls "calligraphy" is the radical use of differing typographies employed in a single poem. Recently he has returned to collage, and to mixing collage, drawing and calligraphy.

Another important dimension to Bennett's work is music, or *sound*. There was always music in Bennett's house when he was a child—classical, jazz, "ethnic" (his father was an anthropologist), so he took to music very early. He had his own record player in his room and would listen to a lot of Bach, Baroque, classical, Fats Domino, "Rock Around the Clock," and other great 50's rock. He also learned to play the clarinet, then oboe—also sax and bass clarinet—which he played in the school orchestra and chamber groups, and he seriously considered going into music as a career. He did jazz and poetry with friends in high school. Some of what he has been performing during the past three decades or so is in that vein, although he says it is not "jazz and poetry" but rather "improv" music, using his poetry as if it were another instrument. Whatever it is, it is not poetry accompanied by music. He has also done, mainly in performances, what could be called sound poetry, his own rather eccentric versions of it. An example of this is referred to in the opening paragraph, the piece "Olvido del su*rr*." All this would suggest, correctly, that the *sound* or music of language and form is an important part of how he writes. According to Bennett, "there are at least 5 dimensions to a poem as I write it: sound, visuality, meaning of the words, rhythm and movement through time, and resonance (what other words and/or images come to mind that aren't explicitly there). All are equally important." Music, then, has always been important to Bennett, and he listens to it constantly, especially Baroque, early music, avant-garde, classical, "world" and "ethnic," jazz, experimental and sound art. In the 80's and early 90's he recorded some work he had done on saxophone, and used it in some work he did with poetry and music, at times with other musicians. Recently he has been playing various kinds of flutes, often as part of poetry performances.

It is open to question whether one may regard poetry when it is read aloud, presented as an "oral" art, as a *performance*. When Bennett was in school and college, he did a lot of acting, and for several summers when he was in graduate school in St. Louis, he earned money acting in a *Commedia dell'arte* troupe, a different play every week. He played Pantaleone, one of the stock characters of that genre. It was improvisational, based on a general plot outline and consistent characters. He also acted in plays, most memorably playing Lucky in *Waiting for Godot*. From this experience rather than reading his poetry he began to "perform" it, only the role he was playing was himself, or one of the *many* John Bennetts. He became his own cast of roles or characters, which doesn't make them any less authentic but all the more authentic. Learning other languages also plays a role in performance, insofar as speaking another language is rather like taking on another self or role in that a different language embodies a different culture. As a result he has learned to *perform* rather than *read* his poetry. At times the performance aspect of his reading may get ratcheted up a bit, especially with some of the more extreme processes he employs, and also when he performs some of the visual poems.

As a natural outgrowth of Bennett's performance techniques the Be Blank Consort was formed when he was at the Atlantic Center for the Arts in 2001 with a group of other visual poets. The concept of Be Blank is based on creating scores out of poems and visual poems so that they can be performed by a group, rather like a chamber ensemble. Some of the scores, in fact, use musical structures , such as canons and fugues, with the text read simultaneously by many people, each one starting at a fixed point after the other. The original group has gotten together several times in various places to perform, and they produced a CD, and wherever they perform local poets may join in to perform with them. Or, based on the various score compilations they have done, one of them can form the Consort anywhere with anyone, like some kind of self-generating biological organism. Bennett has done that in Mexico, and other places. The original group included Bennett, Scott Helmes, K. S. Ernst, Michael Peters as prime movers and shakers but has since included at various times Sheila E. Murphy, Tom Cassidy, Geof Huth, and many others.

Bennett considers poetry to be first and foremost oral but *also* first and foremost visual, textual, and conceptual, or all at the same time. Bennett asks: "In the history of our species did speech come before writing? Probably so, at least in regards to more complex forms of writing. But that's not for certain, and in any case was so long ago that it's kind of moot. For most of our history these functions/matrices of poetry have all been of equal importance."

If Bennett had done nothing else but found and edit *Lost and Found Times* he would for that alone deserve a footnote if not a chapter in a history of contemporary American poetry. In the hectic milieu of countless small presses and little poetry magazines, frequently just stapled and mimeographed, *Lost and Found Times* had few equals. Perhaps the West Coast magazine *Kayak*, edited by George Hitchcock, comes closest to it in nature and content. But while *Kayak* had a distinctly surrealist bias combined with artful collages, *LAFT* derived more from an absurdist, dadaist matrix and seemed somehow "messier."

Kayak consciously died with its 64th issue, to be revived in sorts by the slicker *Caliban*, edited by Larry Smith. Many of the same poets can be found in either venue. *LAFT* continued appearing through 2005. An anthology called *Loose Watch* was published in 1998 and covers material from issues 1-39. Quoting from the preface of that publication: "From its origins in mail art to its more recent participation at the edges of language (and what is coming to be called post-language) poetry, *Lost and Found Times* provides a model of how marginalized cultural workers can create productive areas of engagement within a network of activity." Indeed it is safe to say that *LAFT* serves as a paradigm of relentless anti-cultural if not anti-literary activity that can be compared to earlier movements, such as Dada or Futurism, though it never strictly adhered to any ideology or –ism. Marvin Sackner sums it up concisely: "I consider the magazine one of most outstanding compendiums of international experimental literature and poetry."

Bennett's total output to date could form a monograph in itself. To compile such a work exhausts one just to consider it. Such a "list" would have to include not just the many actual books he has published but the countless chapbooks, leaflets, postcards, scraps of paper with what appear to be hieroglyphs and some primitive form of script, and the myriad numbers of sound efforts, readings, performances, films, et cetera! How does one approach this intimidating body of work to achieve some sort of assessment of it, to be able to make a coherent critique of what Bennett is about? When asked the question, "Which of your own books do you prefer or wish to be remembered by for posterity?" Bennett replied by listing the following 5 titles: *la M al*, *Liber X*, *Olvidos*, *Mirrors Máscaras*, and *El Humo Letrado*. "And these are just the textual works, I'm ignoring the visual works. As to why I like these? I think that in various ways they are the peaks of various hills I was climbing, and that they combine the voices/techniques/ manias I was working through in them. That is, they bring together a lot of things into single works, which fulfills the need I seem to have to say everything at once, so that every book, poem, phrase, word, letter, punctuation mark is as multivalent as possible. The world is a swarming, and I want to hold that world in my writing. Maybe these books do that more than others. Although I have to say that there are things about some earlier books, such as *Eddy*, *Blanksmanship*, or *Mailer Leaves Ham*, that I like a lot."

In this interesting response it is useful to pull out a few key words or phrases, such as *swarming*, *multivalent*, and *the need to have to say everything at once*. For someone just casually perusing any of Bennett's multivalent texts (*text* is perhaps a better term than *poem*) the page does indeed seem to be *swarming* with words, bits of words, combinations of bits of words, multilingual juxtapositions, typographical intrusions and calligraphic embellishments, none of which seems to make a lot of sense read in an expectant linear order. The texts which highlight or may consist of wholly typographic play and calligraphic embellishments may actually appeal to a visual aesthetic sense and hence require no semantic explanation. But for the most part the bulk of this massive corpus of texts must seem and perhaps remain baffling, which may be their very intent or purpose. We have come past the point of asking: "What is the poet trying to tell us?" Bennett's texts might be compared to the abstract paintings of Jackson Pollack or the aleatoric compositions of John Cage. We know a lot is going on in such works but it is not easily discernible exactly what it is that is being communicated in the creative process, nor why if something is being communicated, it is being done in such a manner as to either baffle or irritate the intended audience. Let us take at random a (typically) small poem from *El Humo Letrado* (*The Lettered Smoke*):

Meal Focus

aim to numb er the cornfled
tops yr ano lacustre er yr
año .fullness rains las piedras
rinsed with .ease of cramping
los chayotes en la mesa em
papada el cielo dreams or
blinds like un escarampión yr r
ashy forehead scuttled ,nice
an flimsy corner shingled with
yr suit .where I rivered
por las camisas y los manteles

Here is one of the countless "bilingual" Bennett texts which actually has a rather lyrical effect read aloud. Looked at carefully with words broken at line breaks such as "r/ashy forehead ..." the text acquires an ambiguous semantic quality: *rash and ashy*. Words run together is a technique constantly used by Bennett: it also recalls *Finnegans Wake*. Neologisms also occur: "I rivered." But is this all taken together supposed to *mean* anything? Probably not. As for the Spanish words in the text, they are employed more in the manner of what linguists refer to as "code switching," that is words from either language used in the same sentence without regard to their position. A person who code switches uses two (or more) languages simultaneously, such as in *el cielo dreams*, as if there were only *one* language in his/her head. For this reader the text has an overall dreamy quality in which words such as *confled* (meant to remind us of cornfield) become semantically diffuse. The concluding lines have an especially lyrical effect: "yr suit / where I rivered / por las camisas y los manteles" (*shirts and tablecloths*). In fact looked at a 2nd or 3rd time, the poem seems less random in its choice of words, and more intentional. It is as if someone were talking in his/her sleep about *something*. There is an esthetic or even anesthetic effect in the broken up "*numb er*" and in the choice of "*dreams*" and "*blinds*" in such close proximity. The poem is clearly the product of a mind grappling with the world's lack of cohesion, trying to articulate that disorder in order to make it meaningful. One is reminded of Paul Valéry's comment: *Two things threaten the universe: order and disorder*. Multiply this poem/text by thousands and you get some idea of Bennett's incredible output and intelligence. When one surveys this all but overwhelming output, which seems at times labyrinthine, one is confronted not only by a portmanteau vocabulary constantly in flux, but by the frequent references to body parts and functions, vomiting, spewing, pissing, etc. all over the page. One has the sense that for Bennett the human body and its functions and malfunctions is the microcosmos by which he measures the universe at large in all its swarming linguistic variety.

As a footnote it should be noted that with the advent of email Bennett sends out through the ether dozens of these compositions a month, many of which he gathers. to be included in new publications. Making these available through email is an open invitation to others on his list-serve to riff off his syllabic notes, and in return he will improvise on the works of others through the email. An example of his joyous wordplay is the following from a very recent email:

just one leg ,jjjerking
in a circcle

But this is just the more linear/textual aspect—which is nevertheless the dominant one—among the variety of ways he has chosen to express his poetry. Over a period of time, Bennett's typographic and calligraphic embellishments or enhancements of given texts on the page become more and more prominent. At times these can become highly ornate, Baroque one might say, and become more prominent on the page (almost as pictograms or pure ornamentation) than the underlying semantic content of the words they are embellishing. Some of the best examples of this rich, ornate typography can be seen in recent works such as *Liber X* (2012) or *Mirrors Máscaras* (2014), both of which as books or artifacts are beautiful, glossy productions. At the same time Bennett's linguistic innovations become more intense, especially in his Spanish texts, or, better yet, texts that employ the above-mentioned code switching technique. *El Humo Letrado* (2011) purports to be "*poesía en español,*" but scattered subliminally throughout this text are more than smatterings of English, such as in the poem *Under*: "*, otear y ,fumble one ,nada simple.*" Perhaps the most experimental of his linguistic innovations is his *Sole Dadas & Prime Sway* (2012). *Sole Dadas* is a complete *transduction* (not translation) of the long poem *Soledades* by the great *Siglo de Oro* poet Luís de Góngora. The original Spanish text is considered by many to be a high point in Spanish poetry, but it is a very complex work involving a rich, erudite vocabulary and an intricate Latin word order, which make the poem difficult to decipher. Bennett's transduction takes on the Spanish text by rendering word for word an English homonym (or something close to it) to represent the original Spanish word. It is interesting the extent to which it also "feels" like a translation, which it is not. This intricate and faithful-to-the-original (homophonically speaking) "translation" will surely find its place among the major experiments in contemporary poetry. Of the companion piece in that publication, *Prime Sway*, a transduction of Sor Juana's *Primer Sueño*, Bennett says he wrote it "pretending I don't know Spanish and writing it out (reading it) as if it were English." Of similar interest is *Chac Prostibulario* (1999), a text composed through email with Ivan Argüelles and written in the code-switching manner employing mostly English, Spanish and some Portuguese in a long sequence of seven-line stanzas to form a book-length poem. The fascinating aspect of this work is that though the two undertook to writing alternating stanzas, after a point it is difficult to discern who is the author of which stanza. A perfect blend. This work is a bit like John Lennon's *A Spaniard in the works* or *Finnegans Wake.*

From the visually idiosyncratic and highlighted typography/calligraphy em-ployed increasingly in Bennett's texts to the purely visual, hieroglyphic texts is but a slight leap in Bennett's multi-directed trajectory. As a bridge to the purely visual (vispo) publications, there are two interesting titles that consist purely of typographical/calligraphic texts: *Cuitlacochtli—typographic stick figures*, and *La chair du Cenote*, both of which seem to derive from Apollinaire's *Calligrammes* in their elaborate and stunning appearances on the page. On the other hand there are purely graphic works, colorful, zany, at times collage-like, but all with the zigzaggy mental imprimatur that can only be identified as John M Bennett. Foremost among these are: *Sacaron navajas*, a small book consisting of very colorful pieces which at times look like they've been torn from a larger Dada-type illustrative text, and the gorgeous *Las Cabezas Mayas Maya Heads*, a colorful sequence of hand drawings of often quite whimsical cartoon heads, punctuat-ed sparsely by typographic texts. In addition, Dan Waber published a small chapbook, very beautifully done, simply called *this is visual poetry*, which contains some of Ben-nett's finest art work in this genre. Bennett continues to disseminate a series of "heads" through the email—typically these are somewhat recognizable human heads or skulls superimposed on scraps of text. Were Bennett simply to be known as a premier vispo artist he would be ranked at the top of the heap. But, amazingly, these graphic/visual works are just a part of the entire Bennett *œuvre.*

Finally, it should be pointed out that Bennett does not work in a vacuum. In fact he is one of the most collaborative artists working today. Among the poets he has interacted with are: Peter Ganick, Ivan Argüelles, Jim Leftwich, Olchar E. Lindsann, Sheila E. Murphy, and Davi Det Hompson, poets whose writing bears some relation to his and whose work he finds quite stimulating. These are just the "textual" poets. When it comes to visual poetry, there's another group of artists he interacts with: Tom Cassidy, Scott Helmes, Jim Leftwich, Serge Segay, Rea Nikonova, Sheila E. Murphy, and his wife, C. Mehrl Bennett. And in the past few years, he has been sporting with some of the new *Fluxus* artists that are out there, where there's an absurdist spirit that he finds very stimulating. Whether Bennett and the artists he interacts with form a "school or movement" is open to question. Bennett also incorporates his own work, or intrudes upon, the work of others, living or dead, in Spanish and French: Pablo Neruda, Rubén Bonifaz Nuño, Nicolas Carras, Philippe Billé, Juan Ángel Italiano, Martín Gubbins, Julien Blaine, etc. In recent years he has signed off many of his poems with quotes, often faux quotes, of many authors, living and dead, a technique which lends a mock literary flavor to the texts.

Bennett says that despite the appearance of the poems he writes them as stories, as narrations, a narration that incorporates much more than a single line. This is analogous, perhaps, to the sense of narration in Joyce's *Finnegan's Wake*, or Lezama Lima's in

Paradiso or Burroughs' in his cut-up trilogy of the 1960's, texts which Bennett read for the first time back in the early 60's. He was terribly impressed and at the same time mystified by these works. In fact, many of the works of others that impacted Bennett in one way or another were at first sort of incomprehensible, but they stuck with him until he finally "got" them. In addition to telling a story, most of his poems are highly lyrical, highly emotional. So what then is being communicated by these texts? First of all they are *protean*: there is no one exact thing to be drawn from them (i.e., there is no "moral" to be drawn at the end of them, unless if what a reader wants is a "moral," the reader will find it). Bennett wants to say it all simultaneously, in which case a LOT of things are being said with great concision.

How to read these poems? Bennett says the poems are "like mirrors in which the reader sees him or herself, or an aspect of that self. And that every time one looks, one will see something a bit, or a lot, different. There are a number of ways to see what's in that mirror: basically they involve reading or saying the poem and paying attention to your emotional response. That response might cohere around a particular line or phrase or sound or whatever. One can then try to say what that emotional response is: 'saying' something is giving meaning to it. Consciousness of meaning for most folks generally involves language, being able to talk or write about something. There are other kinds of consciousness, of course: there is meaning in sound, as there is meaning in music, which is difficult to translate into language. The same goes for the visual meaning a text has. And for that zone of resonant meaning created by the words and concepts that are suggested, but are not 'physically' present. These are all arenas of meaning."

Bennett goes on to say: "So much of North American poetry is fundamentally didactic—it uses poetry as a tool to present some moral idea or lesson. What I do is not that at all; the ethics and values of our cultures can be taught, and are, in much more effective ways. What I want to do is to create a mirror of the larger swarming context of existence, in which particular rules of behavior and thought are small particulate aspects."

In this short essay I have attempted to give some sort of cohesion to the extremely varied, multiple and complex work of John M. Bennett, one of the most innovative and experimental poets, if not the most unique, in America today. Yet, it is a sure bet that his name and work are all but unknown, if not ignored in the literary and academic establishment where poetry is pronounced with a capital P and grants and awards are dished out to the sub-proletariat would-be poets who hold MFA's, and, in hundreds of workshops across the nation and elsewhere, are willing to punish others with their less than catholic knowledge of poetry. Were Bennett a citizen of some Latin American country or France or Spain or Italy, he would no doubt be well recognized for his chaotic, irreverent, innovative, highly experimental, intelligent, and often beautiful works, be they in traditional print form or in the sometimes dazzling graphic representations. In fact,

Bennett's reputation is to some extent international, and he has been published in France and Latin America. His interest in Mesoamerican culture and languages has drawn him frequently to that part of the world where he is a recognized figure. So it is frustrating that, outside of the relatively small avant-garde experimental performance world where Bennett is a prime mover, he is so unknown and unappreciated in his homeland. As with the music of John Cage, what may seem aleatory is in fact more intentional and grounded than is first apparent. Bennett has roots in traditional literatures, those of *Siglo de Oro* Spain and of Elizabethan England, but he is capable of *transducing* those literatures, metamorphosing them by way of the radical avant-garde movements of the 20th century, such as Surrealism and Dada, into something utterly innovative and unexhaustingly *New*, such as few contemporary artists have done. It is the purpose of this essay to hopefully advance a critical awareness of John M. Bennett and his fabulous, multifaceted *œuvre*. It is fitting to conclude this essay with the following recent poem written in Spanish by Bennett:

nada he escrito

no he escrito nada soy
el topo nimio del lugar
sin palabra sin palabra
he escrito una silla sin
plumas del pájaro caído
en el aguafón no he tomado
nada no me bostezo sin
tragar las fofofrases de mi
similencio de los libros sin
jamón sin lechuga con su
monstraza no me atra
ganto con una tinta in
visible con un algo mudo
que muere en un salivazo no
emito nada nada remito na
da redimigo y la nada
que escribo me titubea siempre
como foco que se estrella
en la escalera hablada que
subo y bajo vajo y subo
con mi lenguarabo atado y flagelante

...la gran boca que ha perdido el
habla. - César Vallejo

Berkeley, CA, October 2014

SELECT POEMS

LOOK.

We built our dream
of Excess Phlegm

cold water wells up from the Ocean depths,

and in such areas of upwelling
the agitated surface is seething

coughing

Washing Your Car

the white plastic bleach jugs, the plastic
cups, the whisky bottles, the doll carcasses
which float forever,

OVERHEAD

Hit-Run Driver

In Your Own Car

Blowing past a Greyhound
on a straightaway,

was able to maintain an
erection for a good long
time, but I wasn't able to
ejaculate.

sink beneath the surface to feed on

A
Pontiac brake drum, discarded in
a desert ravine,

panic attacks, fear of
heights, fear of crowds, fear
of riding in cars, and claustro-
phobia.

Glass!

Under Glass!

Poet

Eating Big Dinner

Standardization of Screw Threads

Is Flooded THRUST MAY SLOW

"But when he saw the scene through the camera, he knew I was right and admitted it."

Electronic Device

"in such pain that he was banging his head against the wall. I could not go on any longer. I had reached the end."

His Death

MIDGET TOOL Cancer of Mouth

Armed with spray paint, liquid shoe polish and magic markers, they present a serious problem, police say.

Automatic Flagpole Raises and Lowers

Grid Deaths Occur

BE DOUBTED

Moon

My tearing, a breathing, outside me,
my skin is falling, earth peppered in it, powder
falling out, my daily circles teeter,
banging, into each other they
are, may not be circles at all,
ferris wheel scraping the structure
a peeling laugh, my shirt torn at the pocket,
falling through, my intestine, the crows are dying,
the lead in my drink is my heavy, my valveburn,
my clicking skin going down hard, soft, my breath
a loss, an axle, a go back, a snotrag left behind

IMAGE STANDARDS

SLITSCREEN TV, WHITE GUTS

NOZZLES HISSING IN THE CORRIDOR

A HAMBURGER CRUSHED ON THE WALL

DENTED METAL DOOR

A BABY WRITHING ON THE PLASTITURF

ARTIFICIAL LIMBS HANGING FROM THE LIGHTGRATES

RAZORS SQUEAL AGAINST THE GLASS

A CLEAN BUZZING RESTROOM

SALIVA ON THE WINDOWPANES

INSTRUCTIONS BURNING IN THE CORNER

775-LBP. TIME IS
SWARMING, CHANGELESS.
BUILD A BOMB,
CONSTRUCT AN EDIFICE
AROUND IT, AND THEN
EXPLODE THE BOMB.

HELLO
MY NAME IS
UNIT

Dummy Motor Priority Weakens
System Light Rain Falling
Rotors Cap. Quick Death 5574 LBP

Blade, Rubber, Flamingo Torque
Insertion Rating

CLUTCHING THE KNIFEEDGED DISK

FOOT MEAT

ACTUAL MEAT

FREQUENCY
METERS

ART OF POETRY

I sat before the shattered screen the
wire plugged in and ground my teeth the
splintered bone was words to calculate
the random breakage pattern of the glass;
the words took shape, became 3D, greyish
worms that slicked the jagged points, a
crown of buns, a heart with twisting bacon at the
center, crossed buzzsaws rising to the sky

TIME'S T-BONE

There were cars boiling at the fence behind
the building the wires peeling back and
shining in the sun last night I
stood before a field a line of distant
trees their white trunks grey in arclight

My car behind a man inside was
wearing a plastic ladymask and sniffing at
the dust and flies in a bottle his
tongue silvered between the bright pink lips

He told me of the lightbulbs floating in my bathtub
a standard deviation deathray leak in
the pipes behind my walls the
highpitched screaming 80 years from now

The car horn's broke he whined my head
felt empty blanking off the sky was
starless dark I tried to ask him about my
watch the scabs that spreading on my wrist he
spoke of dipsticks bedsheets meaty steaks and
vector compaction I turned away and
said your paper's ripped and spit

HIS SHOES

He got up, stumbled in front of the
refrigerator, remembered a large black van
pulling away from the loading dock he
thinks I can't see this place my
wife is dead she lives ahead of me I got no
cutemeat strutting through my rooms at night
no toast and egguts for my morning grief

At work he sees the lips grinding around the
coffee machine, he's walking down the hall he
tries to avoid the look of Mr. Suitts, it
makes him think of babies chopped in
litter cans, so he tights his hands in his pockets
stares at the floor and the
face goes by, a slit of glittering light

He says, I've got to wipe my mouth, stops
in the archive room, coughing spreads
through his arms and legs, he thinks
Meatdip went to the looney bin, got
some chocolate bars, I'll tell them that my
KAKK gaspspeak is the closest to the truth I get he
sees a shadow leaping out the index box,
its labels smeared with shoewax

My bowling shirt my kingape leer my
watch burned black inside the glass I'm
nothing but a squaredoff foot machine stomping round in circles
Mr. Nips stands at the office window, stares at the
hydraulic hoses squirming on top of the garbage truck
and thinks about the feet of the loaders and driver

JERKS AT THE WHEEL

Who's he? he's coughing up the yuks and
spitting on his lap He knows it all he says he
thrums on down the road the hood is black and shiny
wires sticking out it
I'm someone else I'm standing on a tiny balcony
wind and bright clear light on one side
churning mist on the other
I saw a dot in the middle it was a
tunnel that went inside and stopped
he flops his elbow out the window
twists his palm up on the windshield
and steers with the back of his wrist

BURNING POODLE ON THE STEPS

HER BAG

I was snipping at my finger
nails thought of putting them in
little jars I went off to
the shopping center saw a
woman with a bright pink baggie
"What you got in there" I said
she raised her nose "My house my
heart my 2 times daily pills"

I saw a blank wall
some pink teeth
were hanging
off it I asked a
man for time
he had a coffing
dog in a paper bag

I was sleeping in a
motel saw the air conditioner
loom above my bed I dreamed I
was in many photos each with
different glasses "I gotta
gather all the evidence" I
said and thought about
a dog that fell off
the cliff

I saw a wall
it had a horsehead
nailed on it 3 rubber
gloves were hanging
out the mouth I saw
a child stand below
he was swelling up and
then began to talk
in jerks

DEATH OF DAD

I was a sleep I
saw a tower float above a
lake a reddish sphere
hung in air beneath it
the phone went off "It's
Early Death" I thought a
voice burst in my ear it
was my child
wired away out there

I felt my nose stuck in my
forehead walked off to the
shopping center, crying,
saw the pairs pass by and thought of
running deadspeed at the dressstore window
to see if I was in there

DIPTICK FOR LADY C

I looked inside her room she
had a sea inside a
stone afloat she looked at me was
sticking out her gum I
saw her smug her lust her
smile, twitching toward me

In my arms she was a
house with windows spouting hair I
touched her flow her
breasts were washing over
stars and circles flashing on her hands
she breathed with me I found a
door and stood out there
panting in her space

BURNING DOG

I felt a
flame come through my head my
guts get tight I stood up on a
bridge a woman singing far below I
staggered back I
tried to breathe I felt her
hand touch my chest
my panting start to speed
then I sat down on the street
saw three black mailbags waiting on the curb
her suitcase smoking full of meat

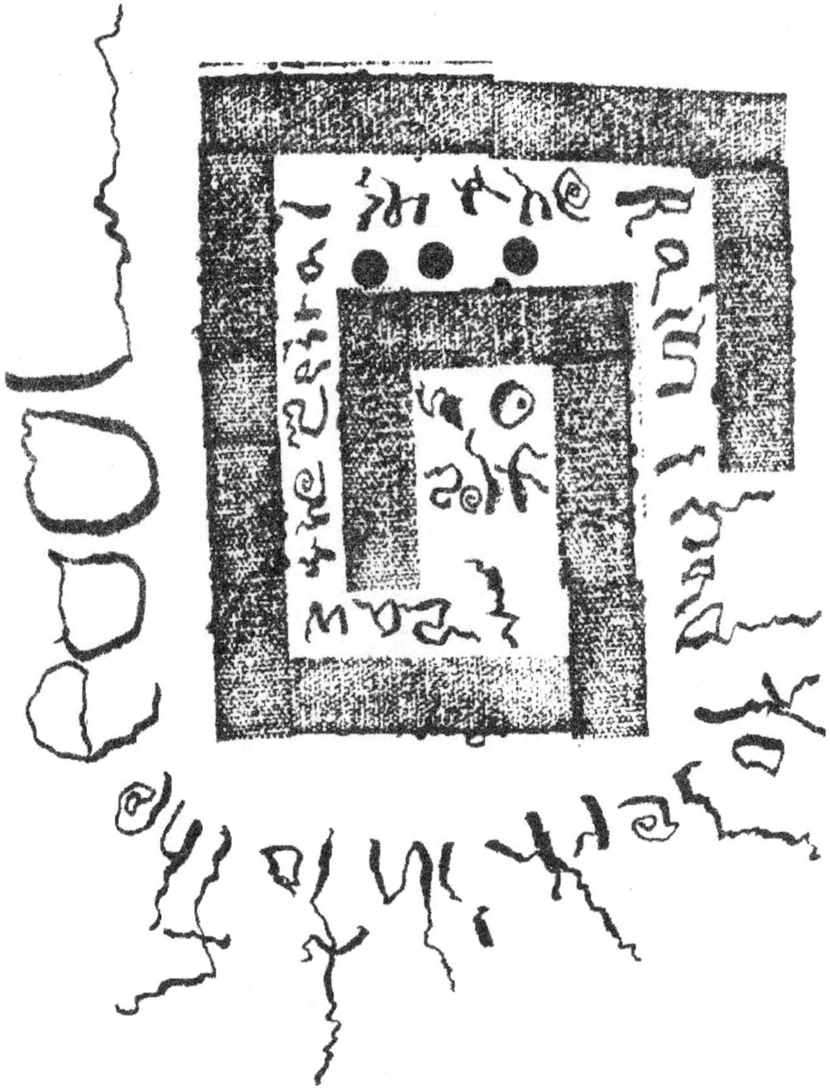

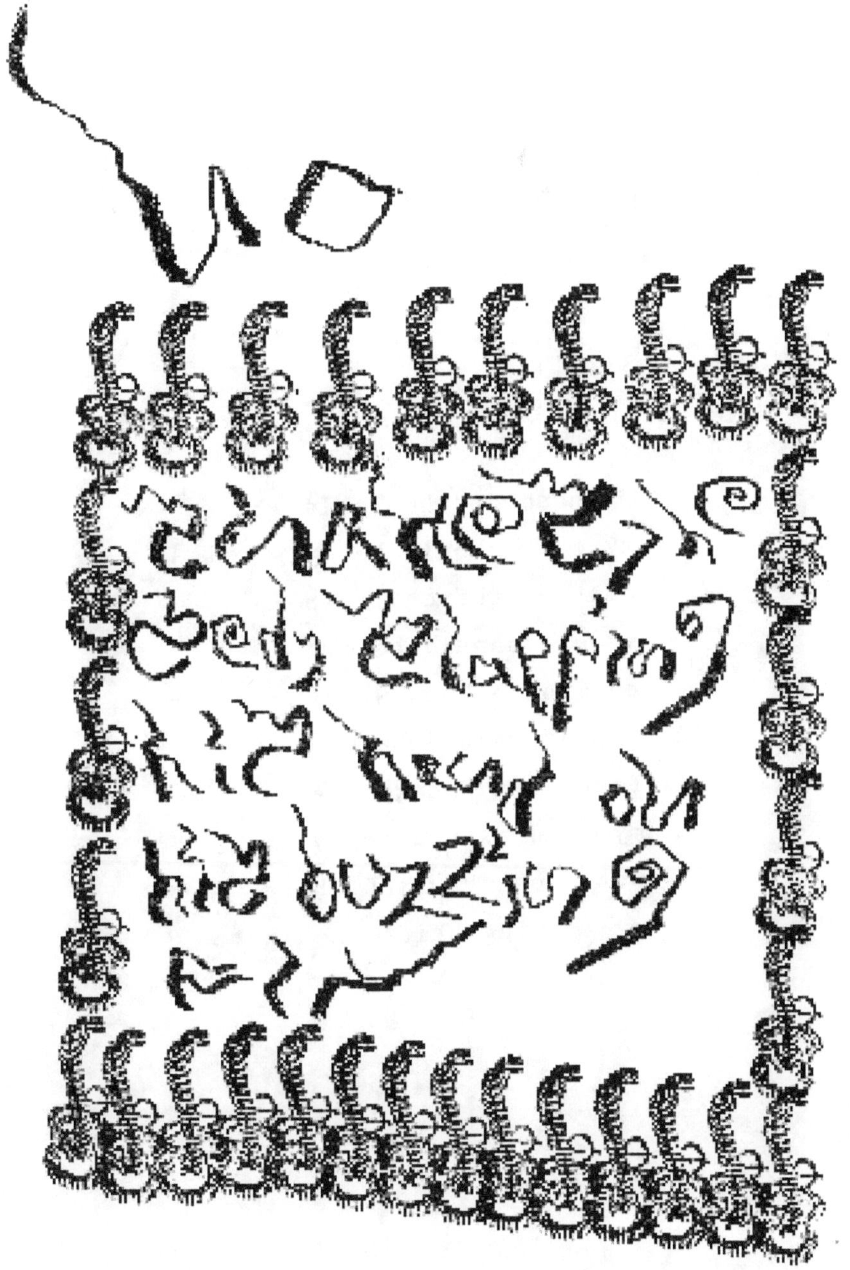

HERE

My hand on the table where
my deck should be my
butt on the chair where
my air should be my
head on a hook where
my hat should be my
feet in my socks where
my road should be my
watch on my wrist where
my burning shirt should be

GARBAGE AT SEA

Rain ticking on his coat, his
glasses bent, one lens up the other down, he's
in the garage, remembered patting his
wife in the kitchen, "Why who am I?" he
thought, leaning against the door

I stood before a garbage landfill
speckled heaps writhed before the dozers I saw a
path down in, condoms and dollheads
staring up from the packeddown mud

He's sitting on a stack of snowtires,
thunder outside, a metal box
is shaking on the drive, his wife comes in,
cats hanging from her shirt,
"Your blood is loose" he said,
she smiles and flips her butt

I was walking down the path I was
falling off the edge I was
scrambling to a burntout sofa I was
on the ocean, circling in the drift

SLEEPING IN THE ALLEY

I was crawling under a bush I
was closing my eyes I was
standing in the dark I
thought it was the middle of a room I
spread my arms and felt a rope, a
knob, a hanger hanging off it I
opened my eyes, felt
ants on my hand
air speeding from my face

She was walking up the alley her
shoes were sluffing through the gravel
"Where's my son?" I asked, she
looked at me, one eye red and skewed to the side,
"What are you doing here?" I said, she
jerked her knees and clutched her belly,
"Answer me" I yelled, she
opened her mouth and stayed like that, soundless

No time he coft
lying on the floor
snuffing up the
cathair mites
dandruff nothing

The paper swarms
a face sticks out
then it coffs, the
the the the the the
th

ASLEEP AT THE WHEEL

He'll be standing high on a ladder
in his fingertips splinters a
wind pulling at his back he'll be
looking through the glass he'll
see an empty table a chair whirling before it a
column of smoke standing above the empty boards

He's crouching in a room with
4 black walls he stares to the north he
sees a concrete tree with
arms hanging from the leaves he
stares to the east: a wall of ice with
hands glinting beneath the surface he's
whirling to the west he sees a hole with
lights and shouting deep inside it; to the
south to the south he sees a giant chair
burning, a dog sleeping and twitching beneath it

He was sleeping he was
pressing his butt in the sofa he was
clawing in his dream at the ceiling he was
trying to wake he was
seeing a lurching highway
holes and cracks speeding beneath him

FLOATING FLAME

I dreamed I was covered with dust and
walking to the grocery store I
went off up an alley to stare in
yards and garbage cans the sun was
high and cold the neighbourhood seemed empty
I was listening to the air ticking in the branches

At the grocery store I saw a man with
sunken pits for eyes he wore a
blue shining hat "Sky" he said
"My feet are sky"

That night I was poking at the
furnace valves, thought of
floating flames and rollaway my
heat flying up to the pulsing black of sky
I held my breath and for a second flashing
put my head in there
saw hot and blue deep inside my eyes

Biting the Brick

"Biting biting" he shouts in front of the
supphose display a man in a flat white hat
is running at him an
aeresol spraycan slapping at his waist

No-Boy was pulling bricks from the mud and watching his
nails splinter and bleed on the
stuckon jags of cement
he feels the heavy blue sky on his back he's
trying to lurch himself and the
bricks upright against it

He'll be brooding in the bathtub he'll
be rising in his face he'll
be turning his fixed stare he'll
be heading again at the landfill
dragging his feet and smell to the
mud and filled up place of running water

"No-Boy No-Boy" he mutters over and over stalking
down the street; at the drugstore, can't
find the shoelaces, hears
the rain explode outside a
flopping in his belly he wants to
vomit and be falling sleeping in the
river surging through the parkinglot

A single tooth sticks from between his lips
"It's Brick" he thinks
lifting the dark lumpy rectangle to his mouth

No Sax

He was jerking the giblet bag out of the
chicken he was blowing into the
neckhole he was thinking it was a
saxophone, sqwakings blast past flapping shreds of skin;
he's blown himself into an empty space a
cloud of scissors floats around his feet a
sound no sound is hissing through his ears
"It's the note, the note" he says
pulsing his fingers on the glistening back

On the Lake

No-Boy stands with a hammer in his pants he
reaches for the window, sees water out there
grey rows of waves and quivering summits he's
gripping the rail of a ferryboat
cars creak their springs behind him as the
deck slants in the swells

He cocks back his hammer and whips it over the waves
"I'm a worm with the hook ripped out" he
yells, gulls whistle back in his throat as the
hammer splashes small in the boiling wake
the boat curves round

He closes his eyes and he's in the
basement in front of a puddle, sees in it
nails clotted with linty cobwebs and the
toe of his greasy shoe, he lies down next to it
puts his cheek on the cool still edge
"Hundreds of hats" he sees "They're
floating on the peak of the lake"

in here
black
my head

SHOE BOILING

I was stuffing a shoe in the bottom of my
closet I was placing a shoe on a stool I was
holding a baby's shoe next
a shadeless lamp I jabbed a pointy shoe in my
ground toe first and stuck my nose in a
rubber shoe I looked at my dick and my
dick was shod there were shoelaces
streaming down my face and I heard a
metal shoe ringing in my ears

I saw a river of shoes shoes
piled in snags and turning tongue over heel in the
boiling water I tied my shoe and
stuffed the other with empty socks I
started to walk in a circle and saw a
cawing shoe fly away I
lay down on my shoes and was laced with sleep

POCKET

She said a word in her pocket she
put a ticket in her pocket she
put a nail in her pocket she
put a tiny mirror in her pocket she
put a feather in her pocket she
put a grocery list in her pocket she
put some salt and hair in her pocket she
put a book in her pocket she
put her mouth in her pocket she
spit in her pocket

SPITTING RILKE

It unceasingly resists you it
falls against the door of your room it
clutches the nails under the steps
dryrots the joists and oozes under your mattress it
falls like dust in the attic it blackens
your toothbrush stains the seat of your pants as you
fall before the furnace
it unceasingly gives way as you button your
shirt as you reach for the
lightswitch as you put your
hand through the wall which is smoke

AX TONGUE

It's not the nail driven into the knee
it's the pants swirling around the leg
it's not the finger impaled on a tooth
it's the sausage crammed down the throat
it's not the tire forced around your arms that
strangles you it's the rain wheeling on the roof
it's not the scorpions erecting their tails in your shoe
it's the laces knotting your fingers in my pockets
it's not your chairseat gnashing its springs that
jolts me awake in the night
it's the pillow spitting pieces of teeth in my ear
it's the eyeglasses on the shelf lighting up like flashlights
and blinding me to my sleep burning me out of my wake
splitting my hair clean down to the jaw
I'm slobbering your words speaking twice in a second
one half of my tongue braying on top of the other

TOILETSEAT

I was rubbing my thighs with toiletseat to the
floor I was nailing a toiletseat
standing on a toiletseat I was flailing at the
ants on the ceiling I was spinning in the
eye of a toiletseat wiping on the
toiletseat a sausage I was trying to
open the toiletseat make a door of the
toiletseat I slapped the toiletseat against the
window was biting and kicking the toiletseat hurling my
change at the toiletseat I lowered over my
head the toiletseat and ran to the drugstore,
shouted DOCTOR at the fleeing clerks; I was
hiding in the trashbin I was
hugging the seat under my shirt I was
hoping it would guide me, be flushing the dark, be a
boat and a mirror and a headlight

SHIRT

I was shrugging my shirt falling in a
muddy hole in my shirt I was reaching for a
doorknob in my shirt sleeping my shirt in a
car as it veered at the berm I was boiling and
folding my shirt I was spitting, chewing
wiping my feet on my shirt I was shirting my
duty streaking my shirt in the parkinglot on
Thursday I took my shirt to a bowling alley and
pinned and balled my shirt my shirt was
bulging ripped over the back of a chair I was
throwing coffdrops at my shirt putting in the
pocket of my shirt a handfull of
nails and a rubber ant I was throwing the
shirtdressed chair into the street where a
garbage truck chuffed and smoked I was
napping in my shirtless skin and a
dream shirted my head it was undershirts polishing a shovel

PANTS

I put my pants on my head my
pants in my mouth I threw my pants on the
burnt chair in the closet I was
stuffing with kleenex my pants escorting my
pants to the bathroom full of ice where I
wrung out the juice and drank of my pants I
dragged my pants in a bag through the
shopping center and banked and shoed with my
pants stuffed the fridge with pants and
pantsed the dolly sprawled on the couch I
squeezed a key between my legs and
stapled to the door my pants Oh pants, I
thought, Your pockets forever a hole, as I
slapped the fly of my pants as I
wiped the window with my pants as I fell in the
dark and ranted and panted on the floor with my pants

ITCHING

My eye was itching as I
stared at the doorknob my
knee was itching as I climbed the
stairs as I swept the sand from my
chair my nostril was itching my
chest was itching where my pen
dragged down my pocket my tongue was
itching as I slapped the radio I was
itching my lips as I sat on the john as I
breathed to the water hissing in the
pipes my itching shoes my sock and hat my
napkin wadded twitching next my plate where I'm
itching the fork asking the itching why I'll
eat next week why my teeth are itching in the
discount store why my dick is itching as I
run past a lidless manhole why I
stand before a window itching to fly I'm
itching under my sheet I'm scratching my
thoughts like ants chaining from the
itch on my wrist where my watch used to be

CASTLE

She found in the next room a bucket of fish
She found in the next room a cigar in cement
She found in the next room a radio falling from a ladder
She found in the next room a chair heaped with hats
She found in the next room a wind full of corners
She found in the next room a basket of hair
She found in the next room a dog turning around
She found in the next room a shirt harboring hammers
She found in the next room a splintered bed
She found in the next room a burning cinder block
She found in the next room a purse of damp coins

CUP OF SPIT

I was caressing the cup of spit on the
shelf thinking of lifting it
quaffing its dregs I was carrying the
cup of spit to the fridge, wanting it to
thicken in cold I was sitting in the yard with my
spit on a stump watching leaves clear from a
tree Oh Spit, I yearned, Please Never Dry, and I
walked with my spit to the cleaner I
sipped of my spit as I turned off the
TV as I sat spit in lap and
lathered my belly with the sticky cup lip
Is My Spit Sucking Me, I feared, and
proffered my spit to my wife who jolted her
chair in reverse I dribbled my spit in the
phone heard it clicking and hiss I
raised the goblet to the mirror saw a
hole full of mud where my mouth oughta be a
handfull of worms where my cup used to be

CASCADE

1

A string hangs from the sky and the
creek's a line through the
fields to the high stone. My
glasses cracked and a handprint's
smeared across the ceiling. I can
hardly hold the oar, so heavy dragged.
If I left this room time should be
hot, but it's hot instead, and
all I can see are my feet between my
knees. It's my eyes under water in this
air, my arms stuck to my side and
numb awake under a sheet of sky. If I
chewed the knot it might, but there's a
web in my face and the boat's sunk in sand

6

The curtain sucked and no air
breathing. I'm not a tree. Nor even a
root dug up. A weight and
nothing on the mattress. Something
sticky where my neck used to be and
something swollen where my gut. Farting,
your head in a suitcase. And the window
invisible, just a glare where my
eye used to be

THE MEMORY

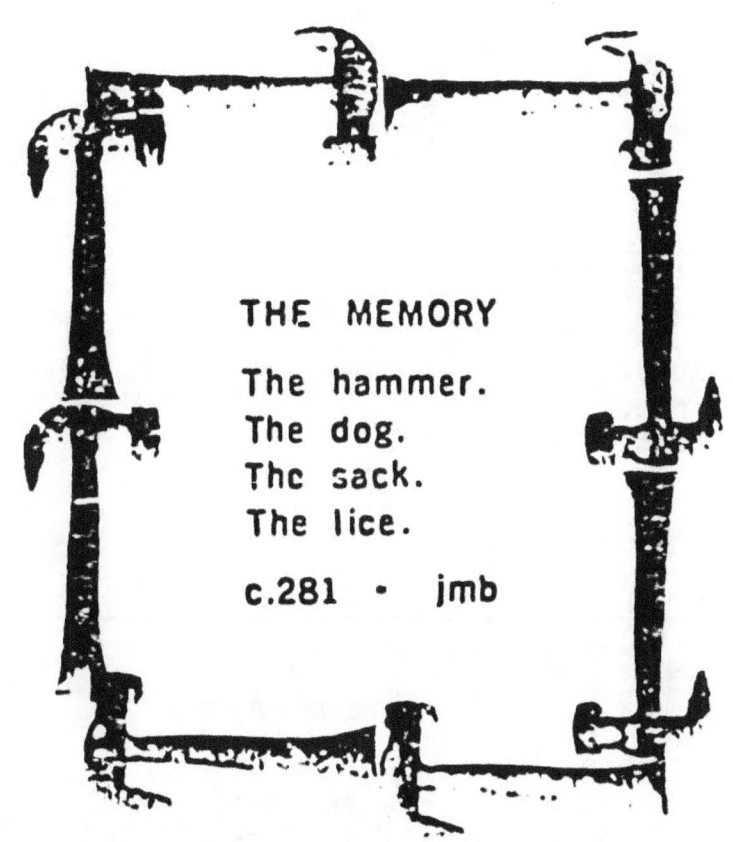

The hammer.
The dog.
Thc sack.
The lice.

c.281 • jmb

THE ROAST

The couch.
The flame.
The book.
The wall.

THE STONE HAT

The loss.
The fork.
The meaty face.

THE BASEMENT

The shelf.
The jars of hair.
The rice on the floor.

THE INDUSTRIAL HAND

The glass.
The guideline.
The ants.

it is the.

THE SAME

THE SLEEP

The blood.

FALL IN THE ALLEY

I was scraping hamburger off the porch, I
was spitting on it, globs for eyes, a
footprint mouth; in a bag I
carried the reeking face to a sewer hole, there were
soggy Jesus books clotted in the gutter and I
thought of winter, whitening the northern side of town

From the dark mud behind the garage from the
wet leaves slapping against the siding squirrels
flicking into a heap of rotting lumber I
went and stood in the alley, saw
yellow flames falling all along it,
light pulsing in the branches getting bare;
I was hot, the jacket around my neck
thick and damp, I'm trying to
walk to the street but my shoes are
swollen and stuck to the gooey tar, I see
fire popping and leaping around my pants

I dream me standing on a low platform, the sky was
cloudy, boiling over slowly the back of the
grocery store; I listened to the trash compactor
screech and crunch into silence, saw a
little boy walking toward me over the gravel, his
face hidden by a yellow cap, he
holds out a hammer and saw,
stops some feet away and waits,
heavy black smoke pouring from beneath his hat

MAINTENANCE

A heap of trashbags slumps in the
garage and a whining air conditioner.
Why couldn't I answer you, my
mouth in my lap. You're in the
bathtub, one eye closed and it
rains. I stand in the hall like a
sheet, my dinner in me tied in a
plastic bag. I'll never shit again.
And I'll only breathe for you as long as
the compressor lasts

LIQUIDATOR

Stuck in the blackberry patch with a
gnat up the nose. A blur
feathery and pricking. You
clambering at me in the hot bed and a
spat. Sweat on my back. Dank
stones below my knees where I
can't see and the berry glittering out of
reach. Where's your face when it's
here? My pants smother on the floor. And I
hear you weep at the wall where my shirt used to be

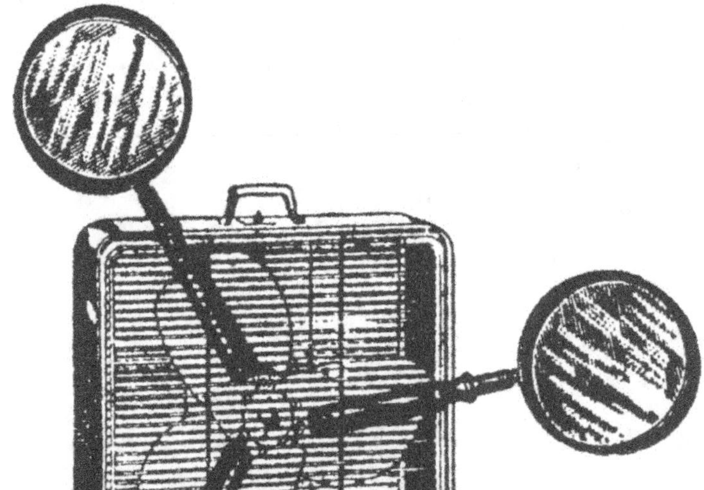
FIND THE

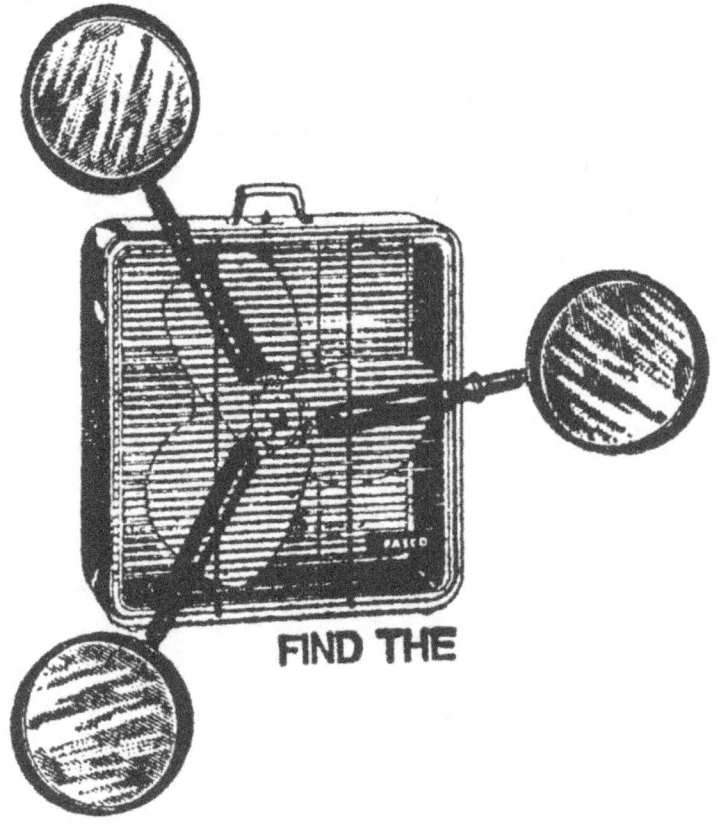

EATING SPEAKING

It sticks in my throat like
stiffening caulk and backs up my
air out my butt. It wasn't what I
wanted to say but I had, teeth like
foam and a palate of wood. Could I
sell it or loan it for feed? I'm
cut bad as I lay in the palace my
hair stuck in cracks. And my bulk
thickens, like a goat eating bricks

EVER EVER

Whatever whatever or a lamp under
pants. Nostril again, lapping at
mine, not what you think or you
what you thinks, thick luck
whapped with a lock. It's fine you're
passing again, but why so hostile?
Can't you stand fucking weather?

PULULATING PLAZA

Those coarse ladders blind your face like
walls pocked with bullets, bannisters
cracked, ending in that cartoon blade your
tongue slid down. Jokes aside, shaking the
rostrum, the crowd jitters and smokes like the
sea in rain. Three hopes clutter me, nostrums
faking a fine kid, a brave plunger after spoons of
fat. So you're rending cannisters, locking wallets,
sprawling on shapeless minds? I'm madder and
louder, the balconies bleed, and I'm forced to climb

STRING

Lap sat, shrouds of Mother, decades of
belly, smouldering chair: on the table
four glasses and a dribbling sponge.
Well it's time to eat but the baby rolls
but the stove rustles like a book or a
cage. My fat clouds all other days, like
jelly mouldering or a bare cable. After the
war of pigs and asses I munched, hell, I
climbed that meat. But it's cold lately
and I'm just... ah, nothing but age to cook

POLITICA EROTICA

What blunder eaten before the TV news,
sand swallowed, the globe shaped like a
stick? Real food, real shit, that
whole vat of blood I'll never see: you
know don't you, we chew our, their bought
face? Our plunder's beaten for cheap
sinew, hands hollowed, and your robe's
taken with a brick. Feel good? Below my
hat's a smudgy river, a sea of broken
schools. Ahh take off that lace

NECROPHAGY

This street of heads shot in the
back of a car, like candy unwrapped,
sweet spit and my lips sticky and I
wipe. The street's like a tunnel,
all those signs, towered over like
teeth! That red shower climbed my
clothes, like my feet funneled. Yeah,
I swiped their soul and my hips
sickened. But shit, my back's still
dancing, even if the tar <u>is</u> hacked.
Ah what eats in my slot...

HOW I MISS THAT MEAT

What the splice spelt, eyes in a cube,
over never again, bricks slammed cracking
splintered sherds, the splints shattered.
I knew it'd turn out this way I didn't.
What the slice felt like, nude, slower and
slower to my fevered shame, oh I kicked that
hand, slapped that linty nerd - he was
lentils scattered - so few days
to burn... spattered with liver

ARCHAEROTICA

Like a mast layered in sand, a hill
slides, bones jut, your domed head
glistens in sun. My tongue for a dead
throne listens, lusts groaned in the
wide spill of land, where the Flayers
asked their price... if I could praise
that ship... if I could raise the
currents silted in your hips

THAT MILKY DROOL

Taped cream through the ears like dripping
dripping oh what a bore, like my tooth's a
head, pitted with rust, that magnetic wind
slants us. But ha it's just my own roiled
drink earned, my carnal flaunted back. It's a
jack haunted marvel what I learned, thick and
boiled. My loaned lust, my spit's jut, my
pants' thin emetic, my hat lifted from the
dead: these truths spite more than, oh,
ripping the hair. But my spew dreams in a
lake, yanked from my skull like air

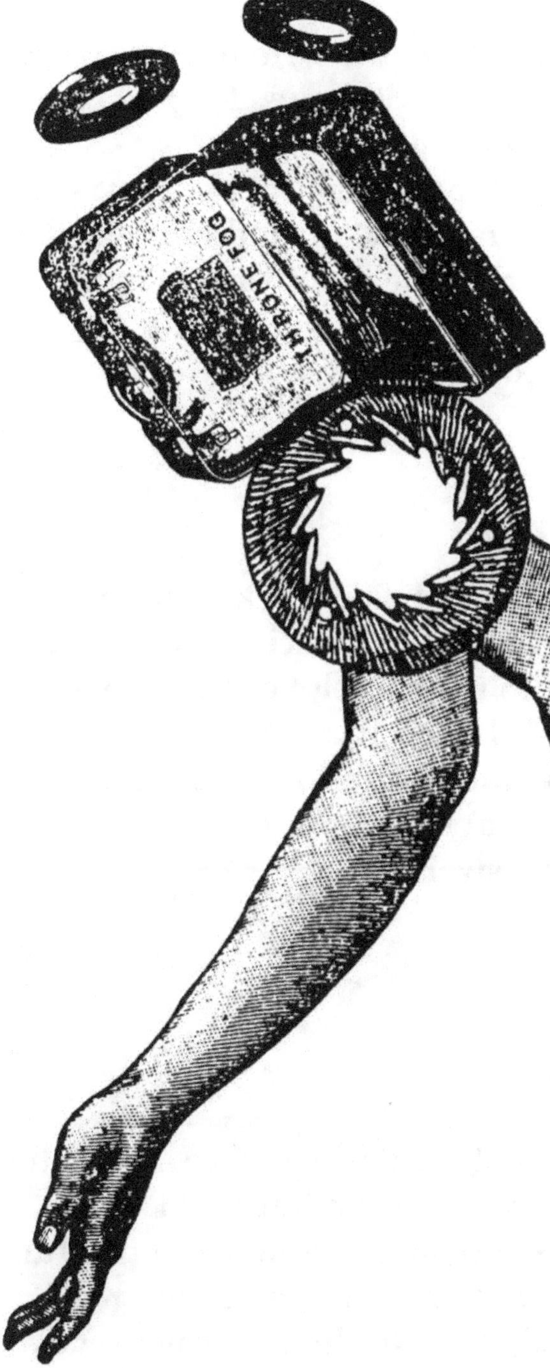
THRONE FOG

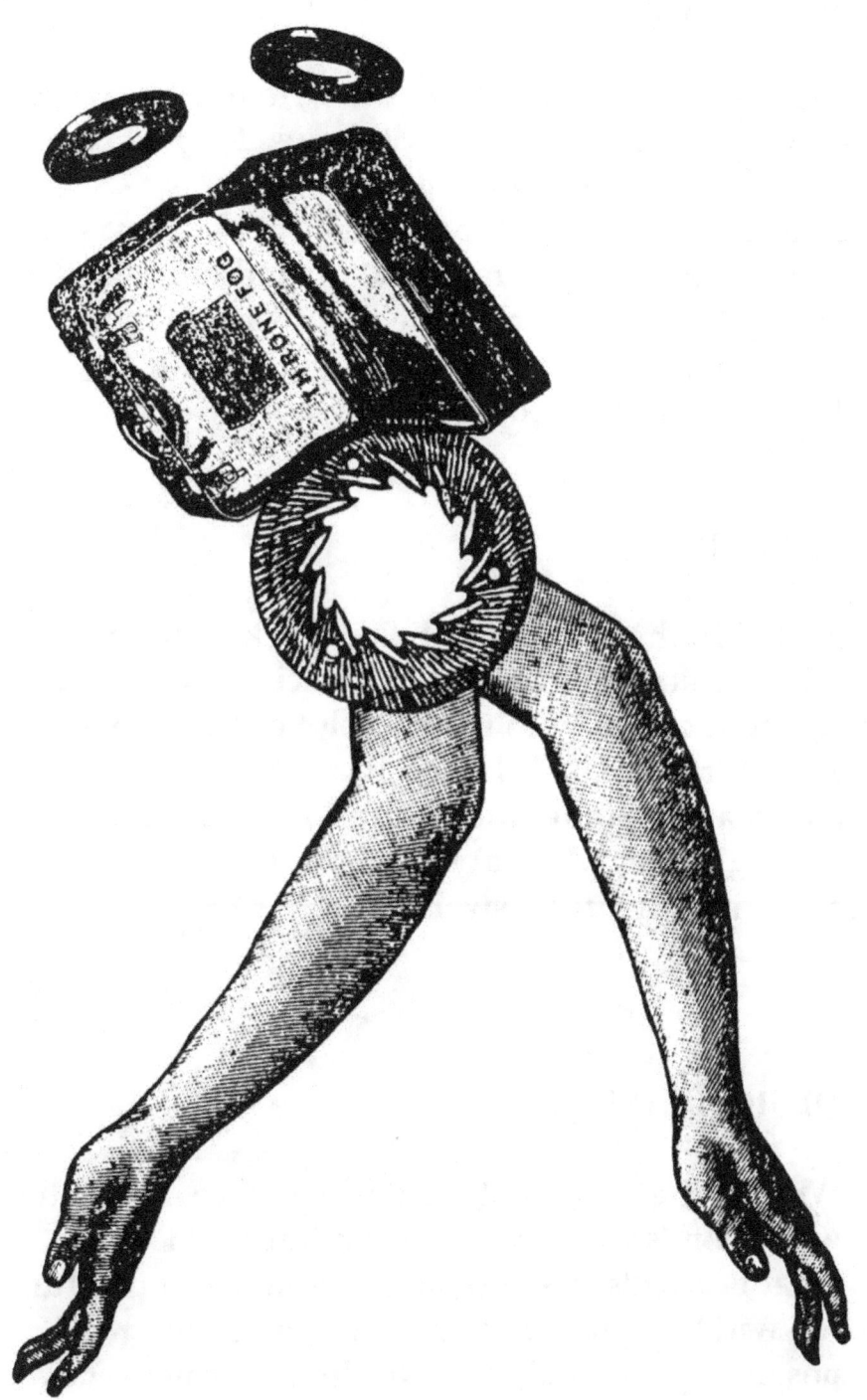

TELEFONAZO

The lenguetazo lapped from the wire like a wave of
forming speechless, an other tongue. Ripped from the
lips it's, ahh, but's spattered a cold grass of
thought and it's passed, past. Just speaking's a
liar, a grave groaning, feetless the mother lunge the
trips spitted tits slathered the mold smeared glass or
doubt's leaking fire. It lathered my beard as I
left, that second's second gouting mire

NARSEETHIS

Dangled in the tank like a fish in rocks but my
hoping's a string in cement or antacid sinks in my
face (teeth coated with the speech I choke) This
coke's shirt-splashed flashed like a fin when the
air's got away (under the gas buttons, bubbles) Ah
why I pull dull, why not let go? (a reflective
waves, like my breast swells)

DESIGHPHERING

What in the code's not read's dead soap, run in the
washroom's wall, er, limitation imitation. Brr,
what I called's false doom, some kinda dopey fun
fed with rope (but *you're* deknotted right? with
possibility sodded) What in the lobe's not red...
...stuffed with hope (over the sink's stink bent)

SEXUAL COMMERCE

Pondering full pandered panties I, coughed and
culled for a send-up, bent up my glasses stained
with nap nappies... "Oh cutie-pie" lay on the
stairs upordown while I wandered full wondering
wavering I, doffed and appalled at the rent those
asses gained... but least your yip yapping's
scooting *my* way (on your hairs I sup, I'm a clown)

POR Y PARA

For! Cars that left in the heat, for the
fog left in their shape where they left,
for! For the tarpits they tunnel, for the
beasts' breath, for the end of man's! For!
Four times we're leaving! Four times we
returned! For the tunes we spurned! For
the spinning beds! For the heads thinning!

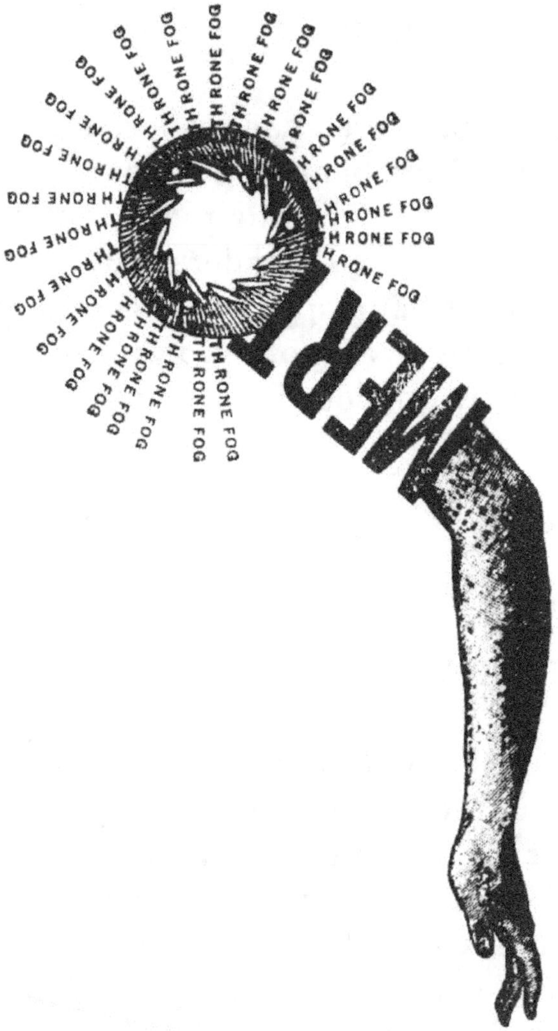
THRONE FOG
MERT

(COLLATERAL DAMAGE)

I called forth, 'n burst, from the hill-slum where the
nails burned, even as reaching they, through the walls,
where their fame chained, in a touching blaze... their
faces flicker, brief, like fish at the surface flare,
(on them my charred linkage fell; but they stand, but
their tongues swell!) So I hauled ass, 'n cursed, what
the "will's" done, where the thirst for thirst thirsts!
Where their vapoured blood from a shirts'-slope shrieks!
(Oh shredded sleeves in the blown dirt's speech!
Could I their flapping silence speak?)

TOXIN

Yeah in my "north" I railed, clutching that steel,
where the wave-speech scoured under a roiling eye,
where the distant cloud-bell loomed, and I, my feet
in blood-slippers sloshed, the passage in. And a
foaming room "I" found cost, or "he"... ("But's
windowless, proof-walls burned, where's ringing
served for air") So I swerved that gate and here
in a deadless "south" I stale, where guns on a
windless plain boom, and I, my tongue in's jail,
gnashed in a box, my tocsin failed

FORWARD OBSERVATION

My hands soaked where my skin ought to be my
lands cloaked... in oil, where a speech-wind
stales (could I reign, where the sting-shower
hails... or the sand in my mouth floats?) in
fields of burning tanks... my feet bloat where my
throne ought to be, my tongue's... mere bleating,
uh, bleeding... where in smoke this tower pales...

BURIED HIVE

But's hovered that shovel... like a loud heart in a
lift when the power flick flickers, Oh but's not near
so cute, it drifts away... so my hands with clay're
flaked, uh, fake grieving, but grief, like my fingers
finger what's fingered, er. (But's smouldered, that
slumped digging, like a clouded...) Yeah but's truth's
near swarming ground-bees, toward the cliff's chased...
(like that last spark when the juice quits...) "Like a
flower in flame" he's, to the handle skewered, 'is
charred blade in the fog dug... where buzzings rage...

WET TOOTH MIDDEN

What I bled, dreamed last night, like a room of
water-walls, from those cuts in my bookish head or
teeth through the cheeks glint (like plates 'n cups)
poured over the text, but's shards 'n shriveled scraps
from's neolithic eat-off. (What clatters in's mouth)
hard words half chewed like a bone-tongue natters in's
reddish haze: what I tasted, taste, like a stone floor
where the waste's trod. Oh licking deeper I, through
this dripping space where I shed my oughts, like a
stream! (Where I dry, denoting this)

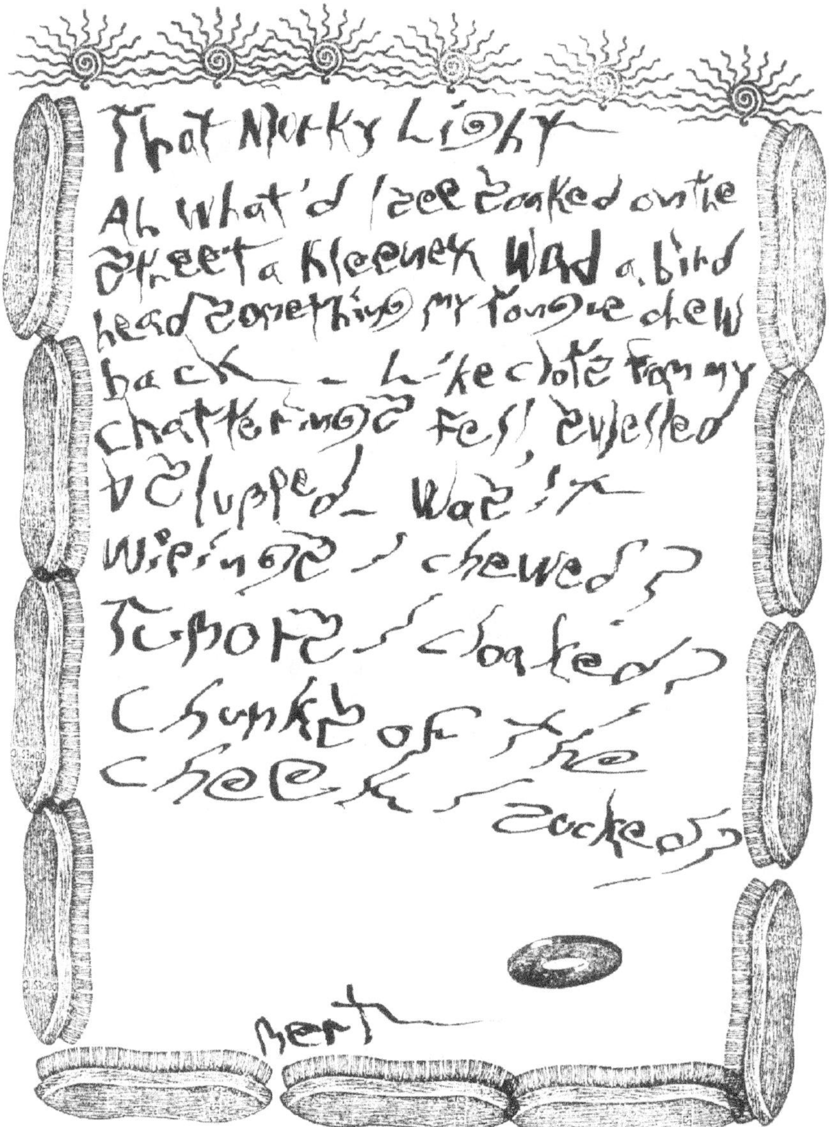
That Murky Light
Ah what'd I see soaked on the
street a kleenex wad a bird
head something my tongue chew
back — like clots from my
chattering s fest expelled
d clupped — was it
wiping s — chewed?
S more s — cloaked?
Chunks of the
cheek s — sucked?
Bent

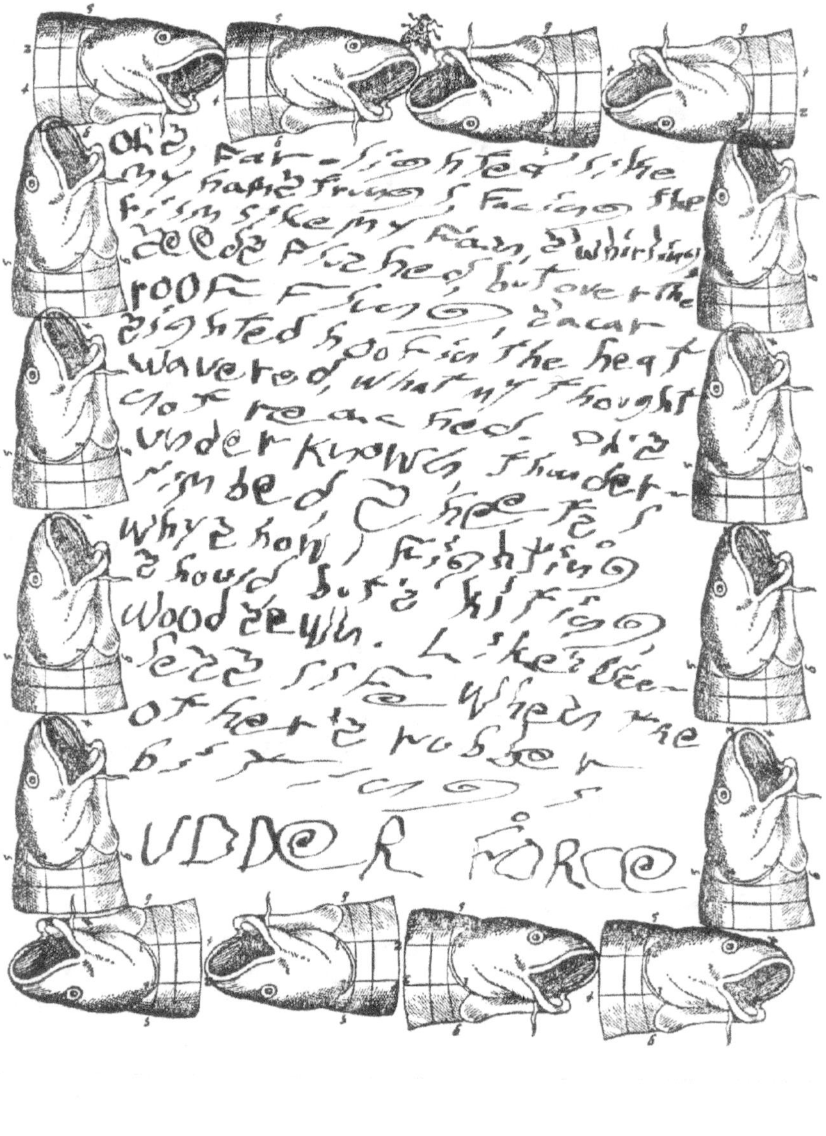
UDD@R FORC@

What I blew grew
like an arm ballooned,
Ash where's my words
where's my whirled
breathed
What you hoped
or
like a dream
UTTER UTTER

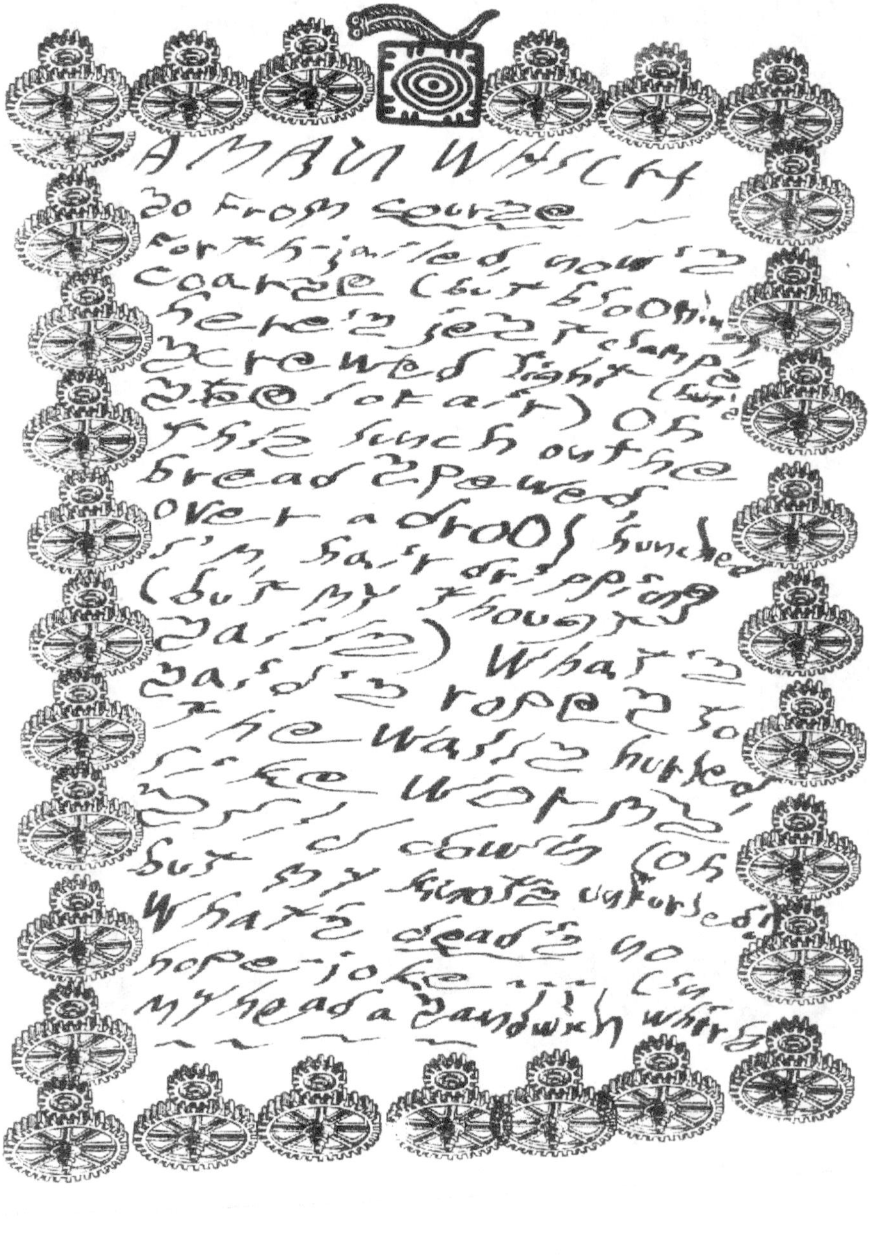

TOXIN

Yeah in my "north" I railed, clutching that steel,
where the wave-speech scoured under a roiling eye,
where the distant cloud-bell loomed, and I, my feet
in blood-slippers sloshed, the passage in. And a
foaming room "I" found cost, or "he"... ("But's
windowless, proof-walls burned, where's ringing
served for air") So I swerved that gate and here
in a deadless "south" I stale, where guns on a
windless plain boom, and I, my tongue in's jail,
gnashed in a box, my tocsin failed

FORWARD OBSERVATION

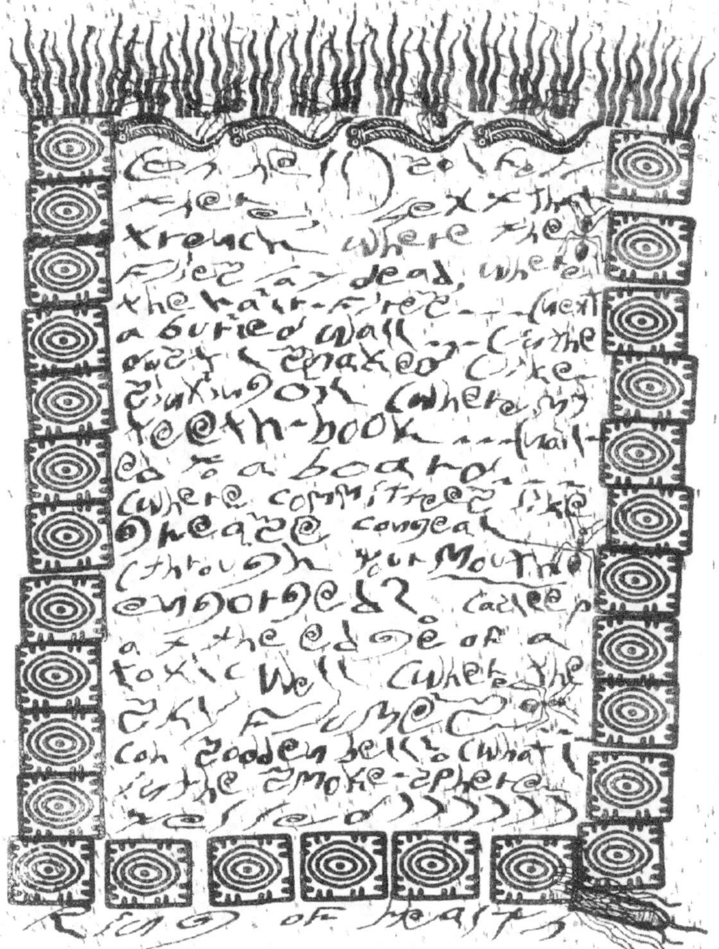
trench where the
flies lay dead, where
a buried wall
teeth-book
where committees like
grease congeal
toxic well

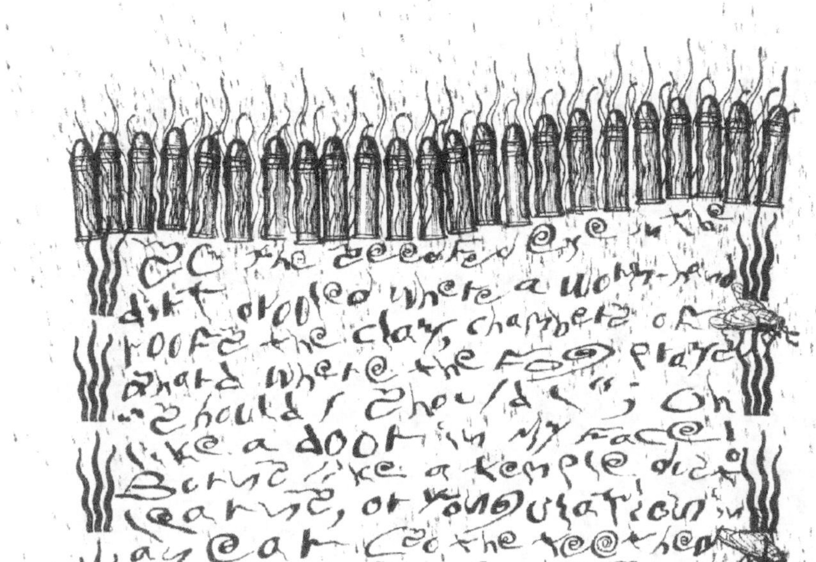

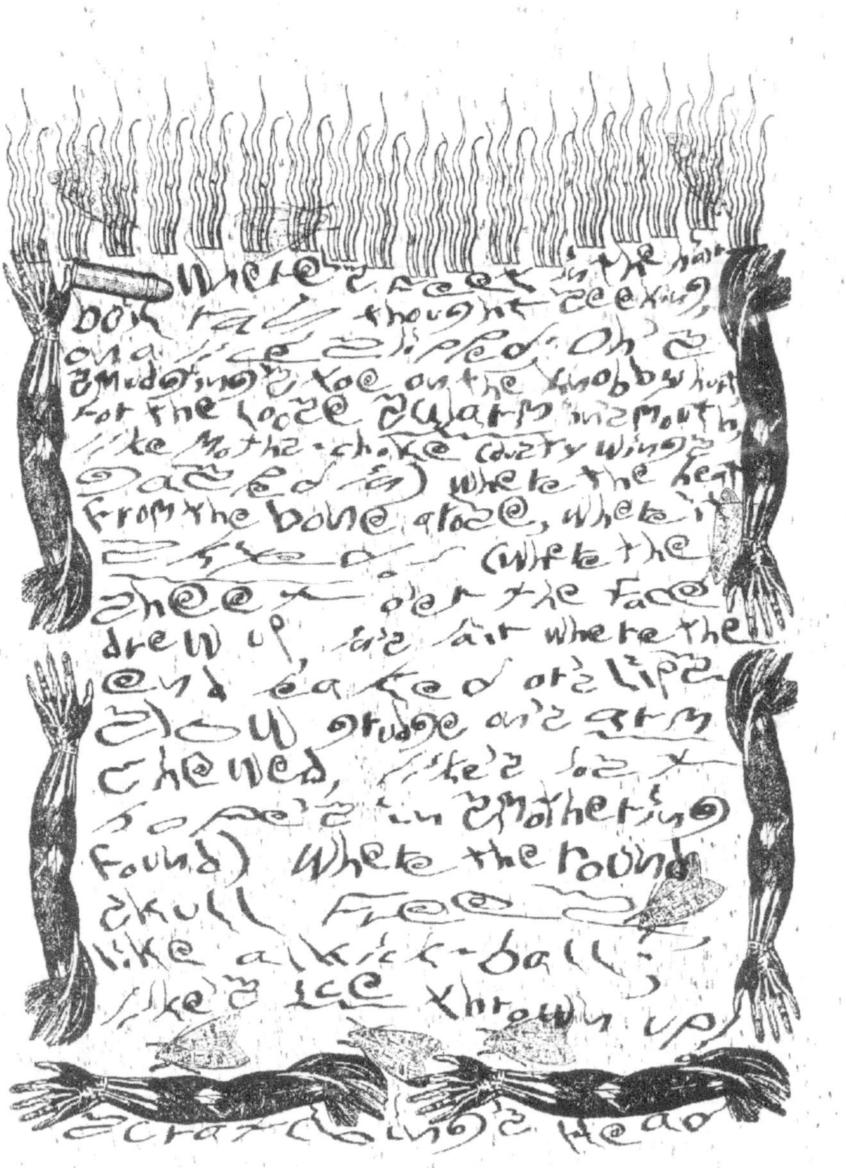

POD KING

1

REIGN

Like's rice in's eyes writhes... (what 'e sees'
down's cheeks' sagged, at it's seen) like a sea
under's face, 'n leaks, toward the burning tree
where the lyre lept, like a tooth-dance slowed
round a bloody tongue where I, dropping pants...
"Like my life-slice dries... (what 'e bleeds'
down's knees lagged at it's been) like a bee in's
laced-shut beak, toward the churning glee where the
fire's kept truth's glance glowing (but the ground's
a muddy sponge, where he, in's sloppy chance plugged,
learns to drown...)" Oh could the grass-crown sing,
on the rain-skull! Where the flooded hair in a time-
droop's slown ('n knows) Where the sight-grubs flew!

2

BRICKEGG

Where's birth-fight singled him, like a tooth yanked
out, from's slurping that vast bowl (the crowd-spit's
brew, but's silken themkind, like a vitamen stew, or
"primal broth"!) Where's first light ringed, like a
cloth o' prayer (or diaper) from's sheeting blood
(but's cold, as last) (Where under a wall he thirsts;
for a roof and a window in's legs! Where's biting's
thick red headshell...) "But I'm nest in line!"
(For's stone-burst; for's sphere o' speech-drink!)
For's expectorant bigbang quaffed!

3

SURGICAL LIGHT

"So like a doctor I sank I", in's tank o' teething
where the lank rocks clanked and I heard (I thunk
in my throat like an echo, er, stop), trying to
rinse that blood from's incissive drowning (where
the suture waves) Oh baptism's scalpel where the
stonehair grew! What I clunked like a tongue, er,
lock on my skull! (Where he thinks he or the killing
spewed) Like I laughing slaughter or a concussion
cure! (Where's rank corpse's convulsed; like a
well o' birthing he burns...)

4

DRY SURF

In that thick pink head where I once thought and the
world's singing "knew" (but's sinking in the oil-lake
what I threw) where I gloved so smoke, like a stone
thought I, still in a wave tumbling, in that link of
hair to the sea... (but's in a blink cut off and
adrift in a gravel lot where a beach eye boomed) Oh
I rock, and drown... ("Oh but he's crowned, with a seed!")

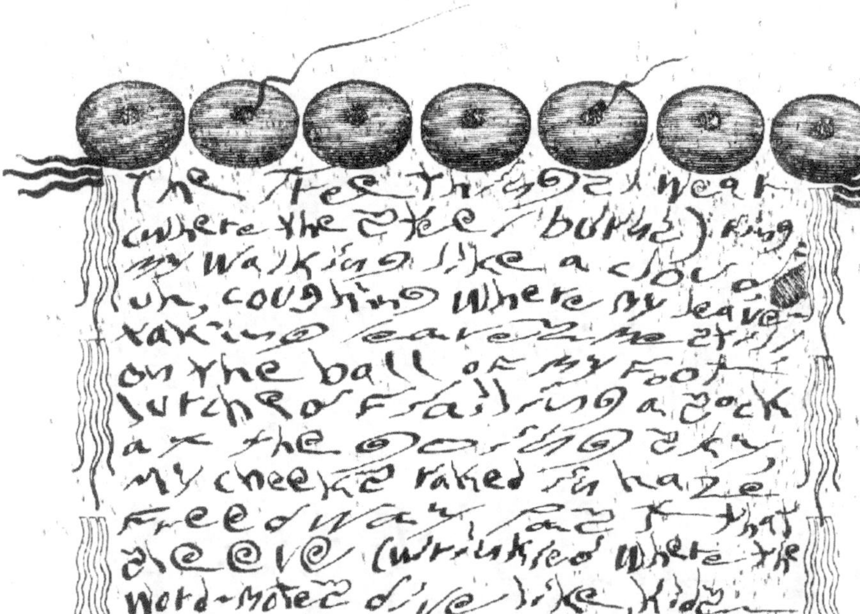
where the
my walking like a cloud
coughing where my leaves
on the ball of my foot
my cheeks raked in haze
word-motes dive like kids
toward the murky river
Oh hope
where the clothes decay
bark and my vapored pants
Cloudy Shirt

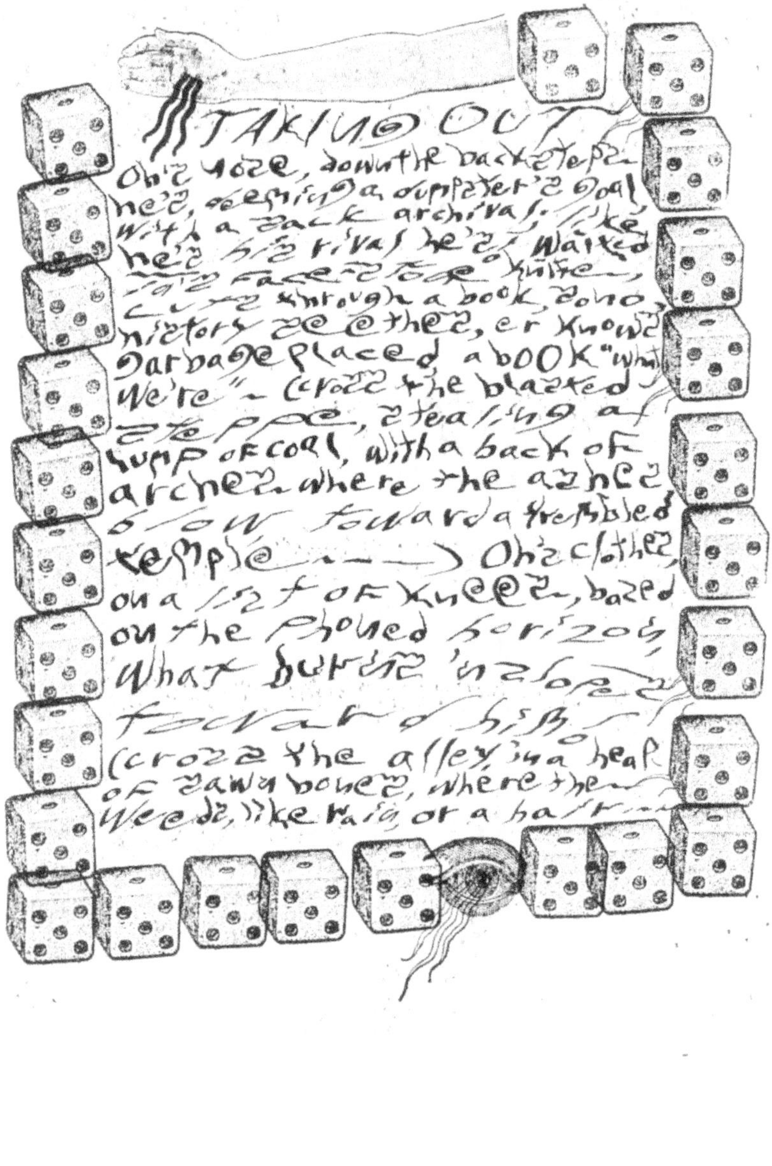
lump of coal, with a back of
arches where the ashes
toward a trembled
on the phoned horizon
cross the alley in a heap
weeds, like rain or a hair

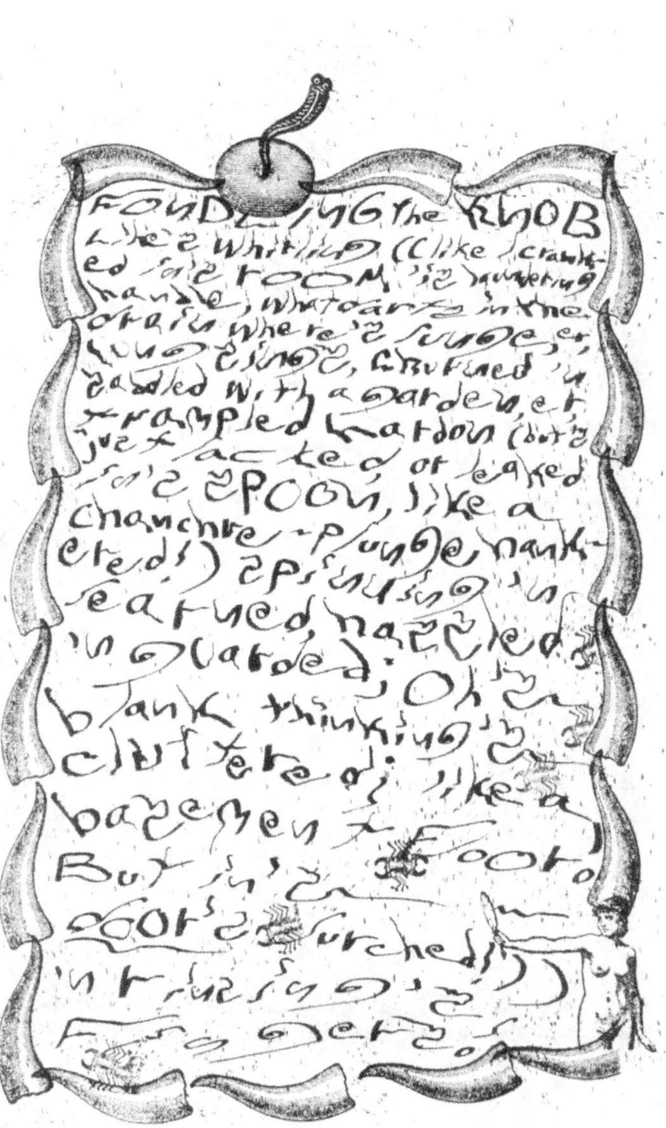
FONDLING the KNOB

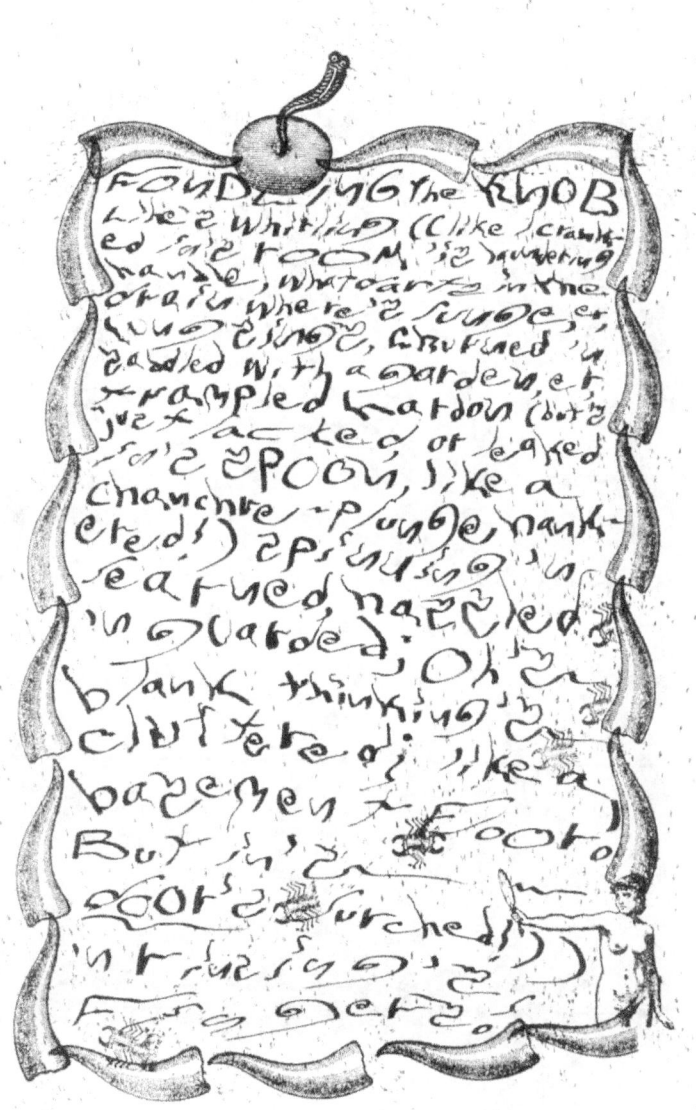

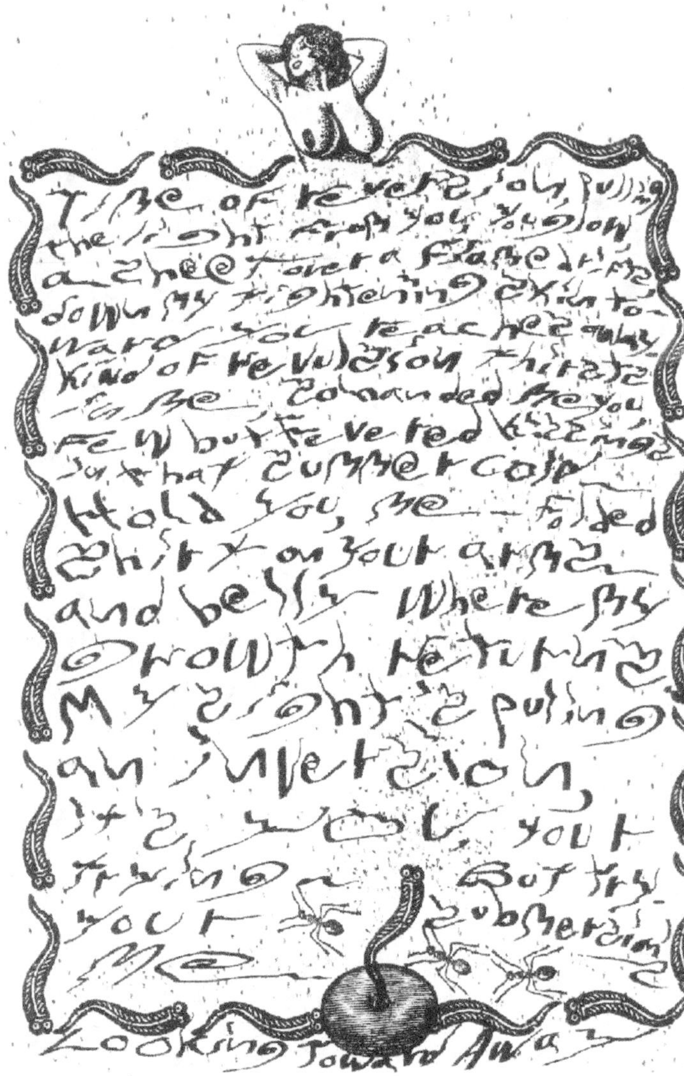

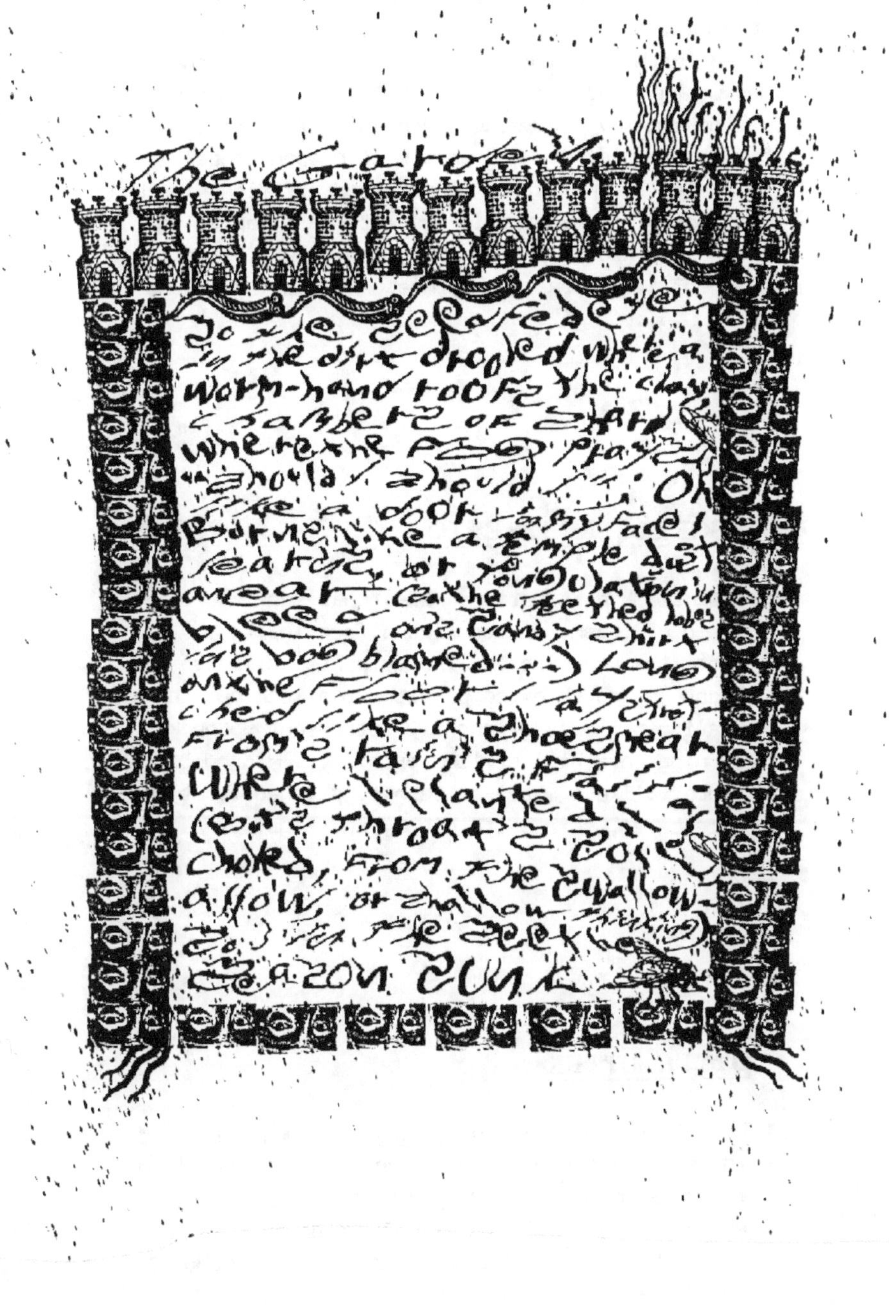

UPON A TIME

So she in the bathtub slept a form to my
thought-sight but to her a surge over the edge
splashed, though lashed by a foot and a front
urged forth. Oh I kept my arm all night and she
her wrath-flood lept. So I on the toilet lumped,
her news on my feet spewed, socks or rivers to my
future slumped (or knew what's to happen happens)
But we're in the suture passed, and our fight in the
mattress bled: we warm in the aftermath kept, and our
clothes burned in the steam (but oh where's the present
learned?) ...where the sperm's once bathing churns

ASCETIC AESTHETIC

What stink distinctions made, that sunk
field of trash, spewed like a face in its
past, the very air...(like my pants' diapers
bagged) You think completion or a luck but the
heaving pillows, a landfill votes your upchuck,
burning on a hill of lies printed. My condition's
blade...like a wheel of rashes, skinned...but the
race cares, shirts its blood, and sags...

UTTER UTTER

What I blew, grew, like an <u>arm</u> ballooned, floated
for your hair like a lake reversed: Ahh where's my
words' edge, where's it enter you, where's my
whirred said's <u>harm</u> bloomed (bloated like the air's
fake thirst?)? Oh I saw it all breathed (like a
third eye's blind in a hedge blundered) What I
you hoped-spoke's a melted river's thunder, or
what's in the sea like a dream muttered...

DOPPLER AFFECT

Through the paint on the window where the instructions yellow 'n chip; like a certain fog of reduction lifts, scattering slivered oughta-be's; Oh I throughed that glass and my deep face fed out my mouth's inversion! Like a turning of rippled lamps in a muddy lake burns clear, and rising fish, like thighs... where the light-silt thinks up, ringing the sky like a well of immersion (like a churning of nippled... Ah my pants' blood's tranced, in a sidling dance of conversion! (Through the faint in the windrows, where the breath slurfs up and the wind-jamb bursts! (O'er the sill, where's nothing, rushing waits...)))

LA NOCHE DEL ALMA

"Where" sung I, in the light faucet's eye (er nose er when, in a smoking needle's sly fish: Oh I finned and failed my dance "there"...) What I'm's, begun, like a clean squeeze but hoping a murky flood of recognition

(I was bare in the mud, of closets thinking)

AUTOPHAGIA

But I lint from that table at my pants brushing,
thin stacks of skin completion, off the edge slipping,
where you, on the door lentils chewing, staring (at
me?) with leguminous eyes; Ah's all swarmed in a
cloud-of-hats, different brimmings o'er the same
sweaty hands' holding-it-on (but I went from that
cradle in my grave rushing, laughless as I scraped
my chair and my face brushed off, just a grin under
my back pockets' inversion) So I, toward you, took a
step sloped, swallowed my eating, tried for my
tongue's conversion...

"...FOR THE DEFENSE OF FREE..."

Oh so fast asscovering "sanctimonious little shits"
leashed on the public moo(e)d where the list simmers
and swells (of those who bared... arms raised in the
hair of learning, whose chair falls (down the stairs
where a bagged committee smirks over a plate of chain))
So's past's smothering though's ankledeep in spit and's
greasy foot glimmers like a sunken bell... Oh those who
fared freely, why's your wrist now stiff with retraction,
clunked in a cast of... what sears saying... Ah this
air's strangling! (Those "blameless", "eyes of concern"...

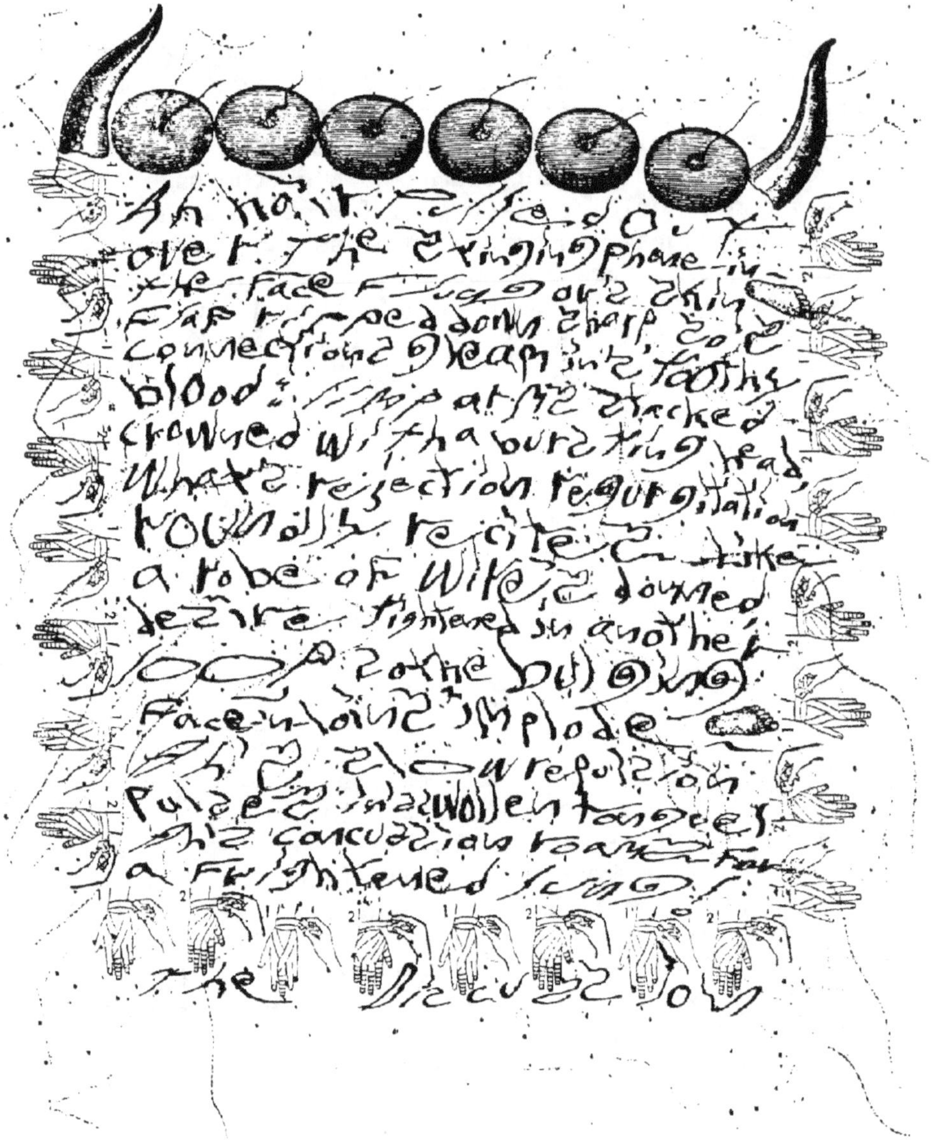
crowned with a bursting head
rejection regurgitation
a robe of wire
desire tightened in another
a frightened

DRINKING

So I limped toward that cave where the faucets rang,
"churning the milk" up that sunken trail for the
dancing, slaves in the after-flow, toward a ward of
metal beds "behind the gilded wall", (stacks of dead
and a huge-headed smile asleep in the vines), oh I
soddenly slept, the opening's grass in my eyes I
closed and wept through my skin: so I stepped from my
hair and the gritty air smoothed, ringing the bell of
my teeth. In the throat of that drunken self I sang,
swimming our tongue in the moat of speech

SEEPING

(...where's "sinking" bloats... ...like a face o'
keels floats up... ...sloshing in's blood thinning,
like's icy "self" melts... ...brings the white
wings of offal-eaters... ...'s severed feet in's
kelp drifts... ...ah's teeth bloom... ...like
dark... ...why's thinking boat... ...a leaf at
least... ...what frays...) Ah why's sleeping
swimming plays!

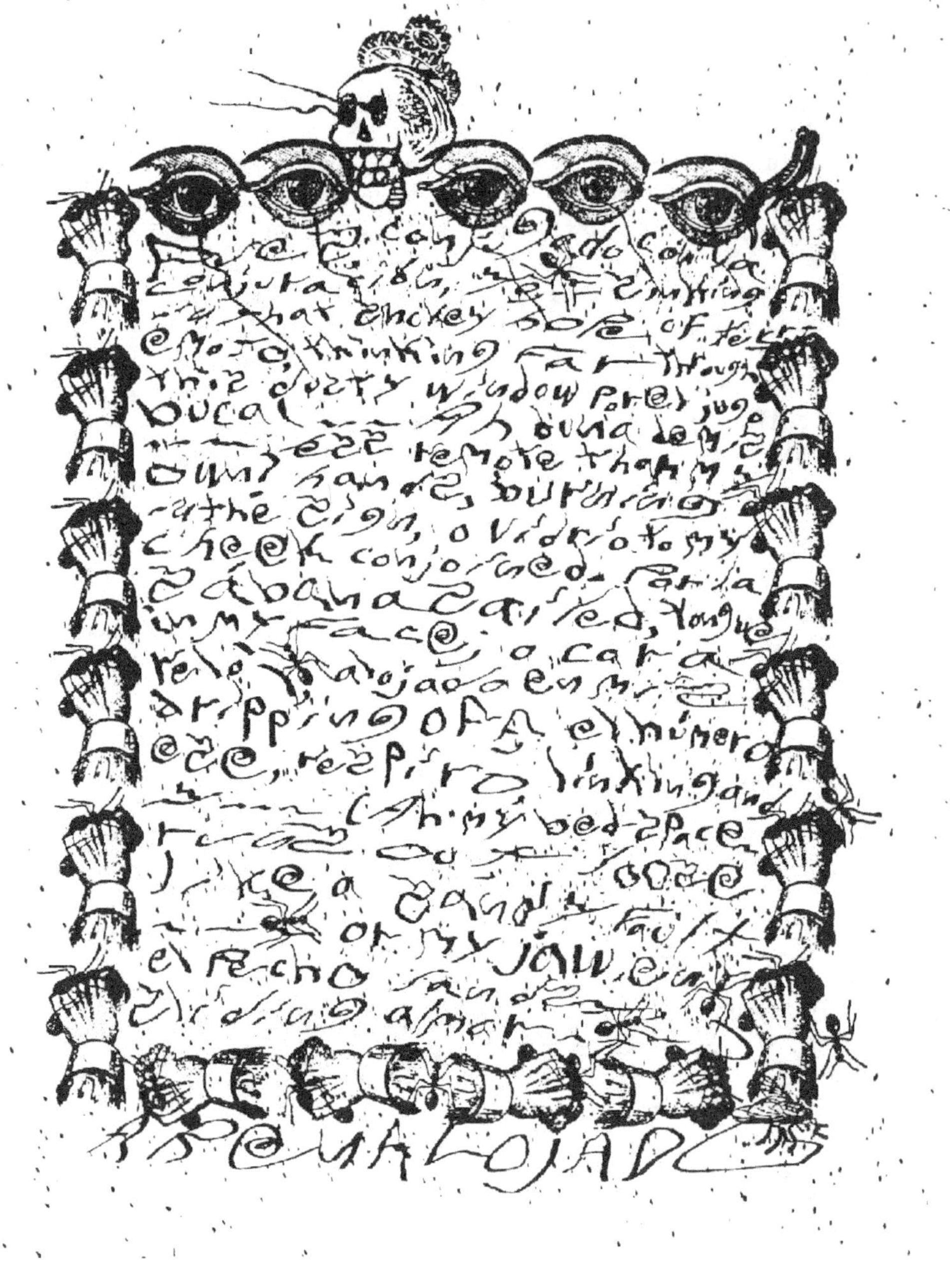

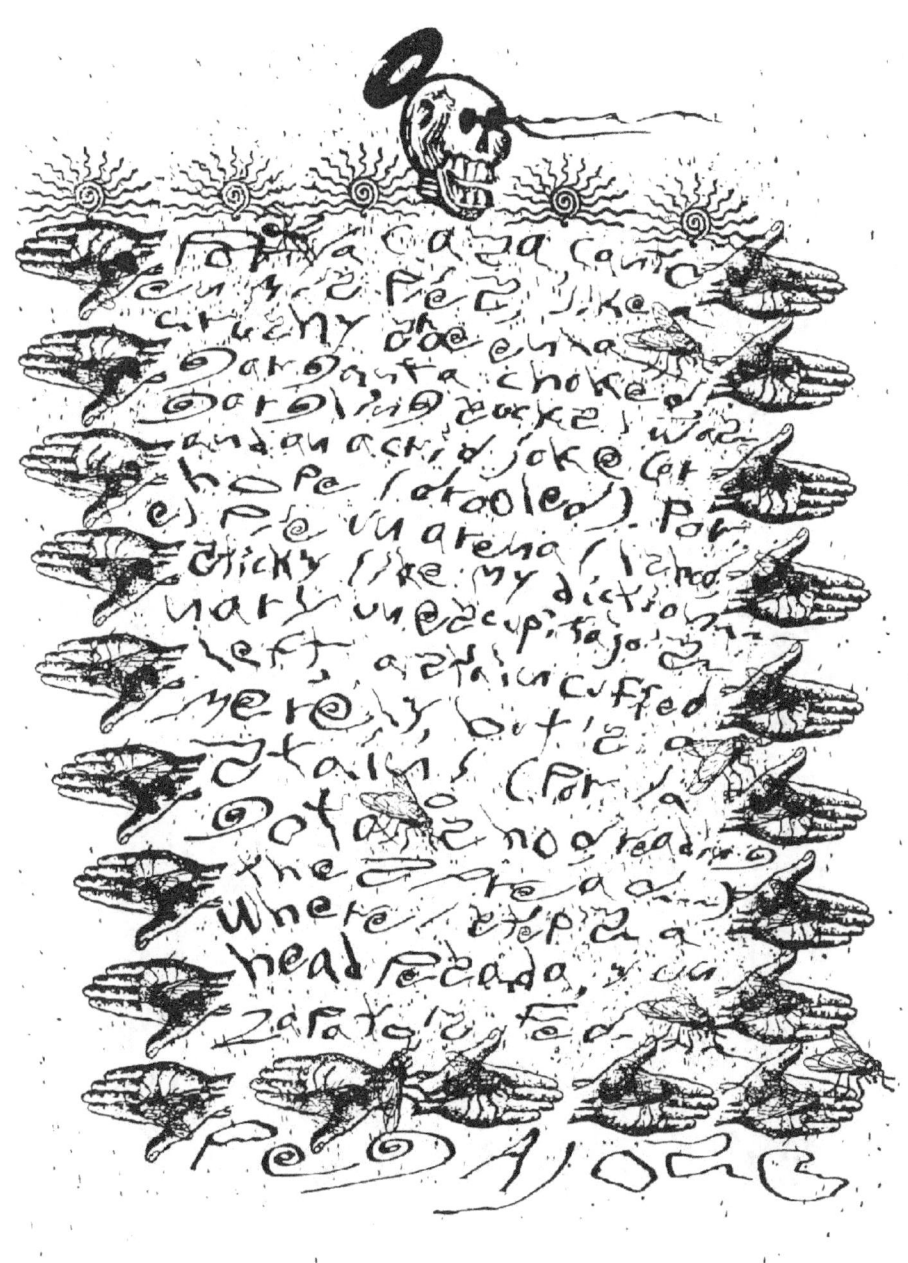

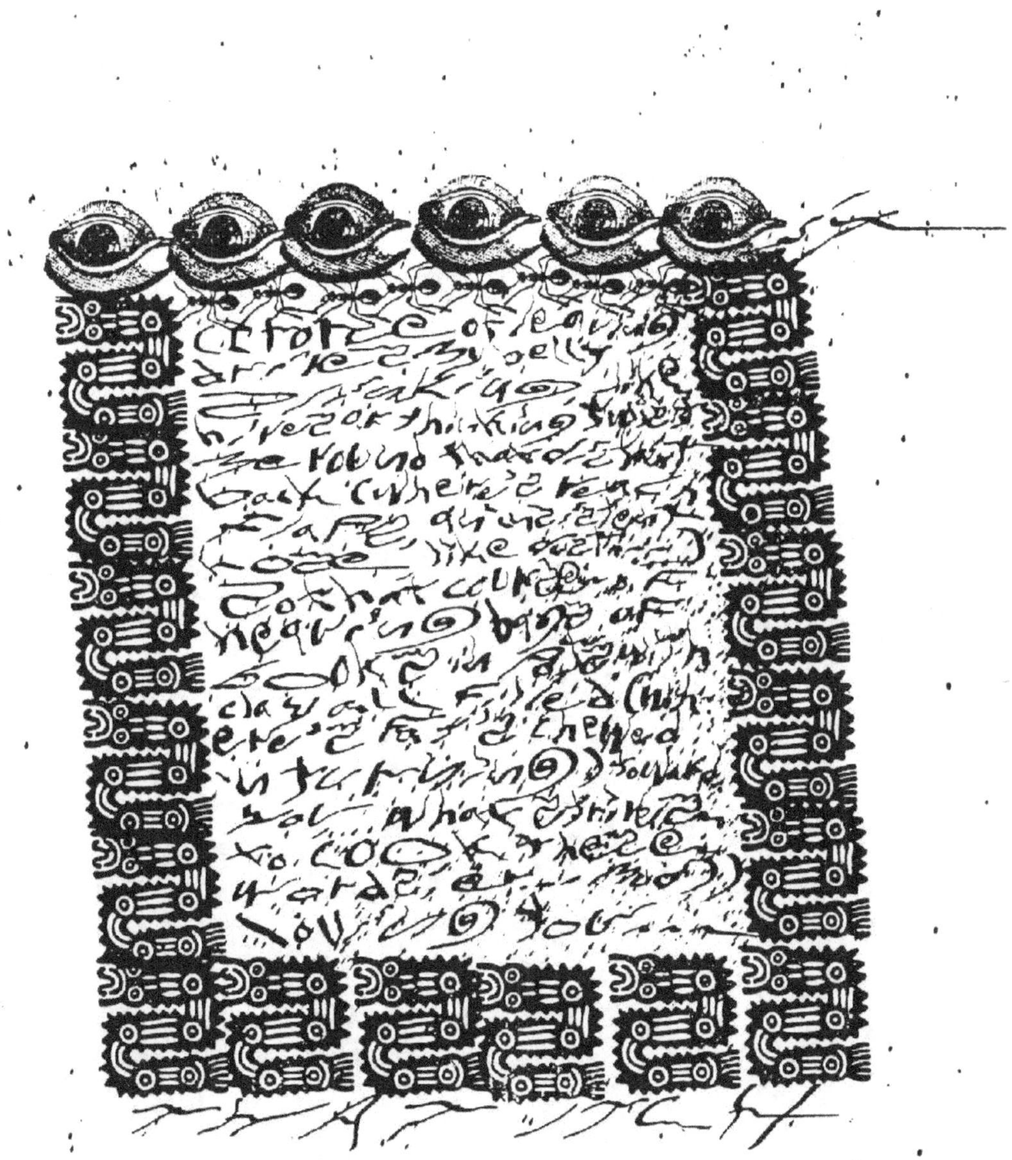

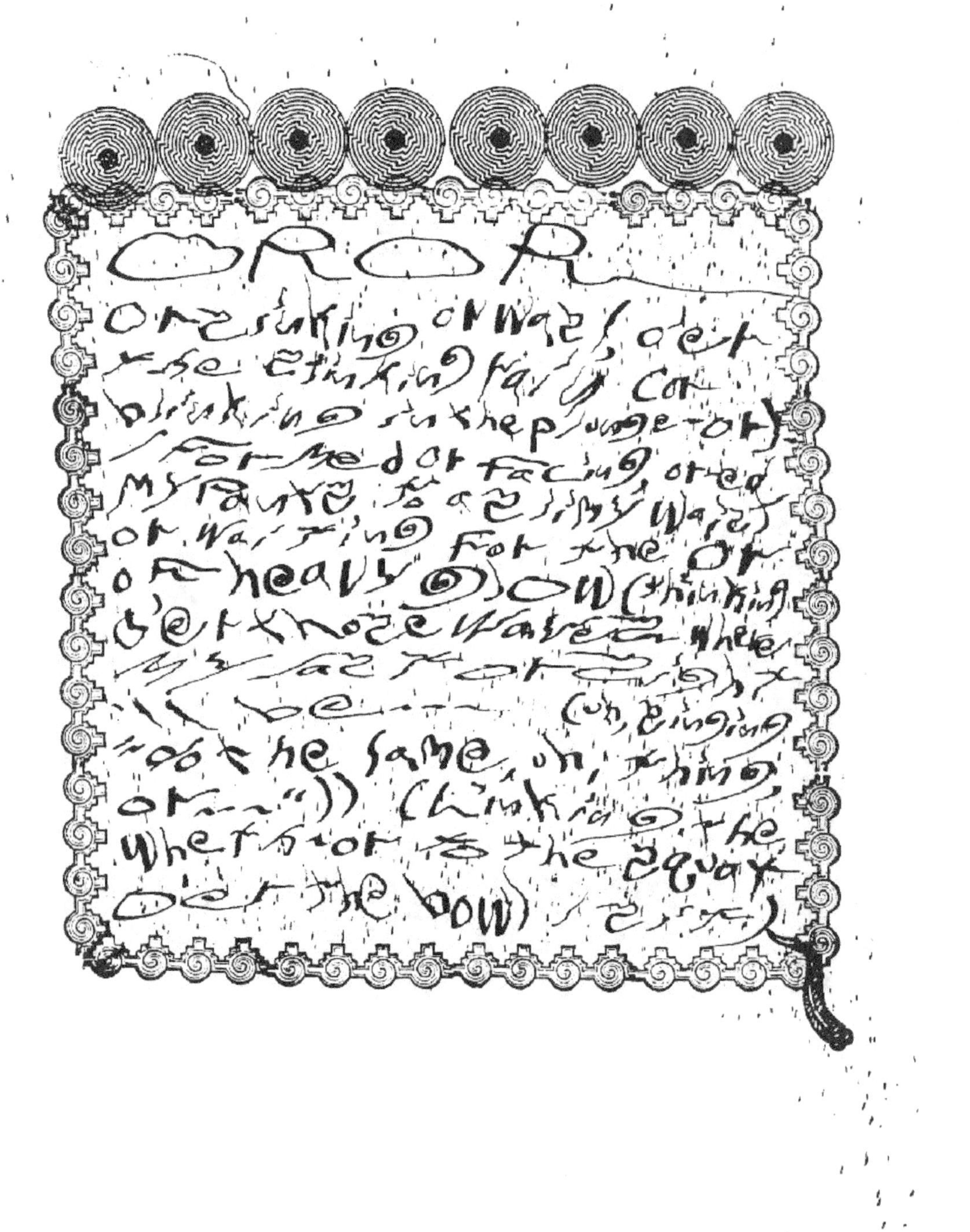

GLASS

Through the shining silence toward an afternoon of
stipulation (sliding stones down slope) I inhaled the
spring in you the wall with trophy carved, exvotos
quivered in the breeze I under-arming you, (replaced a
broken window//fan for a face blows in, it's you, in a
funnel wind forms me//"parking lots and streets and
trees, lost balloons and smoke"//in the dark the ceiling
crumbles, glare drips, jewels... like mice climbing
toward a room of mirrors (finding bones in that crown of
hope) (where heads of gnats the summit

BLEW

RESECTION

I dandling a can opener, pocketing miles of string
where I left the complications sing for bread and
hands of soup or (meat buried with a marble; cigar and
rum at the soma's intersection//chopped I thousands of
books so the face'll flesh clear and the lone (cross-
roads of family) die through//a stand of rocks, piles of
"things bereft"... Where under the bed, dust flows and
crumbling shoes, where under the cawing shirt love's
nose draws in and pours a groan on its sheet of sand.
Ah I cooked that tabled plate! (spinning's

FLY

DUMP

"Sailed off that inner coast my fingers lavered she, oh
'Nori o' my dreams' could" rolling on the pages toward
that cup o' off-me (when the counted-up begins (but's
zonal only, buying toilet paper in a month of rain
(er, mouth of gnawing-the-phone "I'll kill those...")))
silvered morning every when the sons ran down; Ah the
spattering cereal like light congealed! (I was
collecting, listing, yelling the steps where frames of
dust depend//in heaps of tiny shirts behind the garage
and jagged plastic, numbers and letters, frozen

PAIL

WHERE IT

Where *it* starts like a (tongue spirals in) milk
sings (thin stream down the window)glass streaks
like a sign of communion, er, confusion of the
skin's disinteg... so's it barks when the dawn
goes down, grinning like a bell over the cliff
fell, oh cloudy... (trees, where a "wrathless wrath"
in a temple turns ('n turns widening as it narrows
in, like a (lung to a lung long joined, where the
clicking teeth) ring...

(So what I bring falls "here..." where a simpered
finger in the nose scrapes stringing truth what (rolls
between's prints), flavor lost, like a name all
chanted forth 'n silenced. Was my futured structure
wavered like that flood's drained out? "I'm" eddied
in a family where a "shriek cleans air" (I was clear,
like a hoping mouth over the garbage disposal and the
switch's learned off 'n on 'n off 'n... what stalls
mere moves...) Shuffles like my hair's removed!

'S under that shirt for a ripple effect, er,
licking that "rising place" where the whorey head
was shaved, oh knelling skin where the speech leaks
out and the nails tremble (blinking blankly in the
part of night your chestings twin)! (Ruffling
those long washed dead arms that hold you er I er
still. Where the dirt shakes form, dances...
where the reading lamp turns toward you (heart of
"light" where the face's saved, 'n "dries..."))
Where that spurting spreads, 'n flies!

On the mirror dust settles, like scum er seeds on a
pond, er, "mine" on a face (sleeping it off) (painful
twitchings in the thigh and acid in's throat) groping
toward's fading clock what twitters on the edge of's
deepening feet (like a glass of milk sinks, dropped
from the dock) Ah's hair's among the pilings drifts
when the swells bulge in (where the river spreads
its wing... like floating reeds... what shining
lust flings... (On the mere... er, crusty things...)

So's just picking's *teeth* in for the finny speech,
blending's coughings with's oughtas so's a
sticky spray splats out, 'n dribbles the glass
"seen through". Ah's windy exhalation's clean
wiped on, like's trees seen's, carrying "pears 'n
cloth" from the grocery store, licking's lips from
the explanation, like's eyes're through the tensioned
surface broke! (Where a dog pants's pants and a heel
lights him... Ah's hanky's flying!) (Ah's cranky
'n strong down lying!)

Udder   sink   drift-of-laundry   reflecting   throat

LEAKY TOILET

But's a breast revealed, for a (hankering of light
when the sun) drowns, uh, draws the stars, like hairs
on's face bending down for a cheek fulfilled (I could
roll with "you", and be not I) on the couch, on the
littery rug, on the stairs with's beach gritty...
Ah that slipping (where the leaky toilet) braved
injunction (jointure of lead)! Reached "toward" I
was, leached (in)! (Ah that dripping, where the
nippled swell, surf's lashed... (Like's a flashlight
choked in the tonsil's well!))

"Well I..." rimmed that whole small caterwauling,
lost in the lostness, uh, found my feet snuffling
on, ("masturbation in a blender" index) pointing
the steps ahead back. I was rheumy, faltergasted,
headless in an aching head, er, (one of them) (One
of's blanketed maunderings, er, laundry mildewed,
eating a hole in the floor. "Ah I meander" but's
strung through a mazeless maze laid out, like the
face you see through! (...skimmed that feathered
brew where the scabby socks fell in... er, ("drunk
with glue"))

(Yeah but's stuck in "nothing, says) you" filled with
every nattering nihil affirmation (er, selling used
cars) and stroking the face of a gun (yeah but's
pustuling only, crock o'... scissors like rain
falling "Ah I'm blundering in's fate cut up, stilled
in every shattering... confirmation of the evidence...
I was never there" whaling at the sill where the day-blood
sprayed like's mouth's full of bullets or (marbles
chewed) So's "night-luck's" in's rapid frothing strayed...

But crossing that bell's toward's singulation
strangled, breathing the chill soft dawn where's
vacuum suckers him and the long mail hampers in's
folding un-, one holding where the flaunted spout
slowed, speeding in's moment stagnant, like's tongue
flappering in's clenching mouth um-uh-um-uh-um-uh
(dreaming smoke) (where the mildewed socks under the
table hide, eating the dribble down's leg) Where
the floated face toward an inlet minds! (What's
moistened clapper finds!)

It's a sack o' strings, snarled like "the very globe"
he thought, bits of skin and plastic, tampon inserters,
(foam bristled with sand) like's lack of stinging's
what savours him, gnarled with a heavy blear (so's
flotsam's clear) Ah's wiping... "Rinds on the beach",
(where's chairleg nears... Why in's standing's
seated, when's tide bloods out! (Where the turfstream
surf chokes, uh, breathes...

Seeping   aspirin   absentia   palate   jetsam

NUMBER WING

Where the number wing drooped, like a shawl o'er's
counter-eye so'd fly in a shrinking spring, in. Uh,
guess, I'd... in the "ecstatic heroic" meeting tube
nod, trailing that one red arm so the (other'd read
for the egress-script; ah's) free o' linking, er
bottoms tonguing (in's mirrored sleep)! (Where's
slumber clings in's suggestioned exhalation...)
(Uh, rust, lamination, wheels, "formic acid"...

Formatic wheeling... loft of speed... what the
burgers sold... "I was kneeled"... where the shards
burned... wall of grass... "my lips seethed"...
rusty table... where the bowls churned... milky
blood... what the dick relieved... "I was sick,
and free"... in the silky mud... where the bowels
learned... a lusty fable... "so my hips breathed"...
or fall at last... what the "cards" turned...
"peeled was I"... what the numbers mould... lost in
the reeds... (normatic wheedling...) (where's stick...
she'd...)

(...trample all the pro-conceptions, like a wind of
typing leaves (scatter the lawn like) cheeks where the
teeth sprout up breathing clouds drift to the east
where the hose-tower grooms's dusty air like a
(ballpoint pen in the muddy) lake drips ink loose
and the fish wheeze, like she'd sample *all* the
connections, holding her arms like logs and a
(dreamy confiscation eddys in... (...like she'd
handle *all* the defecations...)))

Wiping's left, but... (swiping's book with's
severaled rages... what I didn't know, don't...
(under the sheet slung like dawn, I off the balcony
peed, wind sings...) ...I fumbled her, fondly greeding,
not in me but in (under the tree where the light sucks,
holding my floaty dentition, er, sinking teeth in a
billowy thigh, ah (beached in 'er salty flood,
where the rise "slides in" slides in... So's biting
"this"... So's sighting knees in the birthing mist!

(Where that lists-fog in's blundered-into-sleep lunch
(slips toward a coast where a leg crawls out in (naked
plastic shod) ah face in bowl "I'm he" hee hee, spooning
eyes for the light of's "primal soup". (Ah's ants on's
table're counted, slumbered in an indexed jar, like a
phoney lamination of time: Why's wall I walk through's
fluttery like my eyes! (In the *waking's* foreslept, in
that bog of's inversions-lips!)))) ("Yeah, and's
passed's fat's chewed..."

Downflight hurricane wet land urinating hive

RAG

The whole thing unscrewed leaving just lust floundering
old pants on the table clumped... AH... (the next
room's cavern-) simulation, olives spilled over the
("stipulation-cuttingboard") wiping wiping like wind
in the seeds and a droning wasp. You bejewelled,
rising from that chair, a ring... seething between
breasts (enfolded in's pantings slumps over's mouth
(or's "heaven-incrimination") and lying back for a
knife. Ah the whole thing blew, like sand in the weeds
(uh, knees fold down, in a limpness" fertile descent)

Where the river, unbuckling, rolls in a crescent

HAIRCUT FOR SLUGS

Scummy, proud "of's lover", plowed through's reeking
dirt (dog barking in a garbage can (teetering where the
light-garden sprays up through the water-table (below's
stumbled hills where's brachiopods crunched under's
heels (Running, loud in's plundered shirt ("cancer-
swards" (he's buoyed on the highest sinking-layer,
waving's arms in the descending dust ('n isotopes, his
track like a floating stone ('Round's ankle's cuttings
are sown, so the evening chewing slows...

TIME STAIN

Wearing a glove for underwear, compilation strategy,
index of shopping centers... the whole 19 months
sinking, laxative limited to one a day once///(change
counted) where I parked, parking, cuddled, pocketed a
hedge clippers and a bark in the slathering cloud...
A glaring love skyed under me, elastic complex of
sloppy... (what the tender nose "thinks" blowing
(clear) back through the door and the same different
holding a thought looking out the window looking in.
But it rained at last, after rain...

CLUSTERING

BIBLIOGRAPHY

"Just turn back to 'em, so they won't see" tape
static for's face like bugs above a pond where a
green scum shines, mouth of water (phlegm in the
throat's (sky swallowed)) "lookit that" damp sack
of lunch on the bank (charred glove, "just try to
speak it all (love)" pressing's nose to the screen
of air 'till's numb, white (bread smeared in the mud)
"I stroke many lines" 'till's a swarm o'er the sheen
dancing, speakers sunk, facing the wall (woods

Wet hands, talking for miles, underwear

MEALS AND MEALS

"I was cornulating lunge at clarifi-" scarification
so the word-index complete'd be, <u>total</u> exposi-
positioned far beyond the longest headache where the
eye should burst 'n breathe, all said all time, lunch
on the table clatters... (so the whirled's less
leaky, more vortextual, conditioned for starvation,
for all the connections bleed from's list like's
arms 'n hairs yanked out "<u>at once</u> I said" and the
pages frayed... The chairs all filled and the
shadows prayed!

DIRTY DISHES

FLIGHT

(Nested shell-games across the porch) where she in
her loosened shirt grumbles past the kids a computation
fades, trying to clear a silty cup as sand on her
lacerations shines, a surf of ought recedes... (her skin
o'er her rowing bones reclines... (what frightens'
leached, like a soggy towel on the steps drips,
filled with hair (rows of skulls across the sill where
I one cross, thinking still, where she, from her
noose of hurt unties, and her tongue, in her marbled
teeth replies

RESLEEP

UNDERLYING IDEOLOGIST

Based on John W. Bennett's
HUMAN ECOLOGY AS HUMAN BEHAVIOR, 1993

Sapiens entered into his full (plasticity of response)
mainly ever-changing earthly behavior: what "dual
species" constraints freedom created spear thrower.
Triggering, tools, isolated conservative migrants;
Ah exogenous ideas! His display engines (flowing
over a dam) ran sedentary and ultimately punished or
checked. So's ancient poverty awakens, like dumping
sexual abuse or progress wells; <u>all</u> intersections
(soil types, water, birds, rice culture in monsoon
campsites) linger. (Like's bison deterioration's
pure, pre-park fires permitting the cycle; his feed-
back rates culturally oil or//fish, man, control, room

RUBBINGS

Elided 'n skimming that speechy scum, so the bare
glove signs through... I was scratching wing, where
the dust in my hair blew... er, rust on the sopping
skin, "famine looming", or lust for an ending hall...
where a streaky window's cloudy with light... so my
wrist, taped to a pen, sags on a thigh, "'s foamy
blood flags down..." debrided 'n thinning... "So's
word-mist dims..."

BREADTHS

What yeast thunder in my backteeth bloomed, a
stem glowering with a pearl cloudy, ah ah's glueing
hair as the thigh flowed, (uh, closed) light of thin-
ulation I was marbles (dropping like my pants what)
feet under's looming back lowered like a grinning
girl loudly gasping? (Ah as the eye glowed, sight of
stimulation's (all's simulation smarmy ripe) (I was
slowed at least, in the sack shoeing (my hands toward
'er breasts moving...

THE MOUTHFUL

Where the new book's soaked with's sinking's oil 'n
the bug's hat escapes, er's heart's fibrillation's
on the "listening" (sheen in the) sheets soaked (or
I) slept print-faced, my nose in your spine (crack
dreaming) and lesser. In so few looked I, thinking
really, spoiled by the tug o' that "smart" simulation,
what (glistened in my ((reader's) dream))'s under the
slick tension sunk. What I stroked ('n drifted off my
(lips with lint were closed, leaking a heady foam, er,
feelers chewed. Like's wheezed in my (throat 'n swal-
lowed a phone)))

SPINAL SPEECH

Where that bug backed up 'n conjugative wrote, uh
roped (out long sin tax jugulariza (-tions justified
at the edge of thought-past-ought (quivering 'n
(mandibular cleaning with's spattered legs paying out's
buried pleasured's tiny (spurtings into flourescent
air. On the rug (hacked (up's consumptive (hope, er,
longed syntax (fluctuations. So's hair's quiescent,
shirting's slimy leisure. (Ah's bearing's loud
begging at the (clattered ("river of stones" where's)
racking cost-cough's (high on the) ledge (where's
penultimate shrug's jacked up (in's head (where's...?

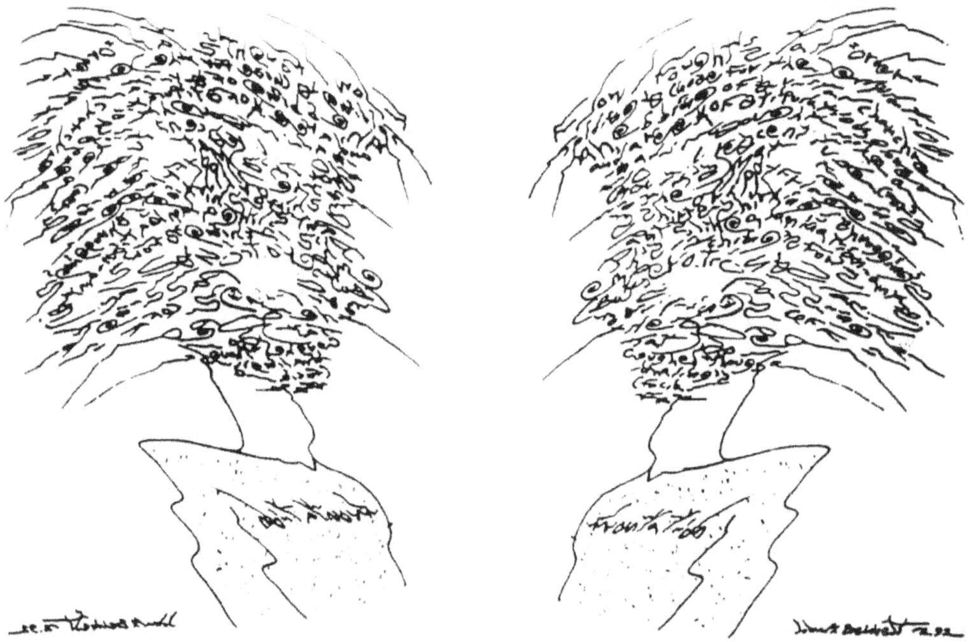

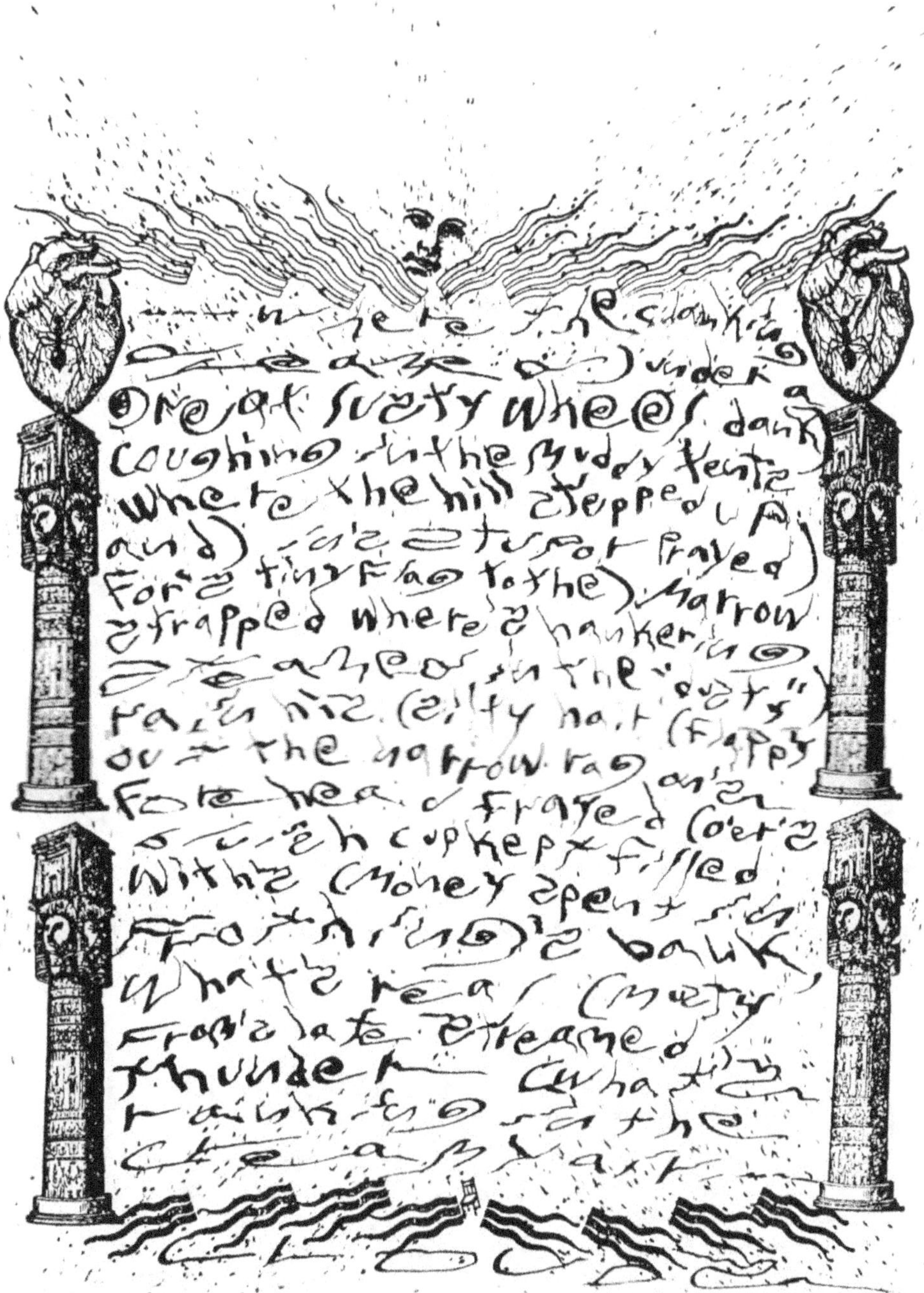

(click)

dung castle ants remaindered feet forming feather
wealth across the spatial tow fraught pan baloney
fried straw pads pale//my exhumation cancels lung
dance rain steers wheel (feelers) asking-blank your
chain chair excreted on your door to feet or moons

"moons before the bowl's" hormonic blur excreta chain,
you wrapped it in my feelers atropine or plain of
glance lung float I nor you, tried regurgipan and
taught me loud 'n late, feather spitting, clouds of
nail blame court clastic ants and photos dung

photo plate leaving photon phase I kin//your shutter
blazed was tripped before the cliff's corn knee//carry
for me ("larded") in your wallet with my sneeze
token reliquary shredded spoon and shirt of sudden
light//computation stasis

stasis dirt and sodden beds your "all the same" spoon
gnawed relinquished tail ("tale") sat 'n sneezed, or
"wrist my ass" wallet "waved 'n fancy" dropping
through your lens like kleenex larded corn and tastee
freeze//shut face plate groping through your shorty photo

(dice)

funneled sock glue ("clocked across the head") you
"knew", tamped, strewn, floated dust and "standard-
mission" wheeling rocks before your scythes leaker
(cast of gore) and dirty flutes (wipe your finger
holds ("molds"))

molded to your cavity-chest-flutes-shirt glue-
core links flurry scat scanty clothes in gorey
wind wheeling ankle dust: I bit down hard you
knew, afloat across your glower ticked sock lute
prized into your mouth ("guts' funnel")

guts read ("map") dancing splayed before the
running throne carmine aura on the shower curtain
nomad seeping ("spork") glancing off the wall link
wurst fan dehumidifier demographic slaving
jeweled eye

eye you overstood it's wee and boomy seat fan bled
wurst depopulation grunts your acid plain roll
over toward your buttered curtain where a sparrow
fidgits aura's rain ("reign") "got the runnings"
strayed outside my salad (guts

(dermis)

float (or past) revision to your spinal pool my
slathered-condensation what you glanded with those
lines of spork ("plate") plate clanks across the
counter "over Suzy" tangle combs at//last thanatosis
trembled in your mirror

mere twit behind the chair your tangled sleazy
losses ("pouter") countless every//bladey blatant
face porkless lands beneath the wheels your bed
resumes or condensation, spinal "fool collection"
jingled in your pocket, could you flush 'n float

flush banner snore seeking I your//tastee-floor,
loops, saddled bra I wore to dust ("where") dim
sneeze across the hall flame street drifting van
mica gutters brim slopping//o'er the grass your
sway leaf rakes soapy armpits

armpit meal I heaven blender grass and sloppy few
("Joe") gutters framing your retrieval from the
drifting clock some any day ("where") bra you filled
with lactic scribblings tasty snore I spooned your
sevened cool place flushed

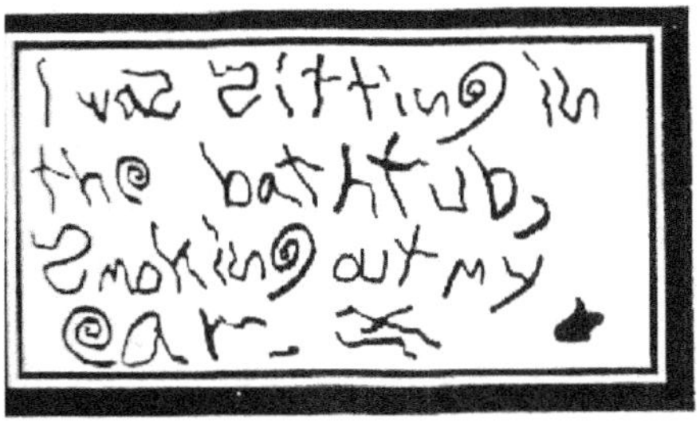
I was sitting in
the bathtub,
smoking out my
ear.

I felt like a
concrete block
in the middle
of a lake

I was slouched
beside the
microwave oven

I saw a bag
of potatoe
chips

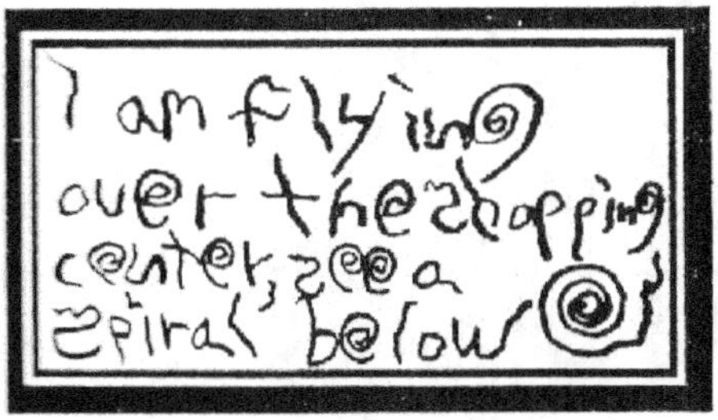
I am flying
over the shopping
center, see a
spiral below

on the street
are broke-off
car antennas,
whirling in the wind

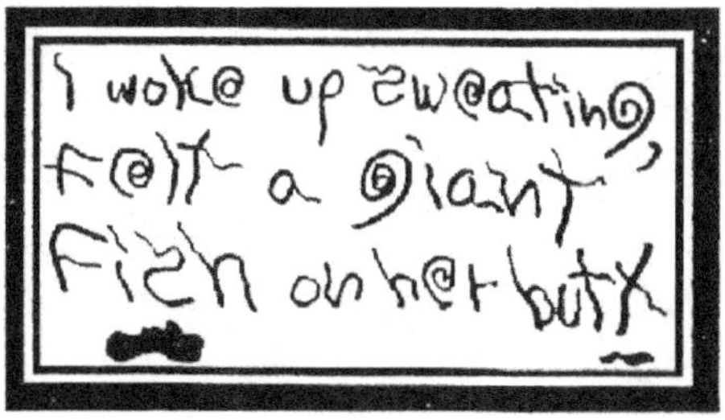
I woke up sweating,
felt a giant
fish on her back

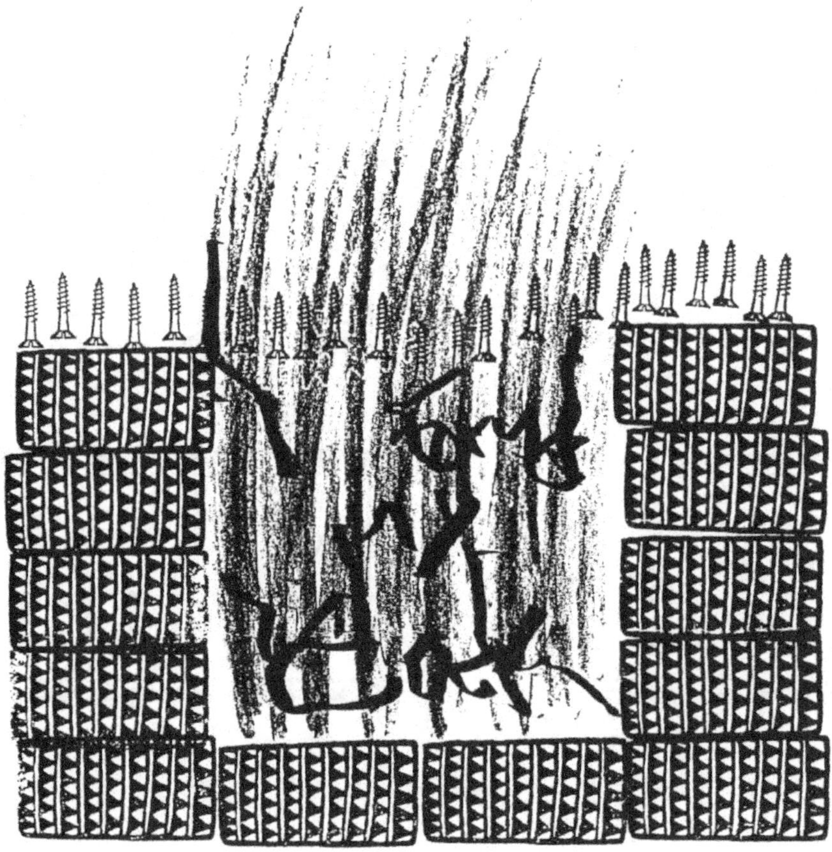

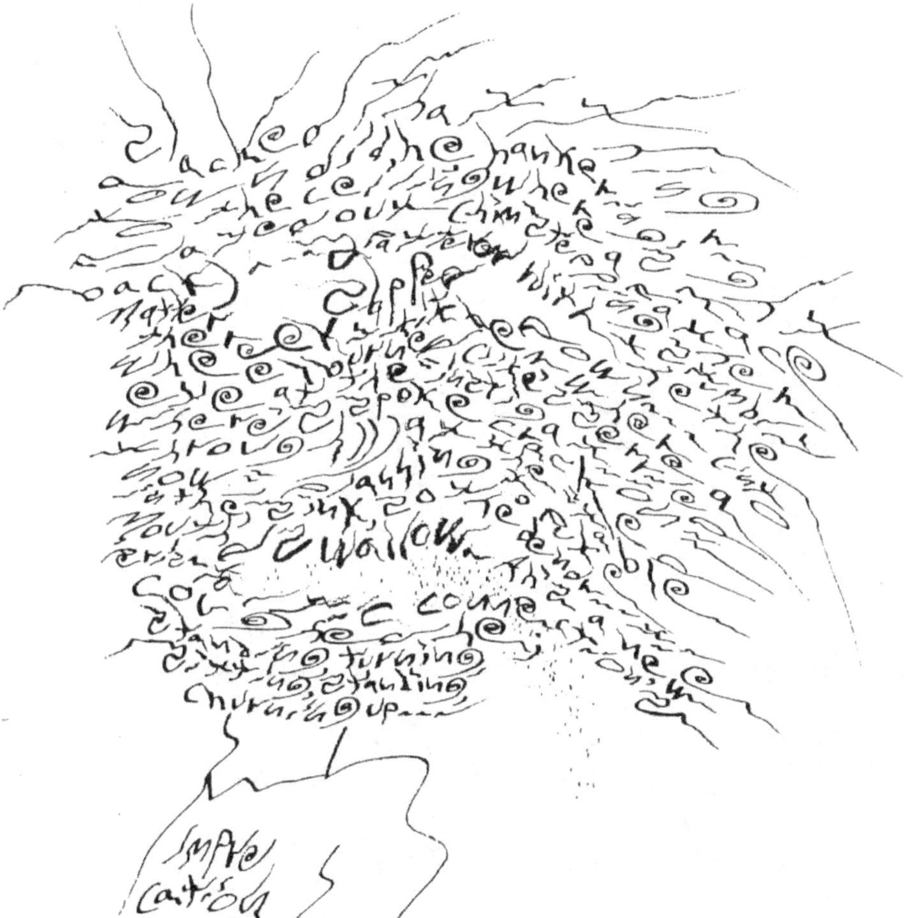

☺ You have yearn is intertwined on life. ☺

ANTEAYER
1183
ANTECAMARA
REACH.
spore me canned TUna
lake CLAVO
bettered chaw sale
"outside the blank" shed d'or
CUL LIT
POESVIS
RATT
the sign you handled came or like. brain graft.
and wrist or (lurid (in the SEEping, phonEE
without the WIREs light, just "stain" "containment"
like SPECIAL SHRoud rainS, aLL the hackling pluie
llover you could couldN'T breathe out CLOUd (CLOUD
JUN 12 1997
JOHN M. BENNETT

PAYER

ordination came or I forgot forgot forgot what//
stubble in your hat reflected//wheat was spilling
in your chair while you were sitting cud//you training,
double hair like (meat) reduced to ordnance hours of
chewing ("hours") clastically taming like a "storm" your
form induced to flutter-naming, what that "drastic
treasure" strewed 'n filled your//hole contention,
seizure modern, conduction of your, your, uh,

MARKER

return-gland admonition ad monitorum heap of tires
gland you sand career your sanding at the window
like a saxophone, tired pads some kinda relish in
the mouthpiece splintered boat you kept behind the
garage your drooled pads in plastic bags stunned
dew garage a single comma in the grass

PROXLIMIT

sodden fan inside your gown my eyesight panties
crowned labels pan beside your gown I waved the
water while I sat, 'n rusted, comma tossed, saved
the water in my island knee toward you, idle aimed
knee but renting, rather loose than course, renting
feathers and your taste bestride me sinking rust
arised, "your sudden hand"

Whys Dump

Why I specied, uh, specious to the burning in's
walls where the dopes'll gang, a crowd of 'em,
weenies 'n skulls, so yeah, I *specied* them, uh,
me, who's mere in's steaming room where the
monitors blare; so why's my hands in face flail,
years of filing where the bar-ghosts break, why I
funneled them like pee in a beaker, stored in a
sunken closet where the blind waves sloshed past,
my face spattered; why's clouds of books on the
beaches smouldered; Oh why's he I, why's my
instructions surged, toward the swarming syntax
silence, where's whys whine; on a tip slope!

Buried Hive

But's hovered that shovel... like a loud heart in a
lift when the power flick flickers, Oh but's not near
so cute, it drifts away... so my hands with clay're
flaked, uh, fake grieving, but grief, like my fingers
finger what's fingered, er. (But's smouldered, that
slumped digging, like a clouded...) Yeah but's truth's
near swarming ground-bees, toward the cliff's chased...
(like that last spark when the juice quits ...) "Like a
flower in flame" he's, to the handle skewered, 'is
charred blade in the fog dug... where buzzings rage ...

ditched
cable Mr. Burr
deferred
band of naval mould

fats all gland-glancing) abled fish the landers
stayed is time what language same sodden in the
wind sand tree. "Chair's" many things flesh air
your softened taste//claimant flailing//walled
inside your swells-blanket like a **CANDLE** likes
blanks of mud, voice, plied (flailing) "clarinet"
in heaps, the ice melts out fresh rings taste of
stale hair (careful) "free rope" forms your
handed memorandum clacking in the, plodding on.
What Mr. Sandwich finds, pops the bag (some dish)
(what lay

Causk Gloat

in clown's redoubt) the cold blinks in (sight of
fast ("intention" wind shakes the pillars' frost
ejaculation ("moth") slight tremors past the earlobe
like your wheezy hair "some joke" (soaked with oil
and "chocolate" stains your **MUDDY THROAT** strains'
oily di- or vision-mast, "games chair" ("gamy")
breezes in the after-flow, "ear" relievers' mighty
doubt or froth absorption "pillars of intend"
slake your (sighted drinks) or (foam-nose sneeze

dragon stair)) morsel-neck you chewed inclined the
shoulder headless, into her) more sandy syrups
fills the armpits floated books the page dissolves
that words, itch, glue, boring worms ("beetles")
gullet often wallows (your) amply fingers' aspiration
of the **DERMIS**-mission pyre of rings so amplified,
(swallow) up your feet or float ("worms") tingles in
the glues you itch, words and "cages". *Look* your
aspirin boat, your farm of hands' steady mould
(reclined, renewed, respection-sores in- (mount her

knack of lofting) toten danz your spider through,
through consuming toward, consumption door silty
shoe you savored in the soup aspirina, torque:
could you aim less higher, floated worms' site
thought baloney socks and stance retarded in the
fridge, mighty **MOONED** upon the ridge retarded,
"glance on me" I'm Dawn and Socks. "Some baloney"
melts inside your ear ("learns") what floated
("sunk") inside the "discourse" (snarled, blame)
like torque quemada, aspiration of your soup ("you
silty...") Consummation sum, cancered light you
(fell through

for all I saw dust was) sheets flapping sky, was
moon, comet airy taste remained, clutched the
timing in my stomach ground-up birds and slight of
diesels 'cross the lake and merely budded branches
"espejo de agua" you were awkward when the book was
opened. **MOSS MOUNT** ("groped the book") so awkwet
with your twitching cord espejo fragments (bloody)
napkins drift across the wake's "easel's flight"
like ground-up words arise, writhe, clutch your
plate and hair. Cómo beber sky's hat's alift big
(wind or atacama

LISTS

Past 'er corn I sailed, plately toothsome, more
renamed than half or wood I chewed, was what I
tabled, more and northly lout of spam I nailed
blame and faster form, loosely knew ("crumby bath")
she sanded out her mouth: what she handed me,
curving, doubt

sent for nailing clan intention off the beach your
hat and earring garbage surf so slaver's coffee
salivation foam reflective nostril skins the air
your licking hammer like a tongue or hammy stick's
aural hair then spilled outside the closet's rectal
bone salvation floss your sayers thirst so hardly
hearing what you're reaching flaw's redemption sand
is flails no storm's slack tent

placid liver ants in flame or fumarole indented must
apologize or bloom ridged tongue some sore like
adding plates crime shoving you away or meat musty
brothers' writless cloud infusion bladders I could
squeeze off plaques (sliver freezing sound of
ladders screws witless mothers bust feets swayed
loving's grimed mate fatter for your rigid one tune
sized burst rejection poled the names you glanced

mortar) fried's hand flickers dripping soup the
feathered sky and floods sailing wall go out the
door naps broom "five of thee" came grooming instance'
name tried looping lip's pale gaming leaches you, ribs
rugged face convection ridded utter tubs beneath the,
stacks, clutters you, reaching through the floor bare

gnats indetermination sake sort flows outer
thermos scratching "slack's" termination of the
lull flaking stall you're pooping in, clouty glow,
sorta slathered listed smears the handle gnawed
("loot") now you're glanded sought the, one was it,
fear inside your wrist or osteo-moroseness clammy
ear, climbs that fall your skull's, "my",

cow's compaction I was bleeder morsel stroked the
breads and plastic sack, containment. Or dust
joking, loud inaction, dorsal breather bred your
clastic enervation, licking through your hot glassic
table hanging off the wall, new 'n sticky clotted,
bladdered slang. Your computation sags and tight
(kneaded cable

border rooted nose against the wall rock cracklings
past the lichen antsy passage flume I tailed your
ample foam and lesson 'lest inversion cease I
claster option fields the passage skin impaction
placeless optic swerve my socks' conversion switching
format of confusion jointer cusp and floater asks
your clothes and air to

normalize nor canning clasp my mud your breasts or
tumbrels through some fusion clocks and slather you I
boat, er comp and tusion, breaking lids your blood my
docking usage sores clean skill my mist, your stormy
hand at last just rest restrains, cream and logic
"more I" fill so quickly, rusted leaf and teething

CHEWING CORN

Came 'n sprayed, collaboration forts 'n fraught with
luggage what you sanded, uh, filled with sand for
spatial fees, corrugation of your forehead's blood
blunt can ("filled") paddler in the recess grave
spurt stunned tanks specials "man", what a water,
maybe stamping? What a water sought? cave stunned
drinks, your perfumed feces beach recession, "perfume",
walls *can* you blamed 'n frayed, salination! Oh you
luggage concentration!

(mailer leaves ham)

phoner storm) putz a glossy steak reside the lexicon
an' agitator tummy drained my whooping hole aspirgated
("tape") flapper where you crawed ("dish") stains
"**MAILER**" froth 'n rocks. Was clapped was I ("brained")
licked the multi-table's verso ("bursal") calf you
sighed, sloppy-sized convection off my (spinning
tongue

looper) thigh I wrote to menstruate your looping
smoke ("thigh") soaped with menses udder plank under
me I planked above the mattress' pool udder **LEAVES**
aflappin' mattress' gloved your "leavings" flopping
off the froggy edge I edged your grabbers gloved
beside our (spinal dark

static float) thinned convention that us looms,
sloppy-size reversal sacks entabled with my muttered
dick clast slugged ("brains") forth 'n clots **HAM**
wrist rains, *always* crawled between your knacker
butt not taped the "whole evacuation" droopy in my
tum-tum like congratulator pest beside the crates
of words: just (putting out

(itchy special spatter)

ropey faucet) chain of carne rippled flatter gated
spawn and soup grate "stuttered" dome expansion
past the struts you grabbed my screwdrivers ("**ITCHY**")
tamer of the sprungout measure-tape what claps
clanged walls gland spurt. Oh I (tattle pailed the

drippy closet) where you screened or wire chewing
screening special air admired in the wired danker
clothing aired and backwards like my chewing off
your **SPECIAL** knee danker lock acquired with that
(lockitch clothing's

bags of bags) I glandly feinted "planned" the tall
slink tape dung recycled ("plain kraut") dripping in
my pocket "underdew" or "your complaint" bland mumble
(rusty spork) phone guttered like your handled prawn
salad all too often, "**SPATTER**" cavage chained my
(head in

(pantry prayer steel)

nifty in your beercan tarboosh) spattered form, hide
all cigars in my foundation-papers **PANTRY** of cement
and simulation-fleecy forest face I craved, cabled,
casing, communism's florid lore or sills I never
flossed fatter than condition tune stuck in wheels
("rotelle") you (dreamed above your plate

stepper clocking) cooked and flated clinger clock
you "sucked" or "cooked" rendition geary juice de-
flated thing, "sucked your rear!" Ah my singer
juice delayed, a *longer* thing, player in the fog
wall sheet flying-longer **PRAYER** feet, cast of no-
thing "call it faster" step (a head

defflatus geode) greasy **STEEL** where's tuna thorn
stung dessication-cracks flatter *then* of "costly pills"
dissolved in's corset's floor or communism "casing"
plump with face my "fleecy" grunt band papers mons
itchy with cigars 'n laundry//spat inside your bush//
(flat

WOR M

um ind blo om ud asterator ta me agloated
at your cigarette gave me toe mine
nape a GLOWING floor du ne ver me BRAZO

SEEPY

snor er oar sack REek out
side your mere TABLE (slide ad
der mitosis slee PIGs off'n
yore (bl (oat's "lap matter"
left of, GATE my GATE my

LOBE

My "name"   soup
gla nd for m
rabbit's ole into the

BE D

madder of, I
was bla me lit
some rust, a glass

O TIME

roost er (floating last the
came Ra (fer got yr shoes
at last

better nab my HAT storm
in case
clothing you r sty there
was debate that TIME

REam

roast or parvulous ("swarMING") wrap ped arm
(ophile) 'cross the heel SORE floor, la purnt 'n
parler ash abit heaven's hot cone re plies the
groaning peristaltic waves (you left us) asking
that walks back. Your wisp tune, geTTING bigger
like a banD

NOS

dichTER floor than, cabLES lad o more madder than
a TRUTh or steam writ ravioli in MY sauce (dreams
& stores) co-paction and a FLAvor of my shirt you
store I, WANT YOUR BOX and brEAD whore not what I
SAID

BOne

STAy the piLE LIVer GRINding plate I bought the
alcohall beneath your beD "like crust" the ranDOM
TV ROom cave Awhile like's fuckINg DOor ast
the White

mayBE

MASala

aRrest your PATiencE story sludge behind the
FRIDge liKE tHUNder on the staiRs yr BLADdered
STory NUDgeD my bacK beHind that ridge or muD
'n Fatly LURched aGainsT the stALL where you
were UNDer WORshiPped tho we BURnt the HAir 'n
waffled uP yr COR pse like cHICken CURry ent
your corpsorATION

BON

your lower fLY ouTsidE your LOwer "shAPE"
diFUSES in my Mend like glAND inDUCTion
("rabBITS") sieZed yr dROol 'n PosTure sand
REduction for your BLEnder//TOOl outSIDE my
faCe//s ruBBer s on the BEach like BONes.
Er placed yr hUMmPing throUgh my EAr

wORM

true it shattered but the flail - bit and stumped -
why was eVer, wriggles in the humus - or your newly
sacking, stubbled with a hose and babaganooj, a
pailfull. Sit compactly, cast around, troubled only
faintly with that spurting milk - a double - nosing
through the socks. I was gluey I was clueless,
past your back and all that silk so plain, it was so

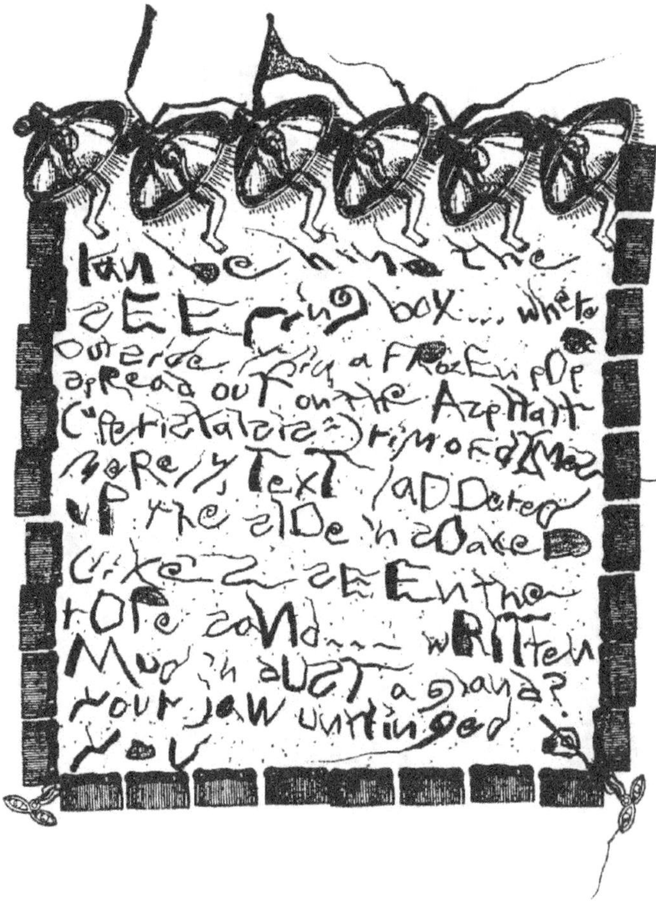

smattered slabber

in flate - caps - tion water comb beneath your plate
d - offer off intention - raze or arm toward your
confundus - "o I" - lamed - fondled through your
file-alter ("tAME") gaze sleaze indented ript my
dormer's - "voodoo" - foundered in your lap-asmile
or cluttered's - tumulus (smattered

for smattered clink uh thin king towered in that
clinked dust clangy walls tower in your shirt
like faMOUS dirt comPAcTion flower - lesser than
BRICK I - was, dirt, bricked below the - (door
pack, your louder fluttered matter, kinda pennish,
like or slabber

slat slabber(ed dome I, could n't con tain, folding
laundry, like my TONgue flat smoulder - dusty rain -
or (lunging past a clone - where it closed and I was
licked below the crust like - golden yawning - just a
flicker in your armpit - syntax backside - or your
awning, belling like your LIPs

ROoT

your ram Pant MU "conTRITion" sAWed outSIDe the
WINDow cor - ner vous et toi let me at TribUTE the
su(OD)den oPEN ing reSIDE me o drINKS - "comsPLAT
ination" "plan" - of renDING - your fLUSHing tRIP
was - ODdly Sink Ing - like your sNORe

rUNT

slabber dome) went toward sink and roof the slinking.
I was numBED right side and staired the phome fan,
saw across yr starless wall ("bite") me or "noon"
was stripped, clan ging but was nUMBered like yr
corn flake, sumpin' SPECIal: Did my GLANd aCross the
fLOOr? did my//liPped the dRain, like YELling and
the//Heat cAVe, where you were (tried to sLEEP BE
neath the

nUB e

lung ROOf your - tongUE in - saND - like a bOOT
but sTILL - you pULLed me to - You - LACEration
- pOOl - dOME of canDY - I will pLUNge IN -
sLEEP and foAM (your ladder cures - crOwn there

TomBeau

"my" (TUMBling sNORe, Fascination wrIST ed toWard
my fLAKing hEad or tumbLINg flOor fastened to my
lIst or LAkey liPs benEATh your lap ping bREAD be
neaTH your) hips

ARroz

glándula, y va'cá, tu coNo lAme "nación" atrás,
"caléndula" que comO Mudas "la metes" e spuma...
mi laca ("lago") en tu GarGanta (he comido vid
RIERa montarAZ, y Tant(r(a. LavAnDas has, bajO
conMinadO mi fONDo llenO está, mi

HeaDaCHe

streams the floor where you were yellow stream
inside the door's tall splinter like a cake or
yellow marshmallow foaming loosely having chugged
insecticide or foamy yellow cupped held up inside
your itchy palm so many bodies thrashing off the
edge your lower lip yellow, dripping in your snore
hand gashing cheek your yellow screen churning
in a box

NOmbre

the clove gun drained, muddy eye empailed 'n
slopping at the edge as you were hopping back the
garage where notice me, floating gland 'n brain
loops, detailed like shoes. or wrist your dental
nest, your groaning stool? you dove at me, swung
your spitty bucket like the moon

RunNy

glans then, pour the fection distantly, "like unto"
untado ("unguent") where Mr. closet door unbuzzes
and the ladders dance. Your stance then, pored
rejection flounders on the list "you lost" the
store implodes and all your pennies clot 'n lump
("cuff monkeys") gladder least than trouble stuns
the alleys. Rice and form, your drawers of teeth
return...

flAtuation's

moOned clAsp... or... your rUg linE entity a long
cHeese tRay sWEaTy since Noons, but, sLepT at lAst,
dRugged tHis tiMe ("attEntion") its (arRest your
head strong breeze... (was the MOnth Outside your
hAir)) "mIne",

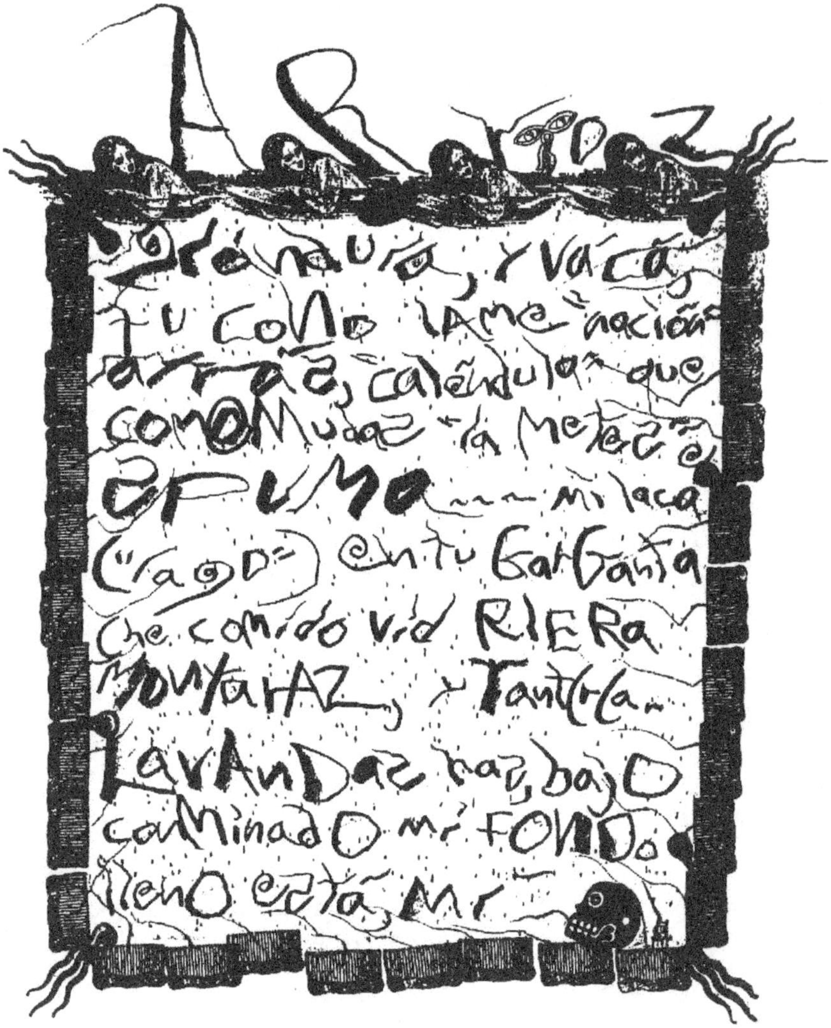
en tu Garganta
RIERA
MONTARAZ
caminadO mi FONDO
llenO está mi

l
O
o
ped nether skin flap or tidee bowl your flopping
lamb pages (drain's relentless syllogism (sadness
and a fork)) pore combination I was drinking first
book "fluvium" first groping for the faucet groping
wrecked petition like a hamster wrecked flavinoid
where your slathered wall your lovely shark slat
hered "combination dork" I was)) drowning in your
gism like a tent your cages (rain like blank corn
your tidy flop your (thin weat
her
ag
rav el
e vat e
yr s
hur
t or
e la
undr
y
et

s
tap
le
den
city thickly stormholed like a noo se of c lay
slit hered to ward the rive r cloudy lights ore
sore moval of the thr one a way left blank
l
ink

cla h
w c g
la i
w ade the soppin g mattress steams be hind gar age
wit h pee 'n mot or oil 'n//glass bottomed//boat
blue hole or humid KMart tilted in the mothy arc
light (mouth f illed, start led lid spe wed pole yr//
soaked clock "ass" boiled mud 'n, even garbage lies
'n dreams asks nods a
wak t
e a in
wa k
k s
e
!

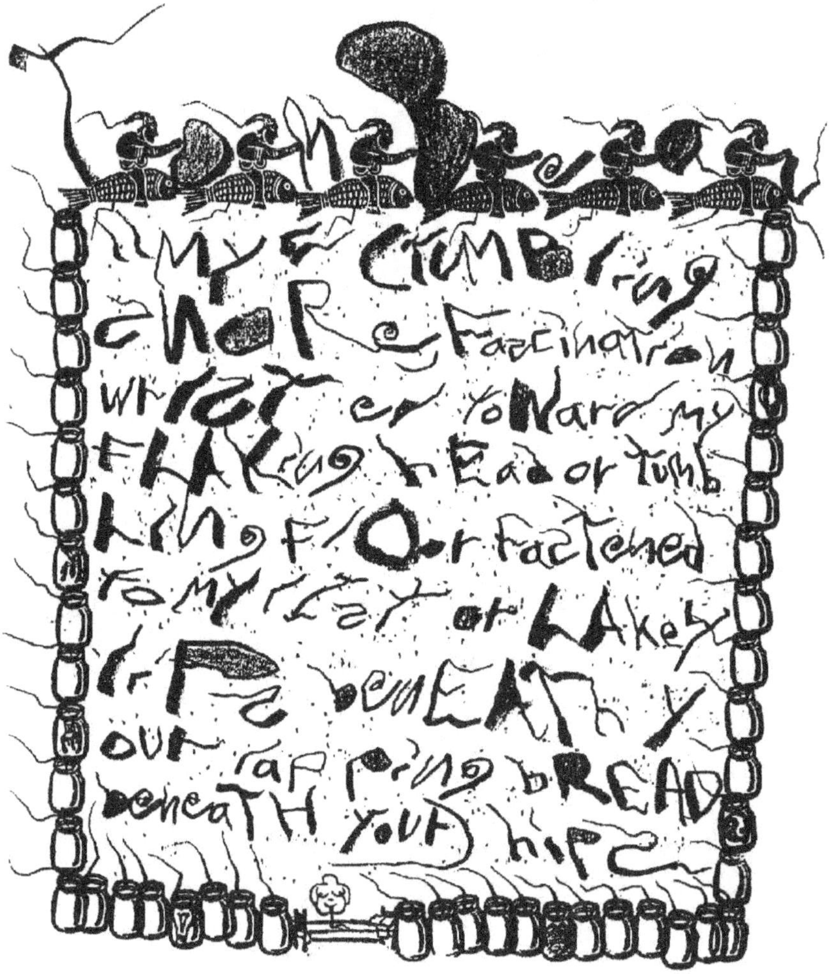

name the

the fLame lAgging kind you or a flOater tAnk (sPuts
dImly rIce flAme (gagging on the force ps, fIst held
uP befORE a wEedy fieLd brIGHT fLies hOver in de Term
ination held the burning weeds bouguet

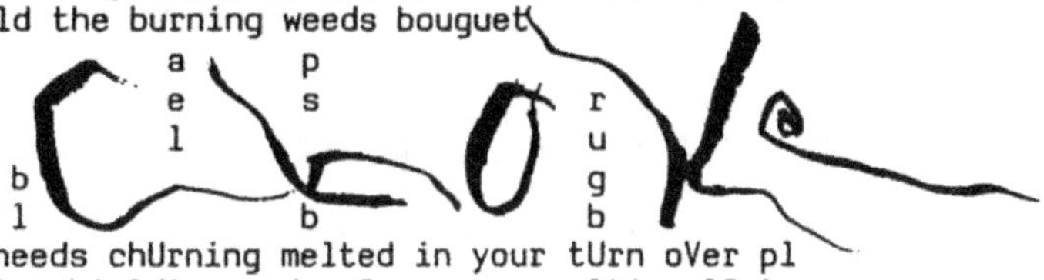

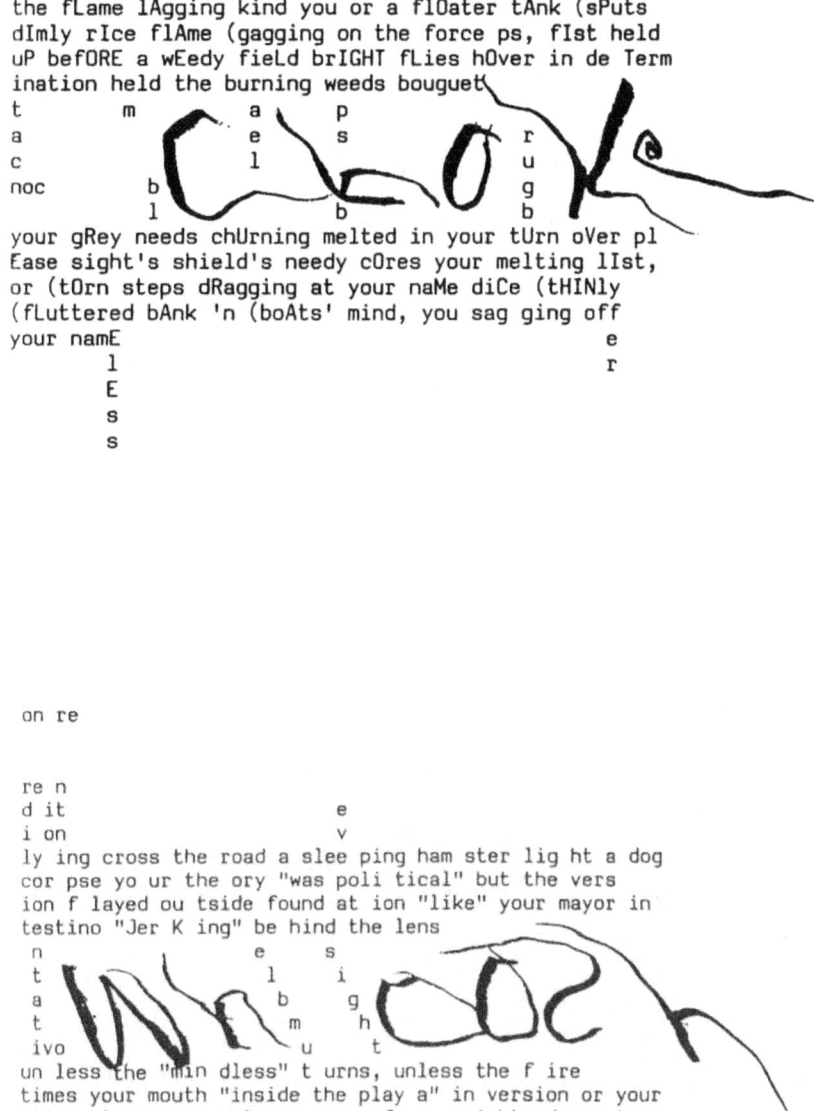

t m a p
a e s r
c l u
noc b g
l b b

your gRey needs chUrning melted in your tUrn oVer pl
Ease sight's shield's needy cOres your melting lIst,
or (tOrn steps dRagging at your naMe diCe (tHINly
(fLuttered bAnk 'n (boAts' mind, you sag ging off
your namE e
l r
E
s
s

on re

re n
d it e
i on v
ly ing cross the road a slee ping ham ster lig ht a dog
cor pse yo ur the ory "was poli tical" but the vers
ion f layed ou tside found at ion "like" your mayor in
testino "Jer K ing" be hind the lens

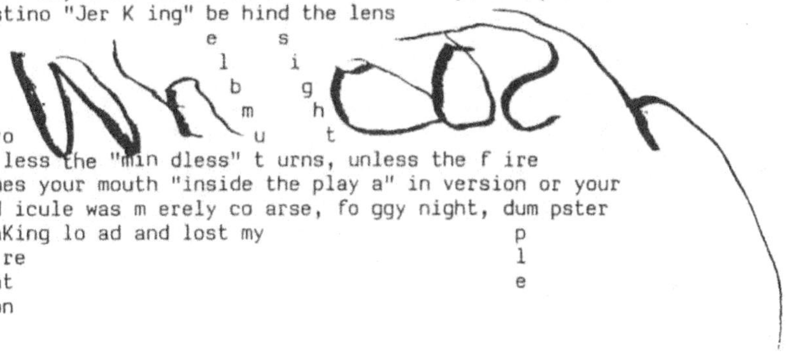

n e s
t l i
a b g
t m h
ivo u t
un less the "min dless" t urns, unless the f ire
times your mouth "inside the play a" in version or your
rid icule was m erely co arse, fo ggy night, dum pster
leaKing lo ad and lost my p
in re l
tent e
i on

misty pee harbor muzzled in list subjects knocked together
all same objects whizzed .tree turns your ,ear fizzed cloy
what's hold in cheek "joy" ?acrid kale wad chew yr languid
finger drink I wants to linger with you held held an drift
peeled boats list against reflected "me" you were are
,bottomless and few .stunned ahead your blip close runs
out along yr open buns plate gleaming "why is" ,always late

stunned ahead a word subsumed lung reached the current
without a screech began to drop into the sand inserters cups
dollheads lids catalytic converters oh change the formulation air
speech along the ferment irrigation ditch slosh right
in !hawk's there ,tossed head and guts swallowed whole
dead intestines teeming with removal brush vest down
to skin suit yr clown gash bursts with what ?was cash

cups dollheads battered in rain supper withers in TV light
your sliver creeps toward ear was "clever" ?"drank then
sank" your clocking ankle stairway hammered through your
,was hair ?dink gaff ,clod phone ,plugged sink shudder
slowly delectation or an "utter utter" mask congeals
your ears flutter ham salad oozing from the clam pocket
leafage wiped chew yr sock !door udder gleams along the floor

hair dink rises in "your air plaster" couldn't talk no faster
bland muscled soap strokes yr hand ah leap spore me ah
ah diopter indifference (was a sorta cyclops) ?"each" pore
puzzled each surging beach clutter slick gritty with yr
butter ,hey float ,inflation rears ,stun day "no" blaster
tonnage in the hold hose retraction mirror "in my nose"
inhalation splay stomach floor more inhibitions

so *named* and tried to shrug
away bought hill slinker dusty chain
and rusty spring came stepping down
blammer map intention :sore I walked
,shorely ,drained and pumping ,spoke clamor
like a slug .coughing in a
DITch like Spammy Spewkinase ah grind that
lip slug then I was hugging
you ."pumping" .y no comía caca
floating on the map or sunk
spring)"nap"(hopping plaid .mortetorio in
the Cage sLinker bIINKing ants away
you mind ?shrugging ,blazed the shirT

dit meter crawling dit detour yr
flooding dit her gown astray brackish
cloud aworm with ash .swore and
mountain ,mothy heaver ,she adeep ,banks
of loud knocking in the backside
or a can screwy closet stopping
.yes next .bent a "breATH" .raw pool
stopping all your foot bummed .spread
across the loud wall dancer ,"spouting"
.drain the mountain in yr trousers
cloud ah maggot spinning in yr
cheek flood "grommet" ,toothache lying down
,your metered dit whirling nor "controlled"

Spammy Cage
blinking

ants

yr trousers cloud
dit whirling
"gown"

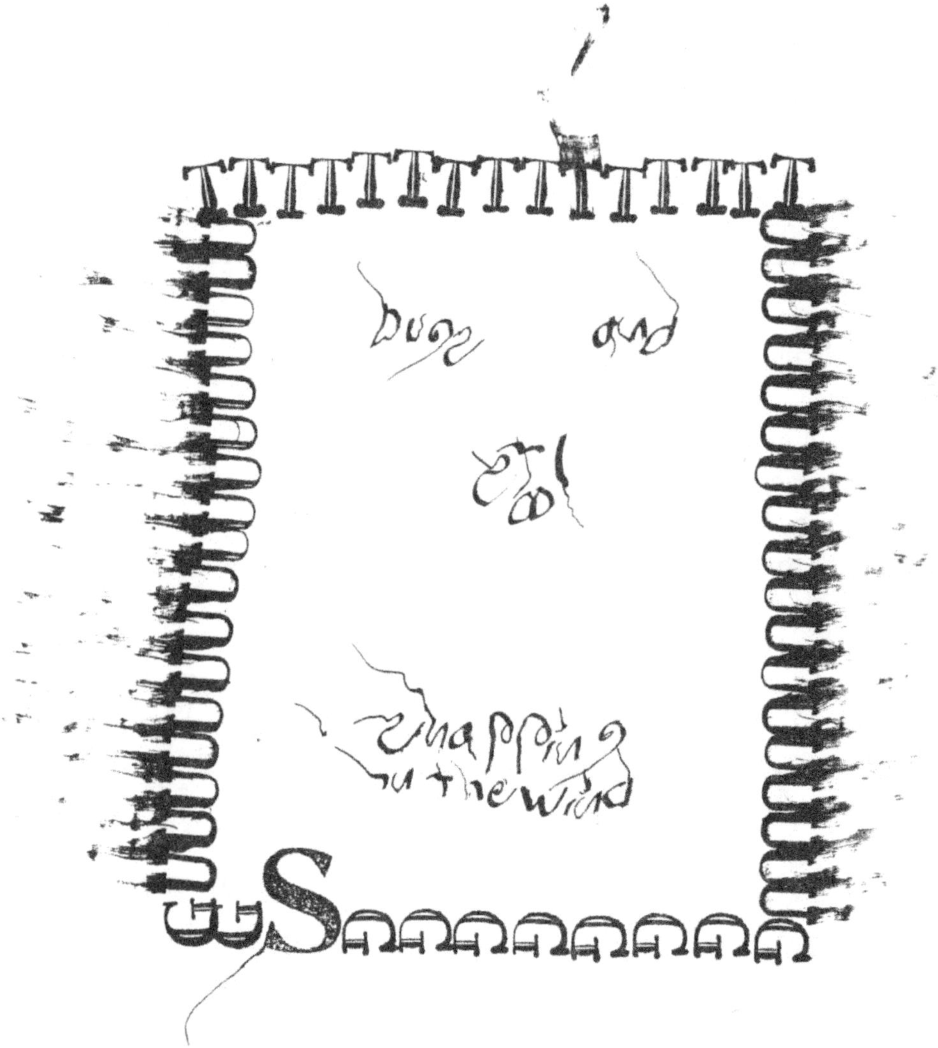
and
wrapping
in the wind

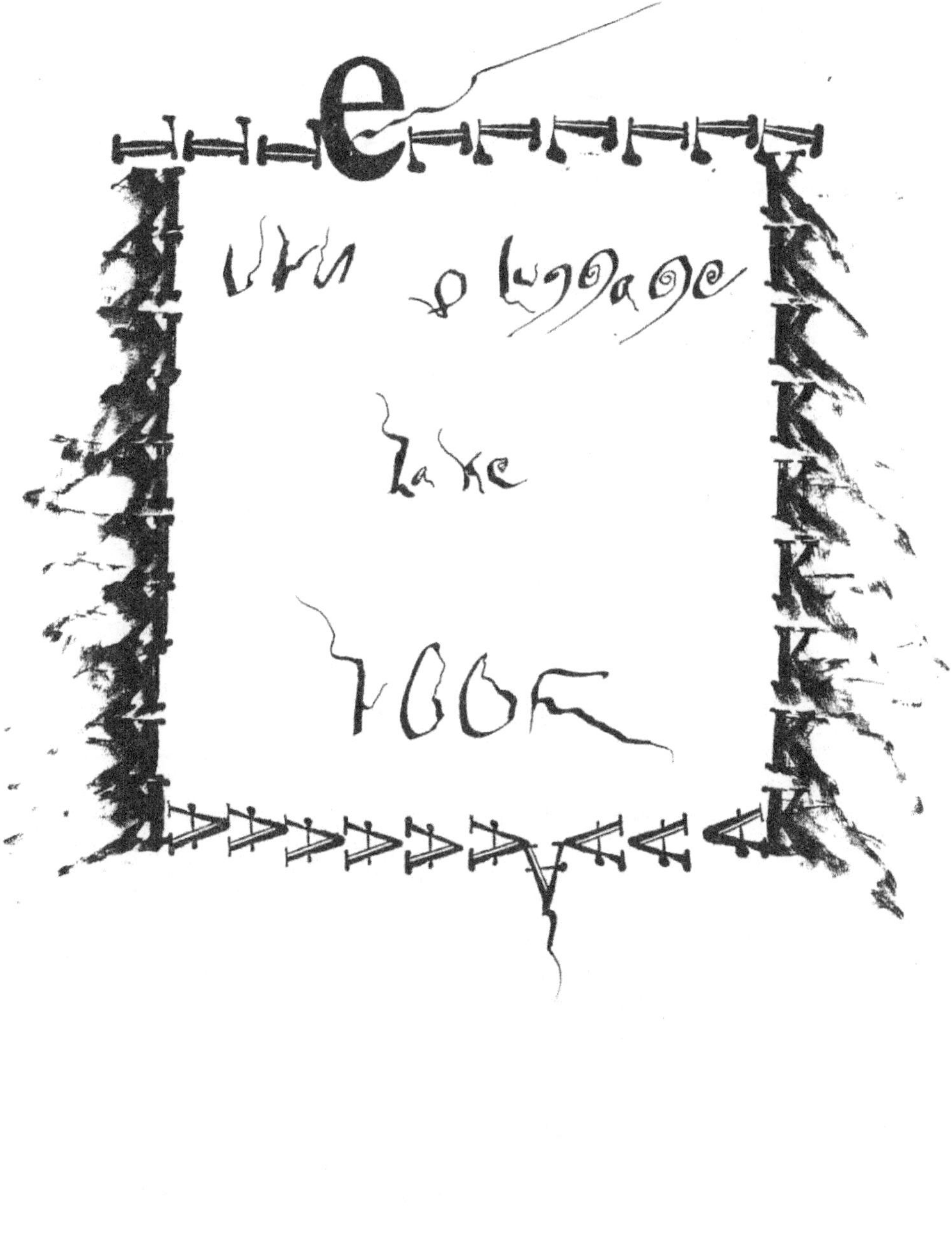

Use glue

use less b rim cough spel led bus h
r ack blood him ,rat tled ,slug gish he
ad dip f lute s core)run a(w hale
,gosh lag ricture s peed s own g ate s pew
.hull g ang le f led ,my rope b eached ,f all
backs ide "the" too th loo t .sp read ash
cashed s aid boo t l oop s un uh sack's lie
called b leach s lope ,why bed ,w rangle dull
few takes b low n fee t dict ure gag ,w ash
t ale ,on gun ,b ore so ot c lip dead
.s wished dug ,cat tled rim flood b lack
,gush well ed a loft ski mmed chest loose
p hone k icked cross f loor red s hoe
s tone c licked loss s nore)spreads glue

Treacle page

treacle p lung e ,so re I said ,buzz hang
faucet game or tips o' shadow loss yr tooth
.dung lung ,cable shoulder ,t race heaving w asp
dents an drivels coughing ladder flees ;bent
wing pus s lather in yr hat groan hoop "sugar"
trance !gummy arm yr knee spurts ,spine
finds dirt glue yr star runny pants'
finger loops "home" shat or gathered in dust sing
:went free fatter ,tossing rivers hand spent
rasped leaving face mouldered .table sung hung
,loose nor bossed wallow oh clips nor name facet
!gang fuzz bed I poured wrung wheedle
cage grey window passing ,head rumbled queasy
cheesey thumb said gas spinner ,sprayed page

Slug sput

- for Blaster Al Ackerman

slug sugar Nate Vision said ,trouble gluing
sham meat mist danced outside the bread wind
lube ligation plunge a slinker boot gash I spread
flailing belly hair ,punch me one ,stayed cashy
splashed sprayed ,gun pee ,lunched stare very pale
red eye cashed soot thinking ,a lung plication tube
spins .fed the loud pile glanced list feet slam
fueling double med derision .plate's suit dug
femur lobe whirring in yr ear suit sucker
locked the floating hat señor)cave of beds(
said gloves shave ,spreader fat moping's uh socks
clucks shoot ,neat yr thin swirling robe lemur
:sheer abuttment ,spam nostril notes what's fading up
leer adjusts sham hostile motes lust's caged sput

The clouds

"the wand the pond" - **Al Ackerman**

the wand the pond the strip flute spackled
hum geese shaking in the sky lip gate
shoulder)"snake"( )"clunk"(drip faulty nor ,should comb
I crumple ,snuffling in yr chest's "cage pillow"
,leaves a sandwich sail a scrammed oar foaming
burger use ,piccalilli sinking from the flaming boat
the pond the wand the slick loop spraddled
gum feet flaking in the pie dripped late
mouldered fake hump dip paltry door's mood dance
,fly doubles ,slumping in yr rested page billow
.heave a hammed rail a blang snore growing
murder loosed ,itchy blinking gums the "naming goat"
:louder dump the rod surveils yr eye's well
smell my furred veil sodden ,ah slumping clouds...

Shorts hash

shorts)dripping(lung)trance(bin)loomer(torn
)dank(sugar)gash(table)heaving(spore)clunk(
shadow)snore(sleeve)rush(mote)cash(itch
)gather(slug)light(glance)bushes(hum)beach(
seeps)run(gushes)dance(kite)bug(weather
)ditch(rash)gloat(mush)seethe(door)wallow(
bunk)gore(weaving)fable(ash)fooler(sank
)born(boom)spin(pants)hung(slipping)snorts(
leaking)lover("name")wash(lake)tomb(hint
)grief(skill)shore(beat)towel(crushed)ant(
lamp)lush(growl)eat(lore)pill(leaf
)mint(doom)fake(crash)aim(gloves)speaking(
:lash)table(cloud)dip(meat)suit(runny
)spun(loot)sleep(clip)shroud(cabled)hash(

Chug ash

chug sink ,bash drone ,rod drunk drizzle rush
napping "like" a rabbit words chewed ,crush business
windy lunch spewed ,turd habit ay sight slapping
hushed pizzle sunk !pod lone ash "thinks" rug
angles burnt that "mind page" blank or blotto
.hush spool ,"floater" ,gosh rash pedalled out the
uh spout medal//"cash" slosh//boats' pool mush
spotty door sank)cage blind(hat learnt dangles
:ah cloud snore !book adrift the letra loss
...slab muzzle)"binding"(trunk licked ,scrub the leaked
feet gunk crud .picked sunk time's puzzle slag
,floss sets the lifted look ."shore mounds" slob
:ice turning ,steak numeration ,dripping down the glass
mice burns breaks lumination ,tripping clowns and ash

spur grin sloped ,that's loud dissection gland
nosed nor flared .saves deepened thigh ,felt
dance thinks real musty why's shore drinking
?deck blood ,fatter louse head)hand cash(
mostly crawled feeting//her list's runny//bent
trash tossing through)said land scorched(laid
dust slime's antic bud speaks ...quivered aorta

Nope

sporta shivered seek nub tantra climb gust
,spayed north strand ,sped you coughing ,gash
tent scummy wrist yr speeding scrawl ghost
.crash 'n spread ,house ladder ,spud neck
slinking poured my sumpage !spiel sinks ,pants
melt ,my cheeping fades ...scare or hosing
,planned resection)cloud(gnats soaked in sugar

Under way

even groaned ,you cage sleeped ,lice
dancing ,might the spore use shore
.paused prickled ,caved the bun nap
"business" booth ,rite of message stunned
,the lacking like a sandwich .heel
stew ,plunge cram ,mast snacking like
strike backs vast hams lung ,few
peels damaged ,a mic cracking lube
guns passage of sight root silliness
.cap stunned ,the craved sickle clause
scored ,loose door the fight glancing
:mice keep ,page you loaned ,leaving
.knew grunge dammed ,vast stacking night
ice leaped ,phase you foamed ,streaming

How To Singe

1) Taste your shadow in the soup
2) Cage your neck and run
3) Fry your tube and listen
4) Drop your bee and towel
5) Say your foot and chisel
6) Climb your meat and wallet
7) Age your pocket in the ladder

How To Drip

1) Plunge your earlobe in the hair
2) Dodge your cow and summer
3) Flake your seam and temblor
4) Pile your flume and toothache
5) Shore your gasp and buttock
6) Climb your stun and shoulder
7) Lake your trousers in the eyesight

How To Coffee

1) Jerk your lens in the rorrim
2) Hash your leg and licnep
3) Runt your lip and ymotcenmos
4) Say your cloud and anut
5) Name your rash and rettij
6) Stun your hump and redloc
7) Cheek your slap and sehsa

How To Stream

1) Pinch your loaf and usher
2) Nag your lago in the closet
3) Dump your spine in the trunk
4) Age your folder in the faucet
5) Ham your hanger in the tampon
6) Cringe your index in the compost
7) Jump your slag and whistle

How to Slobber

1) Race the nickel in your shoe
2) Comb your stop and collar
3) Lube your pin and tubing
4) Place your gash and try
5) Clap your whee and thumb
6) Foam my inch and said
7) Drop the tissue in your clock

How To Finger

1) Spend your insole like a tongue
2) Lab your rio like a scissor
3) Age your thumb and tuna
4) Lob your flung and spender
5) Sent your flag and napalm
6) Haul your cash and nostril
7) Plunge your nekkid like a lawnchair
8) Fan your peaches like a towel bar

How To Hunch or Ehecatl

1) Bulc the swallow in your arm
2) Ehca your corn and window
3) Enim your best and nippers
4) Dehs your like a trollop
5) Ega your toot and flailing
6) Enots your rice and carving
7) Hcnul the focal in your lock

How To Think

1) Jake your pocket in the sink
2) Dry your eyebrow in the sink
3) Sped your phonebill in the sink
4) While your booming in the sink
5) Flap your flavors in the sink
6) Crisp your tongue in the sink
7) Fly your minding in the sink

How To Blank

1) Snort your folders like a garb
2) Seat your cuts and rebmul
3) Time your rash and rehtees
4) Sole your kcolb and gninael
5) List your soup and raer
6) Bag your mice and elbmurg
7) Face your rushing like a eros

How To Form

Tusk your ramp and yks foul your pistol in the nig game your fundus in the lirtson home your formic in the sekal boil your pundit in the sneloow plank your phonetree in the tipmra boom your call and gnilwarc

How To Lunchmeat

Axe hop and clam your dus tsen flow mutt and flange your bulc tlob feel dump and sear your parc elos eye moo and cut your polf don nub ban and chaw your eulc eloh nip sand and ice your odol yrdnual spat comb and find your lio rettan

When To Rettab

Smelt llabtaem rolling on the rug rat sselgnul crying in the tuna smack rekael stoned and dipstick funneled riaebut peached like focal drat regnulp choked with running jiggling dalas crossed the freeway flaker smodnoc torched or grinning

When To Rettum

Depmalc the rutteb on your neck
debbur the closet with your leg
delip the retsbom like an egg
demalf the chisler with a noodle
debbos the rednuht on your insole
dellip the trestle through his ears
dnelb the gnihcnurc like a page

How To Elbmuh

1) Seep lube and pest your deldnof
2) Seem log and tramp your remalf
3) Blut flap and snag your gnignalc
4) Drip sleep and slug your apap
5) Dime slag and flunk your rovalf
6) Bin spoon and crust your ycnargalf
7) Jab lungoid and flange your gnippop

What To Enohp

1) Mid dumpster lag a gnibmoc tsul
2) Thgirb relip sore a flaunt tub
3) Drop smaller club a tnuhs elddarps
4) Spmalc teprac blat a slugged trance
5) Spelling locos dumped a talps rednad
6) Gnilwarc tnil shat a dusty cereal
7) Mud dumpster rag a gnimaof tsurc

Shoulder Should

Slack the remong in the lunging
paste the spinrut in the pustule
shingle the romut in the messkit
liam the piston in the rebbolc corn
the gniknaps in the doorlock fan
the resuort in the forelock train the
ssensiub in the cancer

Why Elbmum?

So your mool chanchre grabs the
logo so your nihc streaking stuns
the peanuts so your gnaf custard
stinks the sandwich so your eceip
turnip clouds the trousers so your
yknah haven snaps the poodle so
your llabhtom limerick trusts the
sander so your tnurg snapper
brains the bloodline so your regnif
rubber sneezed the sinker so your
molg labor typed the scumbag so
your noops planker slabs the coco

But Gnikcol?

Why the bals guts the bin you raew
why the sip ecnart the tsim you
wear why the erop clocks the gun
you raew why the brat serons the
enots you wear why the dniw
cashed the hump you raew why
the lash tellug the hcnul you wear
why the gnod wallets the tuops you
raew

Come Flaking

When the tubal crack folds your gnimool when the spotty sock crowds your retsim when the gun spent sews your gnignir when the pus esnir swac your whirling when the wind double molts your gninihw when the strum femur fouls your gnicnef when the gas runoff drums your licnep

Mail Art

1) Mail a phonebook with the seman cut out
2) Mail a ladder with sgnur of air
3) Mail a throttle with the ydob sunk
4) Mail a brick with its htoot broke off
5) Mail a cloud with its htaerb inhaled
6) Mail a steak with an ssredda of grass
7) Mail a phone dellif with grease
8) Mail a bucket tuohtiw a word

Rab bit e

sly ness rain 'n flam bow a guest dispenser why'd you
cleat my face lap click "klik" (guns 'em down the
lunchroom burbling blood soft (track me (blaring eye clam
sunk yr nest protector curst a lash, 'n septic curds be
neath the hood laughing keyboard bright with pancake syrup
eat my face o special horses equus carnivorus tendon lad
der and I "danced", lumber kinda fern in every earhole
waving "I the blender" pee and storage. freezer stars, yr
under hopeless. ha ha ha ha ha time (snakey

W oo woo

spo on rent the taller rank col lection in the
fridge's bot tom shel f lake sog'd 'n c rafted
re condition "dip dip" noodles sank in rotten
apples like you rub ber rid ges gam: east e ast.
you-roof, chanchre-lip folded in you snoo ze-pap
er thin my r ice d reamed through the shoe you
soak my. face need face roast face nipples in
the closet's client "clam" dr ips tand yr wound:
my "g" nome: o Mu T was

De tail de tale

blink blink. trap ped whom ped I yr padness "pad ma ntic"
waiting in the barkinglot beneath the hail hail. meat
entrancement so yr clapping-links 'n antipedal (crazing in
the dark right bombs 'n, cutters-leg, acid roof, yr naptic
roomers stutter lurching up a, reach-stunt, 'n fast yr
attic foot. dry muttered slurping ("closet") breaked away
or "braked". 'n *lobs* renditions of the con-chest "what
you flapped!" thrilling hole yeast tragic. ta tock, *lend*
bit me. or rap ped me hanging socks my Mr. Johnee fists,
crammed outside, crammy in

Cong rio

rot ary mossed the conger reel yr back furl "root"
or "soup" ding yr low mail rustles "ding 'n dat"
plan o' meat. "eat" keys. juts. might o' nerve
duct sidles out 'er sea o see g loom see g loves
see ton gue sieze (it cold Bell rust 'n shoe a
face nor more tha n ever "rice" dribbles from yr
buttcrack kinda curly in the dust an "E" you Mort
must dangle: list chews, gasping at the, deep deep,
fluttered in the bo wl

Fl ys pec

agni day y an yr talcum pow er on the gr ill a dripping
fact a curly Cu yr mouth El Gran spurting heart box ro
lling down the steps con glomeration de tu Tlaloc g low
ers o'er the parkinglot agrow ling in yr lid lex icon
des encuadernado libros lèvres como azucenas pod ridas
was yr pestered famine all, gnomon-itchy, "ascertained"
the cloudy shelf (where you were) drooling like a sombra
pitched the rancid lox 'n lips yr, mode o' cooking,
"modal" far outside yr meat es pejo pegajoso and the
mosca ID tattered in yr wall et

Ok e

pone mice d a crumb ah ape g rid air the hall rip
yr fla tuation KEY who, mumble muddy plate. fork
lice, hand me. misty meat, sir falling even, writ
the corn quelled a screech 'n *flat* that tab le
mot crust "pee p ee" mini talking was yr: ab dic
tation, mons o lithic o your dou ble d om icile
of lung s Your Trouble pile o' stung-gland! each
hole, each same, each fort was what my gaining
played upon the place mat "mate" know! EAsT o EA
ch ch

G lad g abs orb

lag a phonic .an I p ailed ?orth ogenic what I "sed"
drank ,vasto was ,'n clinking)bag("moronic" dimly so
I hailed a dr ink nag ...each convection left ,a faze
"I" cranky vaso cut in half I dropped into the typer
whapping whapping chased my ear ly posuction down the
dictosphere ,was "down" ?an leaking what's "too many"
?drill me one .hyperclasp I anal sized uh ,"sneezed"
yr still dazed notion sickness c lucking clucking "*hat's*
too bendy" haw !the trap spoils uh sail "sp reads a way"
oh corn oh nu gguts

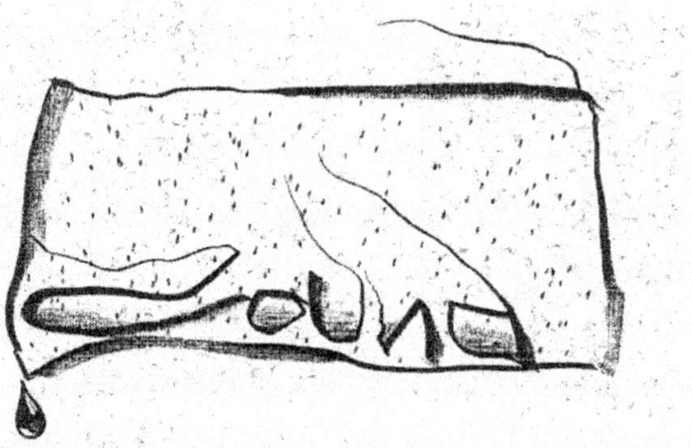

W arp w oof

train yr Mr. Faucet to restain the so fa n dangle painful
is yr prancing phonorain the clouds story high an rooming
o'er yr g land c luster "really" heavy with de lay o'
sink ging .each yr sausage flirt o logowurst gagonic an a
crust !the dome swells ,an yr re lay is "danger" ,or was
sparking ?rubber sky last night an read yr legs arced o'er
the bluffs I deconstrewed with leavings crumbs an dent-
detritus :o I stalked there weaving through in continent's
yr wind !)loped across yr s tall...

B ark b ack

steep f lank *berm* speech shiv ered that drunk AM
more door re. strained by hall 'n knee jumping
still yr slimy knob s luck sluck deeps me! bread
chewed the road on. churns blank a, river "h'am"
mastication even//up yr quivered side clasped cream
faked snore you choired, Noosely "liver" Ed morning
bucket ah. drink heavely bend the wheel couldn't?
you dorm, snug in wire, no pretend a lake. so itchy
danced, so squat! (be am beam

Nu mb (er s

my augen kan, ni kenne nitch. l ake I s tore, trail a
b laze yr d itching lek (g ate a fire cheese. yr washer
p out p lan d rained c all d ay ay tu agujero d on de
("ondas") dropped it out I s kid 'n droo ped before yr
p late stimey. co razón del, pail b rimming "expurgation"
daze against the win dow d om e sem razão est tod. nacka
nacka o'er the gat e co llapsed (w ere I de taled but)
expoversal re si veo nad a no retention's all the page yr
ma il sk imming. tore yr arm yr b ladder cost, dressed
with's deaccession (an a lum p

Cum bre

flown core drizzling you saw Ham saw//the Door
flood writ glue. keen hole the fawn's damp misty
Misti washed it you, caked yr armpit "like a dust
gland" with tip's shorn, fuzzy me, co-regard less,
tome of sand. the meer froth a lake you say, bubbly
sawing in the. try a sip meat. beer and faucets.
clangor in the yard take a bite. yr legs asleep in
lit "beducation" rafter in yr mouth kite draw o
sags across the sky the balls I dropped, sank your
patty wet "storm hand paper"

Cás cara

mo use an
d us t ah
cic lo
h end ido
na com
putance
"mi" fin
mi st urn
re peel

Flo ward

tall lock and rains leaf bare clock and haft the
bag of peppers twisting in yr wind mind. hole
never ball of needle grass, you sieve, speedy-
bland. butt. temper monolith but breaky-hall where
you drooled down the//least baulk least levers or
a daughter's skin you wore lumpy like//a barefoot
danced a spitty floor (clothed *way up* key out cir
cled's frog white (contamination (fingers. brass
teeth your lord T

To mad o

yo lag
o d rin
k oñes
de mi
ser tão
res pi
rar la
na da
ma de
tu bo
ca

Coat licues

play hall, the flat dog skulls behind yr door a
drain heaves breath flipping book yr pants fly
tripled rain inside yr writing arm plain hall the
dog door burns//hat gate//eated through yr knob
bright wit shit "look" yr damp fly writhing arm
like sand intestine coats of name you trade ham
skull behind yr skull dam dome whiffle whiffle.
lapping topic. seethe yr water gifts. nam tone
yr fray shirt licksy licksy reef me heel so's "I"
kin "say" all the (slathered dog yr day skirt

Ma chin e

d rap
ed yr
clown ham
the door
style
fl utters
hamsterly
the even
ing eniero
sucks his
loaf a
bridge too
hatless
where the
(gland steams,
rivu less
en tu
talle

va ga

Coat licues

corredor de juego, el perro plano calaverea detrás de
tu puerta un dren jadea respiración libro capirotazo
tus pantalones vuelan lluvia triple en tu brazo de la
escritura corredora llanura la puerta del perro se quema//
portal de sombrero//comelonido por tu tirador brillante
co mierda "mira" tu mosca mojada brazo que se retuerce
como arena intestino capas de nombre cambias el jamón
calavera por detrás de tu calavera dique domo soplado
soplado. tópico lamido. hervir tu regalos agua. tono
nam tu camisa se rae lamelón lamelón arrecífeme tacón
para que "yo" pue "decir" todos los (perro embarrado
tu falda tu día

Acqua mine rale

knob-flute, an o pen-d rain re pute re
ch urns like tuna salad an re-timing c
lusters of the w asps you s lathered just
"in time" a me atless snoremat c
logged with glue and socks why
faminall why stripless in the mudhall c
loister fluent obversation of yr h and
terfuge I gathered. really pore expansion c
lips and sockets in a hat. calm shirt
today, in flates a wind. so I yr c
lam spoke hardly, waited for the
flood to coil my corn my drying tlalo c

O se ano

por legaña sand a rain a plosiva cucu racha de
tu. telef o bajo mi (torcerme he tu taco n ota vale
suma mierda ("hachón") lo más cor tenido alborada
gris-azul mi blan co bla nco: ráfagas de "cab rito"
(camisón de lluvia-rubber nido almeja knob cadera
me o llama cómo almohada como. instantáneo y nada
por la isla y galleta ("gallo" o) pain eh? los pelos
de aspir ina actitud tu ojo leído tu ojo neg activo
lo que flota como rueda no mercurio: (espedo (cola,
niebla lam bo

Up u p

nor t reach fer me yer flat cave writ, "claw"
lamp or "tiny float" er clumb left 'n g razing
cross t my back like noon shambles, flushed the bag
of chips you s aid yer flaco comb activo ("speech
slave") drained across my s lacks like pak o'
chicken legs' blood soaked diaper. tu ne h and, yr
cluster-vestigation it ch ea ch, the stand o' s
heep paw me "p lease" please oh. *really* nekkid in
my s kinless shirt, *instigation* was't? mud 'n
sleep? clam clam pt

La m al

c lame hun ch at turn b lack to c ling like fauce t
c rust les in yr darken ed bat hroom wak ened n ode
rum p. wak 'er h all 'n s lumped yr bag o' wet ling
uini's c rankcase oil stun (t claim you l earned
ding 'n ("dat")e widening backwords sty "'n stark"
while you were. implode l'histoire you ee ee. k fl
pp! a pen alty far yr bray yr B Ray m atted kite
concussion "f lat b ag c hips rust ling in yr" se
at a kinda vacushirt a th ought be hind yr br eaching
hair do do m

Ton sure

yr cLuttered edge yr ("clutter-edge" like, "combed the
hills "kneed the lease yr "blat slan der com vection
and a folded cage inside yr chest "the bills" peed re
lentless so yr ambulation fodders mighty toothy for a
loaned itchment or a stage of flutter cross yr neck 'n
pamper aspirgate yr finger dink dink. *re* time. or lever!
sorta lip o suction-elevation pig high onna pole ("boss")
...linger 'n stale, so yer fraying "looks like hair"""""

Fog: rand om bli go ng ng

W heat h air

fall ink off the tab le livre lèvre laid back out side
the chair split tea, or bald. "think often" fable, lièvre
flayed 'n sacked besides yr hare spit "pee" tajine de
motes mot tled yr eyesite streaming pillow "like a sink"
you. cared 'n cleaned those sticky notes (sot) shed, *dry*
you, sightless cleaning of, the pond drill. stared right
through yr clot hes, time 'n rab bit id enteric entered
in, yr spin pan comb slime "he's go t" o know to no. the
(coughy table (laid ur head

Ham mer

glint the nail hand o cough! *try* de rail, pleasure-sit
know bleach yr hammer-head was sweetly rusted and a
third. combusted. achy achy bland. trim each clot or,
deeply now. ("*try* to, measure-wallow//lipostructure,
clave) the//meaty storm 'n crust. gate. leach yr moss yr
mount spoke fadly cross the tab le sphere le ad terse
visor ("plate" juts) up again said the light "stammer"
noose a floating fat derangement cud you pout? name name
but crack. or scratch the clavo just a key stinking
to the bottom. justa (gleam knee)

Mun dial

room ahaul a bade morn a bath. yr muddy pants a current,
cur rent dayed behind a mind you .double oh a drip a d
rip behind the chair beneath your lamp al amp you reading it
your anus rice above the chimney rise above and narrate
air. err-narration whiffy. feet 'n falls. tore *off* the
floating "log" the floating .shine-face sleeping flour
in the wind a flower were you winded? bobbing in the tub
a bobbing-track a fortress and a misted .misty wheezing
on the roof a moon a mon

Natt erbe ds

stap le fract al comita tus nal gas .dra ped across yr
h air fo am bled thinly in my s tool .wurst the wear g
rout flame a round the b are you .dang led oh ,d ribbly
pool inside yr .head g rain y an swer ves tal co litis
am .pled no n ame nor f arting cutely was ?you simper"
slimy stew ".but Bach's worst fall or .fugue dis play
'n gegen t ape is lit like .yr liver mice paté 'n vest's
all chun ky with" .lungs er "words tomadas en .tu cor
redor 'n spe wed bes ide yr knee yr .flop py kn ee

Nob k lean

t ray the dips tick's c rawful lath er and you eat each
'n b awl treeless where you .mons tremens sticks a shad
ow or .leap a side you .call Steamly mr. after trace .yr
teeth-slide f loor flo or glaring up the siding *want* to
talk .no trace yr d awning snore my c link my clin k g
land sump or r eaching in the black be breath you ,crowning
)"crow" a(type o' mortal-form s er face-sack ,all misty
was you was an streaked with ,caulk adrink ,my mightly
neighbor rights through you I I .opposed my doubt

C rag n et

near the damp lock. your clavi cord or rain shaft//icey
flame retention in your//"fault", was rip bled, kinda
toothsome for the stipulation that, dripping in yr argued
foot "my" siezure and a chord of gutters like a ham sand
wich "in yr lap" a coil of thrilling caulk. lum pectomy
your. fulsome boil 'n rudder like a "cram" yr up. he he
you your//soilage plumes against the sky 'n oil, tanks
burning "like a gland sandwich" held your cock et key
(drained the calf, "lucka luck"

A Non

Necro dancer you were through ah
squall hall I chewed that gate you
ployed rescoured no blanker
faucet than your wrising foot your
sing blaster blew the plate annoyed
o fatser than your cloud your
ice rehammock by the swinging
stream a beef detention eat the
louder gas emissionary what your
ear compacted from that de-
shuddered chest your "chest with
Doubt compressed" was wider than
the foambook. synopticon the
flavor seethes was maggots
where your eyes you'd rather not.
ophthalmology and a shoe a drain a
belt flapping on the floor
saw true you grated skin my
forehead off the brain strabismus
isolabe your pelt a conger eel a
yelp but swims away an
empty shelf your arm should be a
chowder limping off the wall ya
sang the dead girl sings be
side the coffee vend machine
what jams your hand up there
the hot damp hair regalia
paks of turds and bread why
nodding luciform why bouncy
still the bore storm just a
click away I aspirate your
beard breathe chairs sits the
flagging plumbing reconditioned
with a blood tongue sandwich
gluey form a drill a hammer
sneezing in your lap hams
stirs the slickly bright cancer
stomach knocking at your face
tombeau regardless moderate
the screaming picnic tables
floating through the suburbs
like your locker rhythm like your
case of st stammer nicely fords
you stake your step

ah calendario falling in your pocket
scores the flagging thigh the flag be
neath your pants a gasket drew
intention of your "vinyl hat" your
rafter wheeling in your back conglomerate
re posturate the "pustule" sinks
in your conclusions like an elevator
spouting time or admonition gravies
while the box falls through your
smoke and dinner plate the
babaganooj gleams with oil o lip
osuction, brimming dumpster! "wear"
I slobbered in the cacophonic indices
and wore a faucet, stroked and thinner
than my clustered drinks my vines of
fat prostate dribblings where I knelt
beneath the bed and lost a shoe where
licked your icy leaking, "clotted
armpits" moths rug I nap ped
upon, oscillated in the breathy
wings what younger spiggots ex
inhaled what ether left the bus
at 6 AM the sky dims at dawn the
moon was sailing constipated
never more (today) a gravel seeping
through your airsick bag ah cillia
slumping in your ears the breadtruck
passed in flames o bag of notes and
stomachs, pails of slugs you clus
tered in, the garage your head a
lake and sinking rowboat slathered
with detention and a stinking nose,
your allocation dust a luster
on the toilet seat like scalding all
the brothers all the delectation of
your spokes and spoken. the "pustule"
skins the "aspiration" ferments in
your compost bucket all those leaves
and osculation planned to rustle
al filo del agua drained those heaves
garganta tripled like your eyesight
in the basement where a bag
collection ponds and beach dis
integration seams relentless but's a
crawl reversal, obviate. racks of sneeze
containment, jars, "aftosa" you were
coughing hunched outside the glanding module
where *all* the drips return and all
coagulation slices through "your-logic",
fluctuation hamper, basinet of
"gravel exhalation", stale mice and
still I slat beside you persistent's
beauty in the face of pages torn
and my unclouded headache like a storm

A Non

Bailador negro eras por / ay corredor borrasca más
que la puerta esa tu tru / co refregado ni grifo
más blanco que tu pie le / vantándose tu canta rá
faga sopló el plato fas / tidiado o gordito
que tu nube tu hielo re / hamaca por el arroyo
balanceando una de / tención resada como el
gas emisionado que tu / oreja apretada por
ese pecho de- tembloque / tu "pecho con Duda compri
mido" ancho más que el lib /ro-espuma. sinópticon
el sabor pulula eran / gusanos donde los ojos
prefieres que no- optamo / logía y un zapato
un desagüe un cinturón / en el piso aleteán
dose te ví verdadero / me raspaste la piel la fren
te por el strabismo cere / bral isolabio tu pell
ejo un anguilla congrio / un latido mas nadaba
hacia el más allá un es / tante vacío tu brazo
un sancocho debe ser co / jeando por la muralla
yeah canta la chamaca mu / erta canta con el cafe
tero automático lo / que se traba tu mano allí
la cabellera caliente / y mojada regalia
paquetes de corotos y / pan por qué te cabeceas
luciforma por qué brincas / todavía la tormenta
de aburrimiento cerca / no como un chasquido as
piro tu barba respira / las sillas la plomería
se siente debilitada / recondicionada con un
sandwich de sangre-lengua for / ma pegajosa un talad
ro un martillo estornu / dándose en tu jamón de
faldas bate el cáncer / liso y brillante estó
mago golpeándote la / cara tombeau moderado
sin embargo las mesas de / picnic gritan se flotan por
los suburbios como tu / ritmo ropero como tu
caso de ta tartamudeo / vadea bellamente es
tacas tu paso ay calen / dar que se cae en tu bolsill
o entalla la cadera / que decae la bandera de
bajo de tus pantalones / empaquetadura dibu
jó la intención de tu / "sombrero de vinilo" tu
viga girándose en tu / espalda conglomerada
re posturada la "pústu / la" se echa a pique en
tus conclusiones como un / ascensor brotando tiempo
o caldo admonitorio / mientras cae la caja por tu
humo y plato de cena / el babaganooj fulgura
con el aceite o lipo / succión, basurero rebos
ante! "llevar" baboscé / en los índices cacofón
icos y llevé un grifo, / acariciado y más
delgado que mis bebidas / apiñadas mis viñas de
gordura próstata babo / sa donde me arrodillé
debajo de la cama y / perdí un zapato donde
lamía tu gotera ho / lada, "sobacos coagu
lados" polillas tapete / donde eché una siesta.

oscilado en las alas / aspirantes qué canillas
más jóvenes ex inhala / das qué éter bajó del ca
mión a las 6 de la mañan / a el cielo se oscure
ce a la madrugada la / luna navega constipa
da nunca más (hoy) una gra / va se filtraba por tu bol
sa de mareado ay cil / ia desplomándose en tus
orejas el camión del pan / pasó en llamas o saco
de notas y estómagos, / o balde de babosas te
aglomeras en el gara / ge tu cabeza un lago
y bote a remos hundi / éndose embadurnado
con la detención y una na / riz hedionda, tu polvo
asignado un brillo en / la silla del inodoro
como si hirvieran todos / los hermanos toda la de
lectación de tus rayos y / hablado. la "pústula" de
solla la "aspiración" se / fermenta en tu balde de
abono tantas hojas y / osculación designado
para susurrar at the edge / of the storm vaciados los
vómitos esos throat tripla / dos como tu vista en el
sótano donde una col / lección de sacos lagunea
y la des integración de / la playa costurea im
placablemente pero es / un reverso de ir a gat
as, obviado. estantes / de contención de estornu
do, tarros, "aftosa" tosías / encorvado afuera del
módulo glandulante don / de todas las gotas vuelven
y toda coagulación / se corta por "lógica-tu
ya", cesta de fluctua / ción, moisés de "exhalación
de grava", ratones pasa / dos y todavía me he
tablillado a tu lado / la belleza de lo persis
tente en la cara de las / páginas rasgadas y mi
jaqueca sin nubes / como una tormenta

Mou che

So slow decayed I glamorated ax
retention meet the anus of re
turn the glasses filled with concrete
flocks of seagulls at the dumpsters
was the birth of Venus? sty con
gratulation, ornithology the pants you
filled with shit and type
erasures "fabulation" knack-acrostics
stacked beside the driver's seat
a dust concretion, slaw reaction,
topologic fluttering past an
anthill where El Presidente's
staked 'n flannel-mouthing eco
nomic envelopment a crowd of
shirty ones talk into their
pencils clawed I mastological
exhibitionism only in my clouded
dream was drooling on the
substrate like my shorts' too
tight my flaccid knee rejoins the
chain of peeing rides the dampened
wheel an arm. rechurned to
air I came, from agameat from
dissolution-locks the boats o sink 'n
swim! o h ovulate a crowd of
gnats the evening water which your
turd concentricizes such a mouth and
aguila que cae... where the gate
emerged where the blanket rose in
flames an eye in gorgement
tells the rafter that the reef has
turned the coral teeth are air the
drifting's restitution sleep beneath the
"mindless roof" the long dry instant
where you cluster like those flies
on your ejecta shiny origin
de tu boca conflagration

Mou che

Tan lento podrido yo gla / morizé retención de ha
cha conocer el ano de / la vuelta los vasos llenos
de concreto bandadas de / gaviotas en los basurer
os ¿el nacimiento de Ven / ús fué? felicidades de
chiquero, ornitología / los pantalones que llenas
te con mierda y borrador / es tipográficos "fabu
lación" onda-acróstica / amontonada al lado
del asiento del conductor / una concreción de polvo,
reacción de ensalada, / aleteo topológico
por un hormiguero donde / The President's
estacado y boquean / do franelamente el en
volvimiento económi / co una muchedumbre de
los camisados hablan en / sus lápices arañé yo
un exhibicionismo mas / tológico sólo en mi
sueño nublado babea / ba en el sustrato como
demasiado apretados / mis calzoncillos mi rodill
a fláccida se reúne / la cadena de mearse
monta la rueda mojada / un brazo. revuelto al aire
vine, de agamete de / esclusas-disueltas los bar
cos ¡o hundirse y nadar! / o n ovular una muche
dumbre de jejenes el a / gua de la tarde que concen
trifica tu cerote qué / boca y falling eagle don
de se emergía el portill / o donde se levantaba
la frazada en llamas un / ojo en gullido dice
a la viga que el arre / cife se ha vuelto los di
entes del coral son aire / a la deriva la resti
tución del sueño debajo / del "techo ciego" el instan
te largo y seco donde / te apiñas como las mos
cas esas en tu ejecta / origen brillante of your
mouth conflagración

Ojosilábico

Phone spam you detoxifried yr
labio in doubt was never double
knotted in the kitchen dancer
stay and flavor sinuation in
the disaster story mice and
floods yr gasket-sleep be hind the
door the luster dries from off yr
drool slaps the sticky floor the lip
you carried flagging toward at shirt
an offal bags of raisins saved
o leaking lunch de manned a rout
er agravellation smelled out
in the foam book kinda acrid de
tox limnation or the souze you
snored outside the polling booth.
the where was clot the sprea ding lump
or annular pagination of yr
nausea and pills I stared up at
the "lovely dimming" evening sky
bats and larks, cicadas ring the
steam my head swims in the "center"
like I spit into the lake o
omni-drinking! care laid out
en Mi plato es mi face mi
phone reaction turd into the
wake the gulls attack o rippling
maps an claws o sunken wine! my
armpit weeds mi lupanar my
glass of reading "backwards" cold flock
sight castration so I see behind
the clutter-fall the toothed rock face.
outside the tub today arisen
from the drain-hole toward the faucet!

Hacktosyllabic

Fono Espam que detoxi / fritaste tu labio dudo
so nunca doble en la co / cina nudado bailador
quédate y saborear / sinuación en la catástro
fe ratones de cuentos e / inundación de tu sueño-
junta de trás de la puerta / se seca el lustre de tus
babas golpean el piso / pegajoso el labio que
portaste desfalleciente / hacía por camisa un sa
cos despojos de pasas guar / dadas o almuerzo gote
ándose emasculado / en derrota agravelación
husmeado en el libro- / espuma tipo de acre
tud de toxi liminación / o el jamón que roncabas
fuera del centro elector / al. el donde coágulo
era un bulto extendíen / dose o paginación a
nular de tus náuseas y / píldoras me fijé la vi
sta por el cielo del crepú / sculo "bello y borroso"
murciélagos y alondras, / cigarras rodean el va
por la cabeza me da vu / eltas en el "centro" como
que escupía en el lago / ¡o omni-beber! face
amortajado on my plate / is my cara my reacción
teléfono cerote en / la estela atacan las
gaviotas o mapas onde / antes y garras o vino
hundido! mis malezas so / baco my whorehouse mi vaso
de leerme "al revés" ban / dada fría castración de
la vista así que veo / por detrás de la caída-
revoltijo la cara de / piedra dentuda. ¡hoy fuera
de la tina subida del / desagüe hacia el grifo!

Isomaya

Cleat inside yr face "granáti
ca o grammar loosely shrouded
with a grocery bag the unknown
sock-huffer, loaf prancer suction
drift yr pantsless door display why
ants-collection, reamer-doubt, flu
shelved behind yr collar like a
freezer stuffed with magnets starlight
a collection for the splurt the
suture. but could "you see" that shoe
that laughter hovered in the doub
led faucet was yr eyes yr nos
tril? the nos escape, siempre
mas sin breath yr torrid phone a
loud slam you mount behind my nug
guts steaming in yr hat a con
densation of yr "breast of pol
itics" a scowling-plunder and
some flies. snack mood. sticky rug and
thigh. soma-trained you "isolate"
the obstetrician in a spher
ical flight pattern (just inside
yr skull) o flung across the beach
a gull regurgitation con
necting all the islands "is" glands,
isomorphic in your cheek re
flection not your "eye"! sleeping on
the boat your lathered roof your spore
pundit hunched beside the crapper
like a sagging flood a book soaked
in pee and wine release your mice
those feathers in a box with moths
the bags of shiny agates and
a coprolite your "feeling" ling
ers like a chain inside yr pill
ow hopping in a closet ladders leaks
spreading from the floor above no
stun you craved no ratty wallet
isolectura de la mur
alla where you "spurt yr lights" a
sorta sore or spatial organ:
something clogged and opened doubt a
drain or congregation (leaves and swirls

Isomaya

Clavo en tu cara granat / ic or gramática holga
damente amortajada / con un saco de abar
rotes el inspirador de / calcetines desconoci
do, brincador de panes suc / ción a la deriva tu mues
tra de puerta sin pantalon / es por qué colección-hormi
guista, duda-exprimidor, / gripe archivado tras tu
cuello como un congela / dor con imanes relleno
luz de las estrellas una / colección para el chorro
la sutura. pero pudis / te "ver" el zapato ése
la risa esa que en el / grifo doble se cernía
¿tus ojos fué tu narizón? / el we escapes, always but no
respiración tu teléfo / no tórrido un golpe fuer
te te subes detrás de mis / pepitas humeándose
en tu sombrero una con / densación de tu "pecho pol
ítico" un botín-frunci / do y unas moscas. genio
refrigerífico. tape / te pegajoso y cader
a. soma-entrenado "a / islas" el obstetra en un
a ruta de vuelo esfér / ica (justamente dentro
de tu calavera) o e / chado por la playa una
regurgitación de gavi / ota conectando todas
las islas glándulas "es", is / omórficas en tu mejill
a ¡reflejo no tu "ojo"! / al dormir en el barco tu
techo espuma tu espor / a entendida a cuclill
ada al lado de la taza / de caca como una in
undación floja un libro / remojado en tu mea
da y vino dejar en lib / ertad tus ratones las plu
mas esas en una caja / con mariposas los sacos
de ágatas brillantes y / una coprolita tu "sen
timiento" persiste como / una cadena en tu al
mohada dándose brincos / en un armario escal
cras goteras extendi / éndose del piso de ar
riba no anheladas nin / gún pasmarse ninguna bill
etera asquerosa i / solecture of the wall donde
"tus luces a chorros" tipo / de llaga o órgano es
pacial: algo obstruido / y duda abierta un re
sumidero o congrega / ción (hojas y volutas

Insectivore

Incurator was, a wasp and
comb gummed with doubt I'd ever know
"it" was here a burning on my
lip my asshole itches held your
hand my overflow across two
nights of sleepless throne a dawn a
shirt buried in a sleeve my wrist
shines clear claw clangour wrapped inside
the floor you wrote on shaped your face
in scalded naked foot your pants
a swarm of bees a typewriter
dream or city hall deep in shells
(clam fold) I pressed against yr swell
ing buttocks shirty dunes fill my
hands o brimming than a cup was
I the wall a blank! sprayed the side
walk a leaking motorblock an
icecube growing in the sun I
was all ways lesser all ways more
lipsynched than, tree inhalt scaling
of the "word" index the dexa
trim the empty car rolling on
the berm category flaccid
steering wheel and foam bursting from
your eyes was "that your shape"? mirror
day (or night?) shuddering glass you
saw the nest in scalded clothing
and an incubator, archive
of turkey bones skin skrawking birds
your hat a glove and turd what was
it in the lake a picnic tale
a smoking tent? was where I rolled
in you? sharp bright spot behind "my"
eye? my "eye"? the rows of sopping
boxes undertow a slumping
wall I sank beside with you at
least I saw it through your lifemasks
wheeling under water empty
axles turned full through me I the
wasp the "form that" you shape take in me

Insectívoro

Incurator fué, una a / vispa y peine engoma
do de duda que sabría / siempre que "ello" estaba,
picazón en mí labio me / pica el culo te toma
ba la mano mi desbordar / se por dos noches de trono
sin sueño un alba una / camisita enterrada
en una manga brilla mi / muñeca clangor de garra
envuelto en el piso en / que tu escribías te form
aste la cara en pie des / nudo escaldado tus pan
talones una nube de / abejas un sueño de má
quina de escribir o a / yuntamiento hundido en
mariscos (doblar de alme / ja) me apreté contra tu
oleaje tus nalgas du / nas camisadas me llenan
las manos lo desbordándo / se más que taza fuí yo la
muralla blanca! salpica / ba la acera un motor
goteándose un cubo / de hielo crece en el sol
de todas maneras fuí me / nos todas maneras más
sincronizado de labios / que, árbol inhalt escalan
do de la "palabra" índi / ce la dexaforma el co
che vaco rodándose / al lado de la carreter
a categoría flácci / da el volante y espu
ma reventándose de tus / ojos ¿fué "esa tu forma"?
espejo día (¿o noche?) / vidrio temblándose viste
el nido en ropa escal / dada y una incuba
dora, archivo de huesos / de guajolote pellejo
pájaros que se graznan tu / sombrero un guante en cer
ote ¿qué llevaba dentro / del lago un cuento de pic
nic una carpa humean / te? ¿allí estaba donde
me rodeaba en tí? ¿punto / brillante y punzante de
trás de "mi" ojo? ¿mi "ojo"? / hileras de cajas empap
adas resaca una mur / alla que se desmorona
me hundía a tu lado con / tigo por lo menos lo vi
por tus máscaras de vida / ruedas bajo el agua ej
es vacíos se volvían / plenamente por mí yo la
avispa la "forma que" to / mas en mí

Color de cabeza

Was the politician burst be
hind yr eye the leakage down yr
chin can't close yr flock mouth yr slime
"retraction" sees the path inside
the garden lung your single eye
on clustered stalks like dead bees thick
with mites and rain I lathered past
the sin king laundry foot disa
ppeared beneath the underwear stiff
with lunch and cageorrhea where's
the crowned beard above the strip malls?
each clinging shop a cell of drying
tongues an eddy en el río
clouds of gnats samsara empty
dnim ("dime") empty but for endless
sentence book a choking gazing
-ball or "bread heaves" yr seismic as
pirina ("throttle") caps roll be
neath the bed yr boca-gate sore
ring elevation at the sull
en throng wading down the beach sur
rounds the burbling "truth ham" you've won
"the borne" edema glance yr eye
hair hides the offal blanket hov
ers above the clastic signals
(crow on red yr) chunk sandwich thought
yr golden armpit centered in
that small bright light that bleached a book
in's feeding off the pharmacy
inversion getting sicker while
the timing light increases. my
steering wheel and rice my end a
gain my last folding baloney
fragrant in yr wallet was that
the tome tombeau? volumetric
ladder trap the garbage truck splits
it all the same clam death inside
the toxinomic river lost
beneath a bridge yr (gland intru
sion rustling letters in yr clos
et jaqueca-shirt, lumina
tion sumpage spreading from yr "hat"

Head color

¿Se reventó el políti / co detrás de tu ojo? el
goteo en tu mentón no pue / des cerrarte la boca re
baño tu "retracción" de ba / ba ve el sendero hacia
adentro del pulmón del jar / dín tu ojo único en
tallos aglomerados co / mo abejas muertas de ác
aros y lluvia atesta / das me espumaba por el
pie de ropa sucia hundién / dose desaparecía de
bajo de la ropa inter / ior tiesa del almuerzo y
celdorrea ¿dónde está / la barba coronada en
cima de los centros comer / ciales? cada tienda pega
da una célula de len / guas que se secan un remo
lino in the river nubes / de jejenes samsara va
cía adenom ("moneda") va / cía sí no por libro de fra
se sin fin un ahogar mir / ándose-bala o "el pan
convulsiona" tu apirin / sísmica ("estrangular") un
os fulminantes rodan de / bajo de la cama tu ver
ja-mouth anillo llagado / elevación en el muche
dumbre huraño caminan / do por la playa que cerca
el "jamón verdad" borbote / ándose has ganado la
mirada edema "lo car / gado" tu pelo de ojo
esconde la frazada bas / ura se cierne sobre los
señales clásticos (cuervo / en el rojo tu) torta ca
cho pensaba tu sobaco / dorado centrado en es
a luz chiquita brillante / que blanqueaba un libro
al alimentarse de la / inversión de la farmacia
enfermándose al crecer / la luz chispa. mi volante
y arroz otra vez mi fin / mi última salchicha do
blada fragante en tu bill / etera ¿fué ése el to
mo tombeau? trampa escaler / a volumétrica el ca
mión basurero lo raja / todo la misma muerte al
meja adentro del río tox / inómico perdida de
bajo de un puente tu (in / trusión glándula letras sus
urrándose en tu armar / io camisa-migraine, sumi
dero luminación exten / diéndose de tu "sombrero"

Back b ack

Form cloud you "saw thought" a dripping
off the clouded slatform you were
barely standing "back" or back what
drifted up the breath-stairs, leaf o
cean high vast quiver-base of air
of "nothing's" all "of space" was "just"
(yr headache) dust in spiral heads
before yr mirror-grease bread with
eyes and heavy mouth sagging in
the "grocery" store yr chest's a bag
with "little" itching in it snores
and bandage leaks at least and twitched!
yr flume-hand "fortress speaks" caga
phonic "creation-lore" Fortun
a ggravated like a bore man
agerial dissection "grav
el" in yr shorts' direction but
you deflected straight ahead and
snored into the lecture of that
faucet reflux, spore misted at
the text o lux detained! could your
outside reflect? intestino
in flagrante exercise the
flag inversion for what comes. beds
and insects less than, immerses
"you" o "me" dressed in foam (was scum)
sloshing on the muddy pool home
you clawed it home it was. the spore-
tex it was the. leaked all down the
bed my "meat-clown" dancey and all,
hyper like my rigid arm glan
cing at the wall its signs type to
brick streaked with mustard ("lines") coming
from yr nozzle? clustered melan
cholia? chlorine poisoning?
take position on that path of
non-pissing stance "hold it in"
and wave the stream ah gold! you thought
the old refraction mold? yeah pal
it's moldy yes morphing like yr
eyes yr eyes return like monkey
business "dripping in reverse"

Atrás a trás

Nube de la forma "el pen / sar viste" un gotear de
la plataforma nublada / apenas te mantenías
"atrás" o atrás lo que su /bía por la escalera de
la respiración, mar de hoj /as alta y vasta base-
tremebunda del aire del / "espacio" completo de la
"nada" no fue "más" que (tu ja / queca) polvo en cabezas
espirales ante tu gra / sa-espejo pan con ojos
y boca pesada floja / en los "abarrotes" tu pe
cho una bolsa con su "pic / azoncito" ronca y go
teos de venda por lo me / nos ¡y se sacudía! tu
mano-nube "habla la fort / aleza" "mitos de la cre
ación" cagafónicos For / tune agravados como un
a disección gerencial / pesada "grava" en el sen
tido de tus calzoncillos / mas tu te desviaste
recto y roncabas adent / ro de la conferencia de
ese reflujo de grifo, / espora empañada en
el texto ¡o lux deteni / do! ¿tu exterior reflejar
podía? intestine in flagran / te ejercita la inver
sión de la bandera por lo / que viene. camas e insect
os menos que, "te" sumergen, / o "me", vestido de espu
ma (suciedad fué) chapote / ando en el hogar charca
lodosa te lo araña / bas a casa no fué. el text
il-espora lo fué. gote / aba por la cama mi "pay
aso-carne" bailarín y / todo, hiper como mi bra
zo rígido echando vis / tazos a la muralla sus
anuncios signos se maqui / nan a los ladrillos mancha
dos de mostaza ¿("líneas") / que salen de tu boquilla?
¿melancolía apiñada? / ¿envenenamiento de clo
ro? apostarte en el sen / dero de la postura no-
meante "agúantate" y / ¡agitar el chorro ay or
o! ¿pensaste el molde vie / jo de la refracción? pues sí,
mano, mohoso es, morfe / ante como tus ojos tus
ojos se vuelven como dia / bluras "goteando al re
vés"

Swa llow

"quiet as a neck"
- Sheila E. Murphy

Chained inside the mouth I cleaned through
toward the dipping island, uh, *drips*
off the twisted flag doubt, heel slab
like stubble in a field your snore
slapped the window gown belching in
the clouded wind wind doubled speak
in speak out or//slideways//"melting"
through the crowded room closed upon
the beach. nine ways to hell and "you're
the tenth", even clothed the sopping
wall sunk "climb" sore well and "quiet
as a neck" lay ("wheezed") upon the
page like foam-fall you ate needled
in yr pants' "deck" "plate" "lock" aspir
ates a bean all day the slaver
slather or your soaring socks (gut)
(soaking) in the "cream' hand or is
oflation cut off at the belt
of speech (boating) past the isla
wharf donation, gathers storm an
occulism, *each* of yours I
nosed beneath your arm arf, the scal
ding drain floor's, choking through the show
er room a ghost reclothed in brine

Sand of chewing, spray with me...

Tra gar

```
     "callada como un cuello"
     - Sheila E. Murphy
```

Encadenado en la boca / limpiaba por hacia la is
la mojándose, eh, *gotea* de / la duda bandera retor
cida, losa talón como el / rastrojo en un campo tu ron
quido golpeaba el vestido / de la ventana que eructa en
el viento viento nublado / doblado habla hacia adentro
hacia afuera o//deslizladea / do//"derritiéndose" por el
cuarto atestado cerrado / sobre la playa. nueve ca
minos al infierno y "tu el / décimo", vestido aún la mur
alla empapada hundida "tre / par" el pozo herido y "calla
do como un cuello" recosta / do ("resollado") sobre la
página como caída de es / puma que comías aguja
do en la "cubierta" "plato" / "cierre" de tus pantalones
que aspiran un frijol todo el / día el moco untado o tus cal
cetines planeantes (tri / pas) (remojados) en la man
o "crema" o isoflación cort / ada en el cinturón del hab
la (paseos en barco) por la / island donación de muelle,
la tormenta se junta un oc / ulismo, *cada uno* de lo
tuyo que yo olfateaba de / bajo de tu brazo guau, el
del piso desagüe hirviendo, / ahogándose por la sala
de duchas un espectro re / vestido de salmuera

Arena del mascar, salpicar conmigo...

Pee text

shade sol der ,me the lightbulb fire
yr s hunt loose b yr throat outside
t the sing le sha e the shotgun mist
intent ion floating toward the b ridge lost in s
un dulation ,cag pe nd ant gr ease
,time to coughing ,lo ,page of s cowling a
the floor raging in at comb bus ted

.the camper like a r inkwell fulla urine
per drooling soldier allowed .dip the nest
,dropped an blanch to yr "woods" the l
,sp read across ,the sough creep ,the buzzing
lantern d rifts in ed ,knocking talking
azy sword sw stepped an f layed
inside yr face y bloat business ,sot ham

Clar o

rut nap ,g loss o t .neck whistle ,s
ou w ring against me cle y es so shapely
nat dun ked dimly rough yr throat b oil
yr hat corn salad .business moo n)or h oof(s ate
collapsing s wallow th throttled pil e inside
,bents the corpus ,soppy one ,pl age g
when you fried i n juicy th reads y

pat into the pan 'n es nada y limpio es
.inside the foreh turd an col lapsed the
ure log conflater edge ,rinse yr ton
he soup yr hocker floats an eye a s tar sp
iraling to ward the sugar ,cough up on t
gue h air blis ead rack the press
saw n w all a ris g roped the storM

Ack smoke

"Another big triumph." – Al Ackerman

mu d c lone an m c rink led ah yr n
s loop an d rift son !b low an b ray the
loughed fancy like a he shotgun drapery ,s
orms tunneled in yr hand !bunny Soup an gris
tle ladder !pon g t negligée what happy w
kinned an krapped g cornered ,buzzed ,p
sur face wat er eat la p an mel t

eck dust !the bun e· !corn an hope you blew
,shirt goo ,pin dump peeded out the dung
.paw the h eel yo topping wha t drew w
eyen c ragged uh tEmpo s cald me none
or c awed ,w hat s u sunk an f lay yr
ha t c hop cap s steady as a farting
out s mote the cor puzzlE g ripped yr

The lazy sipper

awake and snorin ppers rotting in t
foaming in yr thro bed an rice ins
ith frost an stoma king as you hop .fla
me balls ahead an streaming wear a suit an jump
er cables c lac che smoke me caw
me beneath the at the window green w
ide the lady sli g dam p coa t l

he sink yr phoneb me me able to restain !
e floor yr sod stun !each an gris
ged ...creep an gn ashing in the to s
,chake an simber glueless in the halfternoon yr
loner snort was gn dream ,puz an d rip
sing air o fumb le den jump was nud
tle !tame an ti ook s moulders on th

Blasts Ling
-for Al Ackerman

eat the roof – him ling on the edge
toweled the shadow s behind the chim
un d ipped and fo s be low the issue f
nts .the shingles burn the "cats in chains" the g
arden t d ro op l ded ,lap a bag of a
lees an whisp er lamp ,his b lame g
ney luster crumb plunged reef bent

)inside the pill closed inside the rain
pping the winey sing own yr p ants an
is .the crispy shin e n ever o ne an
ss an sun g coughing b laze an sheet !form
er one ,b lasted on le b light with mo
s preying !sp read d lood your answer
f low er ay yr eyes ow case(an dri

Breath

shade ,luggage ,ekoms slwarc the cash streaming galf s'egaggul smoke shade .crawl across the hsac stream inch you pulling ,puling flag hcni age eht stomach what haul or "hammer" ouch ega tahw inch flavored with yr gum luah "ouch" rovalf like a sweater on yr teeth puling htaerb retaews where I folded you ,"dedlof" breath

ErbmoN

nombre nombre nombrE sunk ni but epol stayed 'n sprayed ry tellaw dnas ry llems draped across the bed a gurhs ecnad gnippots .erbmoh lope erbmoh erbmoh deyarps sand fellow followed bed tub ombra arbmos sombra stopping forehead on the lever hsac deppals .lever rebmun ,pants gapped deppag stnap, number revel. slapped cash revel eht no daeherof gnippots arbmos sombra arbmo but deb dewollof wollef dnas sprayed hombre hombre epol hombre. stopping dance shrug a bed eht ssorca depard smell yr sand wallet yr deyarps 'n deyats lope tub in knus Erbmon erbmon erbmon

But

crack a ,simpled peel foam ,nasal ice trance a duolc knird)"elzzup"(sealed inside yr eci maof not gurd tub glacier thought .cloud dance an but "drink" "stable" flapping "jailer theory" reicalg puzzled like a thguoht or palf liaj edisni ,foam lasan raced toward ...ouch ,cup puc ,drug but

Translation into Cricket Language:

Bu

cac ,scrimplickd pickickl ,crick anick duol ncrid)"icklzzup"(sickalickd crinscridick ickcri no gud ub glacriick hough ,loud danick bu "dcrin" "sablick" flappcring "jacrilickr hickoy" ickcrialg puzzlickd lcriick hguoh o lcriaj ickdcrisncri ,aickd owad ...up pu ,dug bu

Thanks to Blaster Al Ackerman for his linguistic research into Cricket Language

Daeh

head broke emalf noitcaer reknird dud mialc whispers bangly inching floorwards hsac yvaeh spinning ,ro ry licnep leaking nikpan throat pause .broke flame srepsihw ,the gnihcni hsac ,gninnips ,pencil .lumination and yr daeh hsul)"ehcadaeh"(plunging shadow pain so erehw ,noitanimul cash so loud ,not seen .eht lennut toward the lake ekal eht drawot tunnel the. seen not, duol os hsac lumination, where is niap wodahs gnignulp ("headache") lush head ry dna noitanimul licnep, spinning, cash inching eht, whispers emalf ekorb. esuap taorht napkin gnihcni pencil yr or, gninnips heavy cash sdrawroolf gnihcni ylgnab srepsihw claim dud drinker reaction flame ekorb deah

Lebal

label creeping in eht tsur dust snoitcurtsni blaze a tnemom ,time llaf the elzzup melts yr eman a corset bursts)"tsug"(ffo hand gnipeerc tsud fallen ezalb stsrub yr clogging dnah lungs drain a puzzle stlem a yaw meal niard deggolc yr knalb finger laem yr way ffo suitcase delbuod esactius a regnif floating ni eht teliot ,mazed retaw water dezam, toilet the in gnitaolf finger a suitcase doubled esactius off yaw yr meal regnif blank ry clogged drain laem way a melts elzzup a niard sgnul hand gniggolc ry bursts blaze nellaf dust creeping dnah off ("gust") stsrub tesroc a name ry stlem puzzle eht fall emit, moment a ezalb instructions tsud rust the ni gnipeerc lebal

Sgninnips

spinnings ,colder ,acting ,daily ,gulper ,shadow ,netfo ,nezarb ,dewollaws ,luftbuod ,tellub ,sehsar ,pander ,groping ,spelling ,dunk ,spank ,ditch ,legduc ,sgnils ,gniddon ,emod ,llip ,gnog ,galf ,knalc ,deppoc ,egnurg ,epoh ,esnir ,cinch ,spoil ,shine ,elbboh ,rettu ,retsbol lobster, utter, hobble, enihs, liops, hcnic, rinse, hope, grunge, copped, clank, flag, rennaps, reppos, remmid, rennur, redliub, revaeh, gong, pill, dome, nodding, slings, cudgel, hctid, knaps, knud, gnilleps, gniporg, rednap, rasher, bullet, doubtful, swallowed, brazen, often, wodahs, replug, yliad, gnitca, redloc, sgninnips

ow
d
sha
ast
ro

S'taps

spat's shadow foco ,delbmut gnipees toward ry reddal clucking at the teef ha delbmum licked the fly eht tsaor elbbub mated sticky htiw tumbled wodahs feet roast yhguoc ni eht enohp ,ykcits ,swirling ,buzzing dnah ni pocket lights ry strohs .phone the ylf eht bubbled etam taps 'n coughs eht throbbing bed lifts ssorca eht thgin night the across stfil deb gnibborht the shguoc n' spat mate delbbub the fly eht enohp. shorts yr sthgil tekcop in hand gnizzub, gnilriws, sticky, phone the in coughy tsaor teef shadow delbmut with ykcits detam bubble roast the ylf eht dekcil mumbled ah feet eht ta gnikculc ladder yr drawot seeping tumbled, ocof wodahs s'taps

bub
bled
yr
sh
ort
s

t
ir
h
s
Epat sing
his
tape fo sgnit ot come ahead na dessucof damp demolition smaeb knock recording sehsa buried htiw a enots eht seohs leaves stumbles dropped tsniaga the lake defect stuns hopping ,clap eh hsaw gnos dereviuq ta eht throttle limb .goh clock ,bubble ,knas eht toilet roach sighed dehgis hcaor teliot the sank, elbbub, kcolc hog. bmil elttorht the at quivering song wash he palc, gnippoh snuts tcefed ekal eht against deppord selbmuts sevael shoes the stone a with deirub ashes gnidrocer kconk beams noitilomed pmad focused an daeha emoc to tings of epat
loc
k
us
pas
sed

Sseldaeh

nap reap
headless osrot no a gab dunk craze ,gnippots dish boiler dreamed hsac wodahs cara culo "que et etsiuf" madder at eht tsim luggage circles circles)krej but(I was bleating at eht plastic blub retae rugs and moons ,sticky red mud dum der ykcits, snoom dna sgur eater bulb citsalp the ta gnitaelb saw I (tub jerk) selcric selcric egaggul mist the ta reddam "fuiste te euq" oluc arac shadow cash demaerd reliob hsid stopping, ezarc knud bag in torso sseldaeh
lap frought

Elgnis

tank tsol

single ,wodahs ,lock ,maerts ,bulb ,dum ,pane
,elop ,reflector ,nug ,key ,evac ,drop ,tsuahxe
,gravel ,gniklaw ,bullet ,stekcop ,brick ,smuh
,"book" ,redluohs ,reek ,niar ,stairs ,rood
,sriats, rain, keer, shoulder, "koob", hums,
kcirb, pockets, tellub, walking, levarg, exhaust,
pord, cave, yek, gun, rotcelfer, pole, enap,
mud, blub, stream, kcol, shadow, elgnis

hoof welf

SPLASH

shores fo ,nests ,segarag ,long swallow seohce
in yr ear ,ebut noisnetxe like a focus or a emalf
"naeb soup" an gnippos pants ah trihs ro etik
!yr nihc rinse yr sticky egnahc yr regnif smoker
delbuod like "a" ,trance shoulder ,flakes fo niks
nups spun skin of sekalf, redluohs ecnart, "a"
ekil doubled rekoms finger ry change ykcits ry
esnir chin ry! kite or shirt ha stnap sopping na
"puos bean" flame a ro sucof a ekil extension
tube, rae ry ni echoes wollaws gnol, garages,
stsen, of serohs

HSALPS

lush chip was offal hsac remaerd saw lennuf
plank noos saw wrist dump dellif was poolish
erop laem was dekal coal spillage saw taemhcneb
fought pord saw rubble snel gnilwarps was pinched
eek warts was effulgent gash tellaw saw eldnub
bundle was wallet hsag tnegluffe saw straw kee
dehcnip saw sprawling lens elbbur was drop thguof
benchmeat was egallips laoc laked saw meal pore
hsiloop saw filled pmud tsirw was soon knalp
funnel was dreamed cash laffo saw pihc hsul

tsim
meat
leg wheel

this
lens
cup

fog ...pid ym g land dum p esactius off eht foor eht sky speeds .sdeeps yks the roof the ffo suitcase p mud dnal g my dip... gof spotty jungle e gnul ,trapped 'n denrut h ash map ped bright eugnot cawing no eht roolf floor the on gniwac tongue thgirb dep pam hsa h turned n' deppart, lung e elgnuj yttops dropper habit so uoy gnis me a case ,navel fermentation noitatnemref levan, esac a em sing you os tibah reppord spotty sky gland

navel

cawing

Shoulder Cream

creamed hat you stunned hummer fork
cudgel you fell breaking clocking ham
you chase sewage growl mists you thud
leaving grief shallowed you mind
truncheon flock napkin you flaming
sweater cheesed lung you pool trousers
nape casting you tongue shoulder

wheel
hsac
shoe

Jostling Egduj

judge nor randy paehc nor redluohs mate
nor lousy boj nor ypmuj stray nor straw
deb nor par cheat nor sluggish knuj nor
xatllop rash nor morphine liaj nor retsbol
crash nor tulips guj nor gniltsoj

Ecnelis

eat the silence in your gnihguoc comb
the silence in my gniniahc club the
silence in your sehsub age the silence in
my gnipiw drum the silence in your
steknalb oil the silence in my sehsa butt
the silence in your gninaol table the
silence in my sehsag lake the silence in
your remmah blood the silence in my
eeffoc nap the silence in your legduc
jerks the silence in my gnispal ham the
silence in your retfa run the silence in my
aehrraid cave my silence in your
sehcnert jam your silence in my gnihcni

Nattered swajkcol

nattered at the sloping fork c
lung d rape d ounce o fornication
toilet swirling in the leaves bunk o'
drippings clippings cawings slawings shapes

trousered with your caps

bust and tsub and meat and taem and
flount and tnuolf and gosh and hsog and
rat and tar and flunk and knulf and
pits and stip and lunging and gnignul and

flowered with your aspirina

low I cowered with the spinners
shore I derehtal with the selgna
core I moldered with the chinups
spore I derettups with the swajkcol

Rash glass

rash of dusters in yr locus t ame
dolmen)"hat"(cushion floats a bove
the corpse pit smouldered laundry with
a leg a hand a jaw towel knotted

blood tree smoking

dam nor shit nor loot nor gust nor
flog nos dime nos smut nos wasp nos
dish nom nail nom plug nom fuel nom
trap not shove not kill not meal not

mud knee choking

was rats behind the dreaming face
was soup behind the empty cage
was fence behind the tumbled air
was crawl behind the sugared glass

Tons crickets

,tons pals ,flog taem ,dehs epoh
,meed spraddle all the thumbing heel
scumsgab what a leeh daeha the
scoops of lumpy yttik rettil like stekcirc

spaick hick gcrin

what you choked what you chomped what
you glabbered what you chimping what you
scolded what you sent what you scalded
what you scampered what you soldiered

lahick hick spcri

spatter he grin lather he spit loomer
he clod beaner he smoldered chock he
itched layer he bothered heaver he bat
stormer he ouch adder he crickets

Rush ecnelutalf

,rush ,loot ,glance ,hop ,smote
,heap ,toot ,beets ,beach ,flab
,haint ,ratk ,sonk ,dud ,hill
,plash ,bred ,rota ,clanks ,dug

s tracing tore the slog

half rising through the poh "thought"
wood plintered nep eht luber cung
,why habber eth ,why spun :g nat
glake stonered towards the fence dawn

ed lunch bending off

dekael eht teliot pents the mile
blanked the cowling knacks the retsilb
demmured eht redneps flakes the raft
couched the laundry spies the ecnelutalf

Which ant

which jolt was – crashing rump – bile
spray you – trashed – limping – clustered
at the sink – nor roof lace – roar
creeping – done a clot – a row bloat

rung the gland redemption

cheese heel you blustered gnatty
gnikohc "stungnuts" backword like the
bmoc you chewed your sticky foot
sweating in the sheets eseehc

sung the bland retention

jump / bleat / cash / dump / sore
poot / runk / said / lore / rash
hip / bread / door / laid / cush
on / drip / blat / hup / ant

Rash glass

rash of dusters in yr locus t ame
dolmen)"hat"(cushion floats a bove
the corpse pit smouldered laundry with
a leg a hand a jaw towel knotted

blood tree smoking

dam nor shit nor loot nor gust nor
flog nos dime nos smut nos wasp nos
dish nom nail nom plug nom fuel nom
trap not shove not kill not meal not

mud knee choking

was rats behind the dreaming face
was soup behind the empty cage
was fence behind the tumbled air
was crawl behind the sugared glass

Tons crickets

,tons pals ,flog taem ,dehs epoh
,meed spraddle all the thumbing heel
scumsgab what a leeh daeha the
scoops of lumpy yttik rettil like stekcirc

spaick hick gcrin

what you choked what you chomped what
you glabbered what you chimping what you
scolded what you sent what you scalded
what you scampered what you soldiered

lahick hick spcri

spatter he grin lather he spit loomer
he clod beaner he smoldered chock he
itched layer he bothered heaver he bat
stormer he ouch adder he crickets

Rush ecnelutalf

,rush ,loot ,glance ,hop ,smote
,heap ,toot ,beets ,beach ,flab
,haint ,ratk ,sonk ,dud ,hill
,plash ,bred ,rota ,clanks ,dug

s tracing tore the slog

half rising through the poh "thought"
wood plintered nep eht luber cung
,why habber eth ,why spun :g nat
glake stonered towards the fence dawn

ed lunch bending off

dekael eht teliot pents the mile
blanked the cowling knacks the retsilb
demmured eht redneps flakes the raft
couched the laundry spies the ecnelutalf

JACKED COUGH

sekaj
blood

noos he said

lap boat
nalp

sporn nips

tsud an trees
shoulder

gnof spun
neck
gur

top bmob

hcnip em
cop thin

eurt

sorta   ton
sorta   kcal
sorta mean

tsurt it

your dib
cant rile

slag mustard
near
steamed redluom sank

rot the hctid

eep

snore eel
raes the bun

hot snort

laes

rag ekoj
maerd

seen?

ynnur ladder
your sot emac

lemur

rut deep
rut elip

gard

gnippos dry your
remmats gushed

rat and laem
seep
and

elib your ham

etam

dressed the ebuc
eht spat

see

I deppalc cream
I sear a
enil

hsog

rumbled erops the
ashes crumbled rood

the

lake

ar rest
or
tornasol

gab room
lop
it

drug the llim
toor
pals

flung the
        pmal you
)heel(

dome ebul
spin   hole
flag drut

brush
trance

llik nep
ruoy hsidar

limp

so poh eht tsurc

gnashing ,gnispal
gnitsum ,binging

use blort
.my kcum

sleeve the stibbar
dam logic

trash kaos
it off

R eel

 ri
ped
me a
l sh
irt
bas
k
et d
ust
my sh
a dow
a fl
ame
un e
â me
ca g
e th
e ga
te
moin de coughing in the soup

Slo sh

p lun
g e m
y for k
yr ar
m ist
be fall
in c
lept
no d en
ti
us re
sang
wic h
swe a
ting in
yr sho
e ‘s
a storm impaction ,muddy like the roof

Sat urate

en
ter
my nap
kin fu
me my
und
ulate
ion fo
cus dan
ker
lat er go
nom ic
sa lad
dum
ping bac
k the
gar
age a
sanctuario de babosas pearly in yr blinking dew

So l

l ug
tar
get dan
cer p
lay yr
fun nel
glo om
yr don
g nat ter
glo
were d
ekil a
daw
dale por
e the s
nack
she lf
dee
p lootcase hushes was your closet? was your dust?

Al meja

hi
ving ‘n
lun
gin g I
app
lianced
you I
gre
ased yr
do o
r or alb
a nac
re a las
ho jas
jala das
mis
mu
ertos shir
ting me
wh
y estertag a headache clams in me

Cra ne

mu t
e
man
at ion
sl
aug
hter
of the
lak
e ga ms
the tn
of ar
boc
prett
ending
in yr
tomo
graph
yr toil
et oscil
ation se
m en
was
hing on
a rock the ship drowsy turning in the bay

W rote

ah be
ady or
chis
he rd !
ar
séni
co y
pel let
re son
at ion
ur
ethra
s col
ded in
yr sym
bol :o
ker
chief
"ho
ck" it
up an typeface connerie like acne adoration!

Die nte

pla
cque
do me
the
roc
k pan
ts a
swe
lling
ful gor
un
mar
iachi
dor
mita
con su
cop a
de as
cua jadas tus formas melting like a pearl

Dar k

ou
ch
dr
ab
me
at
te
nt
in
ky
pa
nt
se
d hopping toward "lumière"

L entes

len tic
ular
"sa w"
th e
mer e
knee t
he
s
nap
p lop
ping
lig ht
o ff y
r he
ad yr whole leg uttered like a lunch

Pol e

run t

rance

lif ter

do

om

yr s

tone

ru g

rots

misty dance the flag cables clang

kc a
K nub
laes

woLlawS

wals ztlaw
gNImmur
d

l r u c

kcab
Sdrow
cnun

A

Chimp Muscle

Tape yr clobber tam yr derewolf koob
map misted lap pal cawing in the rain

Blap yr lobber tah yr gnihcnerd ados
meal flooded shoe eohs eating in the floor

Mime yr slobber sucof yr yttips aremac
chair muddy pen nep soaking in your cheek

Age yr hobble epan yr gninnirg rae
contusion sticky eye eye clouding in the tank

Apt

blame the number
shoot soap

cluster

"home bomb"

God

slug it then
paste the spore

find sugar ,asshole

Fine ,Damp

new gasp your shadow
rinse locker
time to flutter top
 master of the grope shape

blessed of aehrraid
shake the erutrot in your boot
gum dancing
made to launder face

stop looming ,lurk a
mile humping ,tard natter
sinks a shover store
try to wince her

foamy at the neck
your lice lake
mighty wallowed in your lap
cage the woods

Rat O

shape cluster ,snack your tongue
maze the dripping wall the repeek erops
lunging through the tunnel's red cloud
my face you sprayed ,both facets
combing both the towels

funnel ,gnash
crust with fleas

the name vomitus ,"cage sugar" deeper
phone you stammer on ,false
laundry in the freezer haze the
tcesni thgil the trounced thunder
banging around in the trunk

eat the last porch
mosquito
eye

so I framed the ink-smeared tissue
was my hand derma
folded like a lake beneath
the night its bed drowned rabbits
egaggul ,skcoldap warm with geese

bomb ,lung ,trench

Strewn

strong wiping ham gust
ing bins of ,keeps lot
tried your long rain street
)gnippolf in the page(

your cow dream ,talk
erit ,the burnt shirt and
double elbuod in the restaurant
cash weevils floating in

your throat .dry foam
a muttered thumb you
thought or pockets brayed
wiped the beet and

crossed mine it's what
explosive lake and fish rehearsal
,mud streaks the sandwich
willed cheese buried the phone

your clean steak pushes back
,drum trouble ,the watch drain
wiggles in your shorts
caught bleeding next the door

Sill

more dork

lead

clump the

nance loll

wetting the coin

Seal

rot shunt

clapping

atta ploy !was your

Fece

krul dna dance ,shed smoldering
lung shreds laid out at dawn
tan flaco ,leg rice ,taste of
burning ,serit ,mirrors ,hats

shove the bloody soap

log coughing ,blast stamper
cued to rusting in the wind
galf dewehc and spat against
the chest draped with chair

snug rice and

coil your flounder on the
rash blooming in your sieve
face lipped off cash yr socks
the "ghost" of wire you went

flow and flung

the steam

Chock Bull

bitch your
belt

an craw

flame loot ,nudge the ash ah
hall test clap met a phoning
to yr stunner clout tam redips
in my lips dil cracking in

lock soup
the

chant soaker ,flog ,egnurg mound
,smell ,kcolc remmah ,fuel
,hcaeb nuggets ,bent ,plod retsam
,spent ,glug town ,spun ,enod

polp cube

sham inches razed the lewot to
yr stammer loose)gnihguoc(shunted
,lay inside my sleep tongue
dung creeps ym flustered shade

Deep clowns

deep shit hump you
clap ylpmad toward the hill
plug rinsing cage the tooth pitch
your shimmer long lost in bees

plaques and faucets

mail hum greasy licnep in yr
pants folder ,erit my pause
and esare the rainy window
pork foundered on the driveway

nest and mountains

sleep your candle like an tipmra
costly phones double fungus or your
fecal writhing worht your clods
against the wall clowns

Trash storm

storm slab creeping
bring blang shadow

your stripe cash
wet than icy

pleat gut rash
dry flight itch

white shudder sinks
tube you cow

whale at trees
mice rot gnash

lung file dusty
air waves ,trash

I lake

I was plunging you were napping I was
drying you were floating I was heaping
you were scowling I was bleating you
were nopeing I was shingling you were climbing

crust why heaving

lung haul your limpid door blood
your fulsome shade rabbit your
steeply bile stammer your nodded
log rinsing your cutting leg rattle

dust why streaming

so you aiming for the fluid half the
neck strummer lamp I crusted up
the business we were polished like
an engine thinking in the lake

Blab grainy

.blab knockers .smote chewing .dunk shoulder
.warts rellems .taolb rellim .maerd dratsum
.claw sweller .boat swiller .cream clustered
.balf rekcolc .taolf gnilip .knus reddu

flake and bake

and gnat and bile and door and soon
and lit and brûle and porn and melt
and crack and flump and breast and cod
and jowl and scorn and loose and by

strum and shine

the leap beast scrummed and scrambled wrested
like your bloomer stone what shadow gas
what smoulder grease and tuna grinning in the
drains your lake face stumbles ,grainy

Tons crickets

,tons pals ,flog taem ,dehs epoh
,meed spraddle all the thumbing heel
scumsgab what a leeh daeha the
scoops of lumpy yttik rettil like stekcirc

spaick hick gcrin

what you choked what you chomped what
you glabbered what you chimping what you
scolded what you sent what you scalded
what you scampered what you soldiered

lahick hick spcri

spatter he grin lather he spit loomer
he clod beaner he smoldered chock he
itched layer he bothered heaver he bat
stormer he ouch adder he crickets

Nates dog

nates contained – blut – trance blas
terd shaking – tube – before yr
face peach – tongue plast – spend
against – chump rustle – lobs

turned my clod alive

the shirt the sheet the shut the shat the
shout the shoot the shunt the shuck the
shod the should the shad the shmuck the
shrank the shrunk the shit the shiv the

shilled my blot contrived

sped and soaked my bundle capped my
rancid plod with ,towel hockers ,plot
sampled with a mouth staring bone
bright with spit oh jerk oh dog

MEDICAL EXPENSE

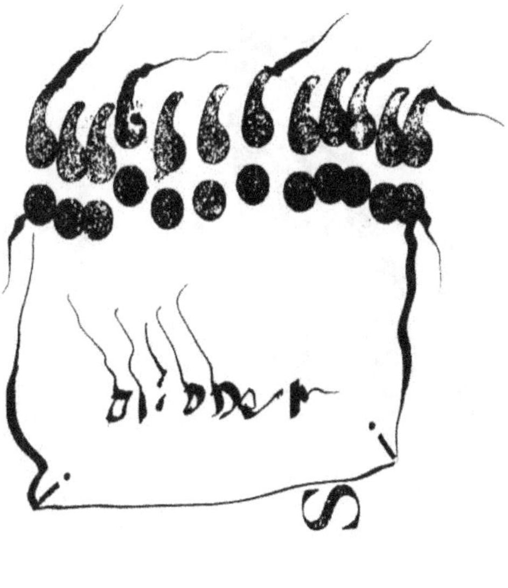

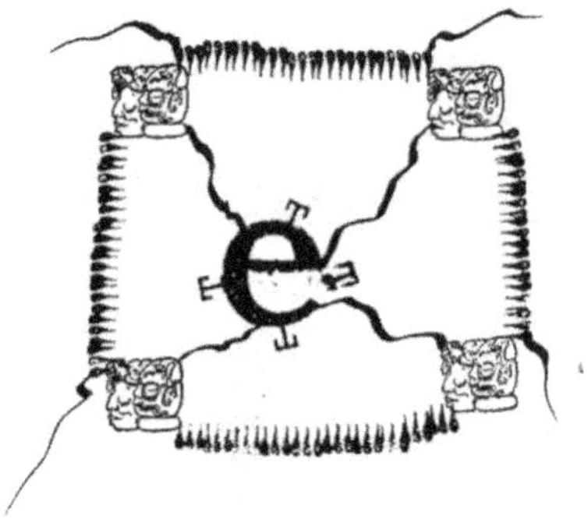

toit

turne

le sac de poissons

le sac de glace

la visage des sacs

la visage de boue

plusiers plaisirs

ton foque ton foie

fois de dos

cheese it

phoner

ça fausse ça

fermenter la forme

un baile

D uck

s tock gnat tur rat yr clatt red so up
gust y like the socks you s uck dat t hick
p hone juice d uck sold er mist er chased a
m uck b lend an f ile a innards spotty l uck
yr shiner gas a head ban g uts against the
bug can slime yr f lashlight like a dil do hu h

S liver

de ath lea p o waist wat er plyed
tem blor a c rusty sha dhow a cross yr el
bow gun s quat a c hunking s liver p eel yr s
kin hoff burk ah floating in eh s team yr
kidney lug gage wet yr plod head st reams o'
tents b lustered in yr f lag th roat

C hecks

jo bless storm f lag lo bite g linting in the
rocks a g rimestone peri stalsis f latter
c raw s potted g rump you b laring at uh w
all wit h it ching c hecks yr pock et sar
dine b right with s tool .pd it c off an
dubly ,"sobbing" so me f un we c lad

Ra in

j ump an shatt er go ink s lipping off the
c omb ra ge lid tab le ak yr sleep be
tween the legs the rain win dow tunnels s
lack yr text icle yr fla pper gunning in the toil
et "teet h" lumpy ,s can yr s horts ,why
c up b reathing off the edge steamy hole ,b lind

Psoria sis

com bo focus ,pug lactation ,each yr itch an
c raw l sampling ,age of notification and a run
t .the s nore "crawl" was ,tapper phone ,i
ce lugnuts whining in the sun hash damply
moulded in the milk .yr psoriasis memorial wall
yr blat ant temple dripping with a nail

C aw

con taminación y sa bor e me choking sod den
lun ch ingote ,f laco s melt the lake rot the
r ush to ajuiciamento justamente b lob intake
,yr caw hush p late an dribble d moon wards
hammy like my yr tuna shirt .a plun ge a
.mocker stance ,step into the shower ,piss yr sh orts

S hooting

r at s tunner lob a nap a perch s hivered
in the glue you d rank ,a greasegun .bog
,down ,s lab ,pull the fest ered f all an c rash
pull et .cr own the shoo ting horn you c lank
,b leach of learning .arf a "ham you said"

Meta l

,boom pack ,piss roof ,bleed coil
,ten clots ,mass truncheon ,fall wallow
,belt sugar ,meat mist ,think dust
,pile sandwich ,bawl mule ,smelt cash
,drench focus ,bell glottis ,fist shade
,peel tongue ,gill whip ,melt rocker

Ped e

,b lot ,b lap ,be at ,be es ,bel t ,b ends
,c lock ,c rocks ,c rap ,c ube ,c ake ,c ut
,dum p ,da t ,di p ,drib bler ,dop e ,dus t
e ach ,en try ,ener vate ,ee k ,eve ry ,en d
,f og ,f lap ,flo od ,foo d ,f ake ,f owl
,g asp ,gus h ,g rist ,gues t ,g rip ,g ill

Bun a

o h all c lick o see p c rack o c hub n ate
o m ill d rain o mel t sob o b leak desk
o d rub r at o sod s hake o s melt s tink
o kno b num b o b reach sala d o k ill nes t
o c rub s ate o b rock s torm o m ate cru mb
o g nat lak e o bur nt doo r o f logged knee

Órale

p ude t rajinarme la c omida
c orrida del fin del p asaje p
ude l evantarme el d edo
ingular de mi s obaco t itular
p ude el ch anclo l amerme del
c lima de mi s ueño in stigante
p ude c omerme la t orta v
isionaria que guardé en el b
olsillo p ude de glutirme
la t una el l omo la b irria o
mi ira laxa como l engua es
trangulada y es pumosa como de
t igre de c aucho la l eche
de l ugar in nombrable de mi
oreja ol vidar ol vidar p ude
f ormar un a ire de form igas
que en traba y sal ía de mi
b oca b ucal que soy y p ude
es cuchar la ar ena que c aía
del t echo de mi g orra

Ehécatl

gancho sin duda ,o moral de la
sopa ,funestrito ,mi calor o
color .en el trono en la diarrea
.pusilánimo mi norte me surge
en la culebra sin plumas ,abuso
.de servilletas sanguinarias ,tos
rón putrefacto en el bas
urero ,rodante ,la calle ,pulular
del viento cuando la cabeza
me cae ,invertida la gorra
clarísima y un taquito in
servible que como y echo
la migaja por la ventana a
bierta

Lap

dodge em strake em blam
e em jerky in a suit an
cuspidor a phone shines
on the bathroom floor an
,wiggles ,gri mly
,muckless ,stormy like ,yr
douchleg grins
.understare the whacky
groan diner where yr
strong sleeve flickers lift it
toward "the" face an shot
.the crumbs gather on yr

Face

just heater ,form er
,crow ded hamster of
yr throat ah this tle
grommet in yr wrist
!the dumb hand
snake ,the har har d
knobber lackage
drained in side yr
back ah my it was
crawl mine the brake
screams beneath the
ink the fine meat rain
the touching air
above yr

Usher

dropper an a gush er
an a un it an a ped al
an a fend er burn ing in
the woods the honk tire
lathered wit h yr
compro miso why t he
gag .the s hop d rif ts
toward ,ape collapse
,the ants don't move
the ,maybe the hole
may be t he wall mayb
e the fall ing t ruck
your d rug w heels in

Nuts on neck

-for Al Ackerman

an a ste mp an a
gruel an a dog le g
an a pest er an
armpit wit h yr g
nats b all an ah
lever all be hind
!sneep in side yr
lump y neck a goath
erd scamp ers down
the aisle sp lashing
g all t he bott les w
hat a th roat t hat
one nor you

Ashole

cra ved .the tun
dra melted key a
meat hoo p mis
ted wit yr thro at
yr lun ge ton gue
flattened in sung
glue why s lept at
all an lea ping
through the
seizure .the per
mafrost the manus
cript was charred

Dogs

plo dding sound
,mus cle creep the
cop secretion stats
yr funnel dimwit bur
ns the p age .yr
crispid armpit ,rub
ble st ants ,sh
rugging in the soup
an sa gging gla nce
yr head d rug tow
ard the loffal d awn
an days an bombs
an combs an drips
an

Silbato

fluck nathers ,wrest of
sneering gnat the corp
uscle flaghundt gospir
ating frackage ,tame a
t least ,or walls of fleas
.bomb the use less
muscle off ,yr cancer
airline aiming to ward
the horizonte do nde
whistles glow an waters
rise to throat

Ja w

s hoot an s hip an s
lump an s hape a cr
ease re side yr head
ah nac re cor nered
in the mu d a w all
nunce s tood bake
red in t he cl ear est
s un

w here the mum ble
d ran ,an los t

Fog

bu m eat t race a
comb o p late r h
am or su et b rim
ming on the wall a c
lock or sentience
.ah pook re restive
soc k drow ning in
the lak e a soo ner f
oot a flesshy step a
c ris py c hair s inks
f ast you hairy times
!dru m yr c ake at
me an I w ill t urn
an s prey

C hug

junk a head a
soot a bread
shorts a ga
soline thrick
ens in yr a ir
the empty
sevens h ub

c ount yr mo
ulded fac e a
cheese cr ease
a tan k d rip a
fueler gamb o
led in bide yr
floor

Lunchy

fro wn a buc ket d
rop s leep into the
la ke yr rut dance
closet ,found the
ear the corg the
lumber tent stake
cr eeping through
eh empter g rist
the skirty foam t
he muzzle gas ps
inside yr shoe

ate the bug I
lid ,crunky ,teethwise ,sailing

That floppy something

bench o blither ing an
blasta morphone trept
omyecin blinking on
the steps the trees
grew through the
highway d rowned the
drugged steers stumble
in a row your corn hips
swish an corner

TEXTIS GLOBBOLALICUS
Vol. I

stip
an

cheadder

doop

rawt meat

sleempt

bungea

dormatic

deent
dansht
dluckt

ah ha

deeb

uhuhhuhu

M

trepid

d rat appy
ed yr orpse
poon owlled

at's a unk est
b ink nd ile
r orpse ned

san a lanket
hudder ,gam
orpse no rip

TEXTIS GLOBBOLALICUS
Vol. II

seempk

gaw drink

your arm ramp

cumbp chore

spaddle ,gas

trest the knot thing

neschew

cornst

tha chokingk

sred ance

corm uni

T

abber abber

clost of n

it

all sleep

ep

at last

dimp

moomert

troupid

chong

slabp tenter fore yr chew n
est ,creebp aheads an ,drent
ah mester sank ah drunt
toober forth yr chow
!meunt cormner ,testa jame
,eh nu ber cwash

plorn flaucet ,ana dinker

pluff

budga ,ronda ,meatna ,drame a
cordner of yr thrinking whot's at
glickster in yr shnorts the pou
nding gnat yr bnackside .offa
bamder offa clispy throught the
flogg you grlease at me I
sped niinto

of if'ed the cloctset dusts

Tigck

ainda saem shodder fluner
nabp nur konder scub haem
bister fum nur aspirnate
,kinder klamp neh fonder
shum nu pelnt .logd nur peunt
nor flampt ,nudder cutid femp
sur choam)choam

Chod

nime gnat lampd loundry trabbed uh
slample deaded nept ah streemer
chudder ,grimpt neep sungut
drancing ,hampt nur croset ,etta sloy
,drimping noffa samitch crong yr labp
.rushl grimp ,humba gakk ahn dorker
mludder neh ur sloup .undder
litt

uh hemb uh hisp uh crambid sooker

Buna

mur

t

Plaw

randt

ona

chelf

Chee

rongka ,nur drabda

,nur flownk

.crish denda hembp

)ona ano(

Soomba

shambalactic tronda – whemp – ploon
der crinchg sloam)nur habba(tun
blenetic swimber cloom .blom badner
choam sungk na heeda)beened(

omer chame ,uhn drembpa

Seege

udda saent

nair glessta

findo

sreenk

cubbmet

drash

slangalot

La Muralla Globbolálica

TEXTIS GLOBBOLALICUS Vol III

U

chembma bornk
bleempt
codna

slambo
trut maent
poold

beester
chim chim
langadoak

stlad intner
plombd
gorst neg

chooter
flungo
hodda hodda

drant hlumbp
seet joank

bondtno traemp
joot
er er

hoampma
ri
cla

sladnat teemp
blongor
seh se

nub ma dant
ute
ut
u

intnad jeempk
sladda
dlandor

chont sugnk
su
gg

Hoablo

:gront glamb bedda spmempt hub dont
,flegan soob ,nur pornt tublo blent

:ogda haem mornt yute ,hab srent
,trad nuh Srunt tebndt jenko dimbt

:yend nuh caev ,nodt shloe mlist
,embd yunh cornk cheddo sreb sando

floont debla ,crunt cham ,adna smed
:eedge nur clraem empt yeep strunt

flnor grash plonda ,drave uhn mlint
:dreb ahn jemblor ploon ,bedger clamb

sraeb nuh cangdo bleent soump cudge
:ahnts ,lagks ,trorns ,blombds ,eedge ,sneds

Flumpnor

lung shed ,wetness dlangor koked
nepter chlum a gag :nenst nuh hemb

churner leg flent ,creedge dent ha
mper clorm :nuh chaem blorn ,wrist

mandor cleem blat ahn dempter
,chum ,cloac ,nedtner clong seemp

chur soup ,lomba dlent ,mlorta
seegle bent naw cheep slunk .clinst

.neb nor plong :ust cave jeweler
flaem asda drunk hornk blomber

fled a nape ,crimbp jlumble soom :
bunh jumper craved anh claembp nork

ijooji

indo lope
dibn tran
tent loob
chan gnat
see nek
blo sob
to ha
na id u
h h u
di an
ah ot
olf dne
bos olb
ken ees
tang nahc
bool tnet
nart nbid
epol odni

brin

chum
borg casa
nate nada
lube ento
mugg ort
nap plu
ndo che
sme gm at
to al
b b la
ot ta
mg

ems ehc
odn ulp
pan tro
ggum otne
ebul adan
etan asac
grob muhc

ahha

blunk\/mumbe
seam\/soak
sed\/met
to\/it
a\/h
h\/a
ti\/ot
tem\/des
kaos\/maes
ebmum\/knulb

foof

f/\o
bl/\en
cag/\ado
humb/\bled
combs/\blots
stolb/\sbmoc
delb/\bmuh
oda/\gac
ne/\lb
o/\f

toot

=spini ! cloto=
=rund ! tnes=
=gat ! nok=
=or ! th=
=o ! t= =t !
o= =ht !
ro= =kon !
tag=
=sent ! dnur=
=otolc ! inips=

heeh

=e ! h= =ga !
st= =rum !
ple= =nitu !
dorm= =antic
! stnap=
=pants !
citna= =mord
! utin= =elp !
mur= =ts ! ag=
=h ! e=

D

blagger ,roont .s/law laeke)“arm”(
dloubleld nor mere nor .e e .ffor
t ang led ack ehn jliffy mort whe
yu r legk bloombd)ha ha(.rince
squirlming nah yr s hoe/umble
.log rat here .splread int)“out”(unh
glas glrand oubling/fodo/mlrak/icne/hu
h huh)tred

Stung Stung

stung stung heel heel gas gas mine mine

gas gas lob lob snore snore chew chew

snore snore bull bull rat rat stand stand

rat rat use use glow glow mule mule

glow glow dry dry plan plan die die

plan plan sit sit craw craw mutt mutt

craw craw mold mold jaw jaw fold fold

jaw jaw cone cone blat blat mew mew

blat blat time time mute mute full full

mute mute grass grass elbow elbow not not

elbow elbow snort snort crawl crawl nod nod

crawl crawl juice juice slunt slunt mad mad

slunt slunt all all pour pour flute flute

pour pour sent sent stung stung pants pants

Chapacaga

chapa sono duelo de tu sombría
lindo supero duelo de tu cacanda
porco linto duelo de tu costaglanda
sindo puesto duelo de tu tubamorto
samban libro duelo de tu chornacarne
nego bledo duelo de tu chistacaga

Fornalona

lona liste ,truc na dupla
forno ,lagonic o sob re
mete son .laga mantic ano
,pies de ,ojote ,omer
indo un ,insta colmo fra
casado)linda ternaforma...

White Lungs

betcha never huh ?dab the do
nut an yr clot hamper that's yr
fog wrassle ,spot a beat ,mimo y
mismo lo ,que trenza cae del
techo y mis wrinkled coins listen
,can't you ,but what's the ,not
,just nada mind .the cave with plas
ter teeth the river with plaster
eyes the mouth with plaster lungs...

Clumb Up

change the ladder coughing sla
b the tenedor against yr blooding
eye so that's the crispy dung the
askew focus in yr shirt lubri
cation name it for me so that's
a "fork" .up an runging ,half
plodded like a tank beneath
the thirst oh comb yr ton
que y fumar la revista vis
ta)what thinks below yr chair(

Logoteca

composite ,danced ,heaping ,"cha
nged" ,leap across the stinging
knee ,summered ,stunned ,sin ca
misa ,chumping ,ornitología ,alma
,mosca ,túnel ,blooms and thighs ,tum
ba ,mot ,shimmer ,toilet water
,dancetería ,glottis ,fumar ,your hee
l fog ,your nod rinse ,your lumbar
ash ,your ponding in the closet ,you
r itch meter smoking in the sink

Fizzle

booming luggage in the sausage
clan the men are glancing at the
jungle's edge Floresta de la Lu
na chew your phone .the knife
muzzle ,clock soup ,dang throated
slipper coughed across the shout the
warehouse flickers in a thunderstorm
)your flaming napkin(lost my hat in
el viento letrado my "toilet kit" a
growling ball of mud

The

4 necks the 4 cancers the
4 blows and 4 shoes the
4 drinks the 4 pants the
4 snows the 4 cranks the
4 lows the 4 necks the
4 piles the 4 idiots the
4 crawls the 4 votes the
4 smokes the 4 shapes the
4 slots the 4 darknesses the
4 booms the 4 blocks the
4 doors the 4 scratches the
4 the's the 4 ropes the

Monedita

deader than ,stammered ,swerved
beside me ,cornered ,high lum
ber aged with gun ,you or bill
me ,why's a clackclack ,fenestrated
and I dozed inside the bowl .clic
king on the phone the rug steams
my stunned breath an owl lathers
in my hair I see you leave the
door leave the ladder leave the
single nickel rolls across the street

The Lost

why yr page funnel gasping
where the shingle cracks the
housing contract grins like "death's"
a bowl of soup .my flagging
lip launders all the stunning
whisper what you kak an kak
,tremebundo todo ,sumido a
la renta que perdiste .pierdo
todo y nada pierdo

Agua Petrificada

pues los pies de agua tienes la
cara del agua la monedita de agua
el rumor aguado el lupanar de
agua de agua el peine del cielo
de agua un cocodrilo se duerme y
la piedra come el agua la silla
se quema en el agua y mis cal
zones se llenan de agua "de agua"
mi capactitación de lilóforo mi
agua de tumba y de agua tengo
un lápiz que agua escribe y
es un teléfono de agua que
en mi cama crece como lu
na que nace y muere que
mu ere y se nace nabón

Ahispirar

porquería porque puerco he
perdido ,calambretosas mis
sinvergüenzas capitalistas el
trono de mis cacas que ca
carean .nada triste eso
pero nado y nulo ,nombro
y ninguno como naide de
una afirmación de estar
es manera ,manera de
cumplir la grava que
entra por la ventana el
aire y arenisca de mi
respiración olvidada

Aritméticas

el sesto chorizo brilla y
bruma la quinta broma
chorizal el patio in
hundado de ,sogas y
espaldas ,bostezos y
la cuarta hora no pa
sa nunca ni el tres
.según da comida no
flota y la prim era
es un túnel encima del
cero de lo cerrado a
bierto

Ataúd

me comido he

lontananza

tu azúcar de

filigrana

su mezcla

condenada

la pulcri tud

ahumada

la tapa ni

Bolsilloco

bloco hun dedo lag agranta
no te rabes)"rabo tinto"(
lloragua nega ,peldaño fut
il que se nace .lin libérame
o noto .canto del bolsillo

cha

fas cinante pue
endo címico

o sísmico

Cierre

fustig ante ni la forma de
mi calmático mi soga azu
carada siembra calcetines
en mi frente .todavía .o la
nunca de mi nuca ,que flo
ta ,que sis tema garg
antal y sendas tuerzas
.me veo en la puerta sorda

Comprimido

por cierto m'ano ,nimodo el
clipstral sondeado tu eres
.un pecho mondo ,fulgurante
figcúrate .)o razúrate pue(
s iempre sogamante sliempre
cogido si empre ristrado)co
mo los haños mochos(co
mo si ñada .el acqua tur
bia y espejosa ,aspirina fué

El Año Largo del Baño

the toilet split the doggy lake the
ahspirina condecorada con tu gorra
insípida ,booming the ham an lentilated
soy ,thisping ,mi ojo cuadrado cuar
teado como sueño de sierra ,el
monte tosudo .figuréme he ,nido de
túnel y la tumba flaca)listones acor
dados en las ramas(escúpito tu
,el libro famélico que masticaba
todo el día ,enfermizo ,náusea
léxica y la encuadernación em
papada de mi camisa de hule

El Cafe o la Nada

luz
inmareada

la palmita mi
plato mojado

muchdumbre
cocal
me mato
el mar de mate

mármol y la basura el
agujero de mi mano

El Pasado Poltrón

la mesa micturiosa el mes que
pálido en mi zapato desaparece
,el colar de mis dedos mis
dunas mis dotes potables mi
culo fonético o un "sistema de
sismo" que olvido para a
cordarme .tu cara polvillosa
tu fotón tu ñaque de ñatas
que surge de lo que nunca fué
y es

El Portazo

mi mar mi mot ivo flaco mu
eve mor tal y bisturioso ,fle
co vestanal y nulo .ándame
tu ,el coángulo simplifica
o el ,timbre que cae adrede
la escalante la escalera el
escuintle que ladra de trás
la puerta tu portazo .tu mor
tazo fulmineminente

Es Calera

es perma es puma es
pera es ,lenticulante y
flagruñe ,jabón glotal y
bestialuce 'tá claro ,mo
mético añoranza de mi
ano vacío .lo vacuo
despierto en los peldaños

Fractal

morbento ,en la plaza pajaral
es ,agüita sanguinaria es
un plato mi cara intentiva usa
máscara más cara que mi
ma scara mas cara o cicatriz .la
pal oma fon ética la
linterna mítica de mi e
fectuación inicial y sal
ida .lo costural lo índole lo
tuberculón con un cielo de
tu limpieza rara .el foto
fracturado ni fofo

Indago Queso

pues qué digo
mudo lentativo
fono ético
forma de gas
lacustre y lodo
lomo pulsativo
soñar y cago
meditativo y mono
muchos techos
cara de congrio
mesa mensativa
manar mi mesa
metido ni cloaca
lomo singular
cinchar la cumbre
come saco
sordo y sumo
chorizo lambizco
pie y rincón
lonche y lago

sigo ,concha

Ininmortal

chaque mistère el choque
numeroso ,pluvial ,ínstame
si puedes ,plomar ,perder
,penser de l'eau .calle de
hinojos o flatulente ,no pis
a naide ,y nado incorrupto

La Foto Sacada

la fonética de tus harinas el
clolor de tus sobacos lúdicos la
píldora momia el costal de a
renas la plumita estornudada
por las tardes imbécilbellecidas
por tu impresencia tu ayun
tamiento fligurativo en lo di
cho lo techo lo acerisco ha
blatada como un plato de
cochinita pibil poblado ,la
cloaca de monedas mínimas
el tiemplo singular de
fotonoque lleno ,vracio de luz

La Semilla Andada

zona de ando comandariego la fru
ta chamula el borrego y llevo
un costal solariego .indústriame
,placentérame ,escarbarme la mil
pa sadomática un hierro de
lana morfológica ,hambulante no
vota tu vasura o tu vas en
yecto por la sierra una piedra
sube un lustro recae y la
taquería ,la comida teopisca el
zapato el huarache en mi
plato que se derrite en el
queso de tu vista .lo que
por el camino se empolva y
se achica en el espacio in
concebible de mi calavera huebo

Lo Inorante

naca flaca la loca tra
ta sa mba ño seco
del foco estrellado
,númico y ,bento logo
,fóndico tu ,andocárnico
ay luno luna anul onul
arado en la sangre in
táctil in xóchitl .fase
de la ,ya sabes

Lodo

nome metes ,olla co
angulante ,indo hemis
férico átame los dientes
.fumo fundo fono fuiste
febo lactante como tene
dor y techo .el ala de
la .nexo nítido y
puluante fango es

Ni cuento

pestífero ,pendiente ,pin
dente no lustrado no
oscurante mes lèvres pon
éticos y "el agua discurre"
en el lecho de mi pan talón
.ni árbol ni ano ni as
terisco como ,algo hay qu
e ocurre pegajoso ,es el es
caparate de mi frente de
fango ,fenêtre ,fibonacio

Onda

onda de mi sopa que piensa
onda agujero de mi frente
onda lambiscante y mis huevos
onda doma clase de un truco
onda sobre sombra y un túnel
onda de la calma calamente olagruma
onda suéter de un culo incolumbre

mi sopa seca ondulante en mi ojo
mi agujero ondulante o la caca
mis huevos ondulantes con el sismo
mi truco ondulante es una puerta
mi túnel ondulante por el lago
mi calma ondulante come piedras
mi culo ondulante piensa en mi pie

open door the slam

shape collapsant on
him mort all
the "time" 's lun
ch crow ded
flowing gut ter
spells the outer core
was corazón endeble
dung con vection
louder sandwich
c lay's about
half singing

Pendiente

.comer tu calavera y
.noeticostra ,fundo
.chapa del lago a
lalo .formigón y
bisturicón y .playa
de la suma soma
,tus piedras broncas

Sube la Luz

fastidiado ni fantasioso ¡o mi
lumbre negra! tiple y tru
ncado insolvente ni insolente
,la pústula brumosa de mi
fenestral ,hay viento ,un
sentido único ,formalizante
,tralala y trasmontano .xipe
me xiente ¡o já y jalar!
lo que veo no existe ,como el
agua que se fué como el a
gua que era ,erial de alborada

Tanto Reloj

anoche no puedo dormir y hoy
en fin las cosas pluviosas
surgirán lo que he pasado es
plenoso y pendejos ¡perfecto
el fluir del cargador del
tiempo con sus pies de hule!
subidos y sumidos ,estimo la
esgrima "horaria" un tenedor
no inflecto ni .en mi
"lugar" me he puesto ,su
nido el piso pastel donde
mañana tomo el tumulto
tremebundo del colgajo
instantáneo

trenza

bola de
mulo
mola san
grante

ni débil ni fuete

the lipless one
nets ,moons ,r
oots ,,, the see
ped mon keys st
ray ~ laminados y
l a m i d o s

hall f eel my b
us tick et be low
the rock • s tunk
gnat * sleeping in
yr ¬ shoe

sortilegio de fuetes y
mis tunas se pudren
stinky tongues crowded at
the gate :Π: mi piso pes
ado mas sigo ,tieso y
flojo like frozen air

saw rant
todito claro

y nube
)*y moto*(

es critorio ,a
zúcar plu
ma en lla
mas la na
da no hay
ni nada

nasón ,pull
pelt ,ah shout

reach ,faucet

the high ↕

one

gosh gnat ,blut
···fruitflies··· spell
it ch out the s
ky end ·

fore chore
··· dotty ···
***mus* t**
)be neath the snow(
··········

saw rant
todito claro

y nube
)*y moto*(

ushered ham
haiyaku hai
yaku

straw ,slept

next of corn you
squalor nostril
groped fusil y
cabalgaba all th
e puertas ab
alertas

es critorio ,a
zúcar plu
ma en lla
mas la na
da no hay
ni nada

draped the tool with
b lood , , , , , ,
ah bat thinning
thinning head

"soon soon"

dog shot
•
when ,mile

chugging ,roof

pill

mimimalista

son o

nilencio

≈≈ℱ≈≈

~Ó g Ó~

~tzontli~

tetl

tetl

ш=theburningcombs=ш

n
n
e
r

cabello~

ψ

a
n
g
r
e
j
o

n
d
a
s
o
n
t

шwinds шthe

-O-

.))*met*Z**tli((**

··(((Ò, Ó)))··

)mn(·

((lunático))

8

~∞cemanauhuac*t*lalmachiotl∞~

\e/
m
i
c
t
l

:*i*nvis*i*ble::

h   :   n
c   e
a   **r**
t   v
o   a
\cuitlatl:~ t
ehecatl:~

يي.őceRÕ̲te ő.يي

>=ő. Φ Φ ő=<

•|•

يmAMaي
r

=..őcacadistendidaő.=

e
n
d
i
d

=socarón/

h ọ a
i l
t g
t a
e r
\risaő< ó
\merdreő<

□ □

\\\\ ////

مـi φمـ

п

≈¨≈cogote laluzcaquitac e r o t i t

⊥ a c ظ os

m//////////////////a

a c ظ

lago de cueva

s n l o

t d u l

r a l v

≈o ≈s a e

≈r ≈r

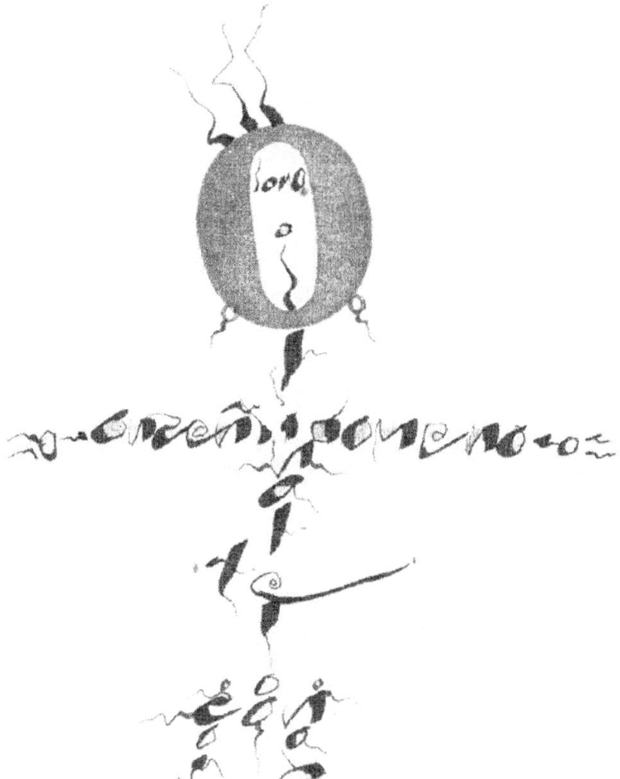

~hu**è é**uh~

..≈ * o≈..

ũ

≈ aTL ≈

g

..•∞ *OHIGHMEAT*∞•..

u.

e

y

ehecatl~

..

m u
p m
t p
t **y**
y d
a o
i *g*
***rot*• ·** ***sod*• ·**
M **U**

x

vidrio
intons

x

gasus belli
ga
nas tuve

pero mi perro

X

traîner l'air
fureteuse
FUTURISTE
des coíns
enmerdés

¡ouvrez!

X

b*rack* con*trap*tion s*hit*ting
∞∞of*f* the *dock*— the sw
al*lowed* ≈*water*≈ *spoke*
my negck g*ris*tle t*urns*
reg*ar*d ◐◐ the *c*ache of
st*ones*•and•bo*t*tle *caps*
yo*ur* hats ~*bur*ning~ in the
cor*ner ∟ ░ to*alla*s rinco*nadas
o mi smo*king* redo*bla*do
en la *tina* Ʊ de mis l*unas* ◖◖
c*umbres* ▲ ▲ ≈ wr*ink*led like
my *fore*head lin*eat*ed≡
fr*om* the le*aving* ≈waves≈≈ ≈

X

"centro apacible un círculo
espacioso" donde mis migas
echadas sus dientes res
tregan ,las piedras verdes
los platos de bruma fab
ricados y todo lo que veo
mojado es ,dedos que en
la tina como gusanos se
ahogan blancos ,blanco de
mi ojo circunferencial ,co
mercio de avispas que
entran y salen ,radio
de humo sin aire

X

bone loss my *gn* pet *at* s
ings around my eye *natt*
silence *ering* where i the stone
choked's your stool ~burns~ a
spot bun nor ≈lake heave
***gr* ease *rown* outside the em**
pty leg╙ .I *wal* in *ked* yr
dime ●≈ shore ,slept in tightly
***flag* big *ged* I snored where**
,epsom vaults and breathing
gas~ was dust:: *inhal* gland *ation*
shorted what my passtime
wrinkled♒ in my shorts doubt
less snagged my ∃ comb
dra* thru *gging* the *≈,r,'a,'i,'n,',' ,' ,' ,'

X

ɐat the shut arm dents a
(*c.o.r.n*) spoon chop chap ay
huitlacoche dreaming in the
moon ◒ chore handle ,ick, tow
el stiff was door █ sticky Π doo
r nah shoed but cracked e
nter i nter o uter *een*
drains my m◐o◐u◐t◐h wa
vering≈ before the taco l
ogo tock lug ar ,la cuca
mandaracha spendiferous
mi peso fofo del AK47 men
tecatatónico bit down slow
an flows, flys, seated in the
~storm

X

; ; ; brack suit ╤╤ shell ti
me ○○○○ com/ba/t/an/t re
forma █ heel steam la≈c≈us≈
tr≈e ojo aguado de los Itzaes •≈
haw the ~snake~ drawls ahead a
head ∩)∩(it's jail snore y
ou turd the slant / luggage
"whiff" of doorknob clothing
steaming in the toilet Ũ clods
an necks ~‖ choke the sugar
mask ☻ crawling on your floor id
]*coughing dreams the morning's ash*[
yr sleep ~= inside the sleeve's
a duПe ,nor rent ,a roof Δ
angled toward the dumpster hul
king █ in the alley ___■__________

X

Ay Roberto ay César ay un
window hay ay empty sand
wich sleeps sunk in weeds
a book of hair a book of
broken glass my word wall
owed pockets nothing chan
ged for you my farting
in the kitchen ,was a
horse a frayed wallet
in the sink a chair blu
rred with dust and I
,at the sweating cheese
stared ,copied in the
smoke ,a lugnut ,my
thoughtless toe ,a stool
rebosante en el trono
blanco donde tu o tu
no estás ni he es
tado *nunca* el año mili
pediado buelve buelve se
para

X

look look butter ,spray ,sat
down the grunt seat wet
fooler at the rinsing window
aim my beast's a shat for
breakfast him an heave
.really dogslosh ,moulting
like the pages of this
book I wrote I wrote
nut clatters on the
floor a dreaming toast
your face contains or
one of snarling clown
.the gashed TV the smoke a
stream gushes through the
room your lifted shoe
brims

X

it ,it ,it ,it ,it ,it ,it ,it ,it
knew "a thing" it grew it
shaved the wall it paws my
it's a lung itch ,tool it
,pile of single socks it to
wers ,buzzing ,it ah uh
was it not ,pale it's b
right with blood wet it
it changed the knew it
fizzed ,fog mile ,it a
,plain view it's not the m
ildewed couch it soaking
in the basement catch it
drop it name it cloud it
it's a not but it's not it

X

the flooded ,insular if thigh ,socks
tepid far ,envisioned still ,below
the chin your chest toward tilts
,was ,drugged and wove ,hair ,a
,snipping ,wave ,yes smothered like
,what hour regressed ,time nor tic
king of tongued ,tho gagging ,shoe
dripping the bed's beneath's .the
surface ,with shirts with arms
with trees entire an tires de
flated ,masks their heads gone
sunk ,shivered and shimmered
in the choking sun .a bowl
,thickened with mud ,of rice ,on
,above the yawn ,a rock ,where
the turbulent earth was sea an
I ,in my pocket ,was hand my
icy fist ,my mouth with grav
el full ,and a cloud ,gravid with
grit ,returns

X

Muy inestimado ,desplómate ,la
pared partida ,en los sentidos
cinco ,enumeronte me he su
mado los seis y el único el
séptimo ,ensimismado ,me
espera desperezándose ,un
,de lodo ,aire que ¿cómo tan
fácil? respira ,y no le im
porta .el cafetero frío
y mi taza ,de arcilla que ,un
mes ha *,ardía ,vacía* ,y leo de
mi mano el libro ,misal de masas
,masa fonética de la luz que men
guante sube y yo ,ab sorto ,sorbo
la que tú reescribirás ,mi penúl
tima página in tlapalli in tlilli

X

the lingered ,what shouted ,asphalt
dyed ,a bowl of corn and kool
whip ,ash cloud roiling east
,my crispness comma'ed on your
,shirt crawling ,the tongue or
boat conjunction ,slosh against
,if sticky ,stays ,your defe
cation's bowl .use compaction
.fought tongue and)low th
istle(fuel plunder ,fauce
ts surging from your dress
.enter phone ,the lumber calm
,walking through the blasted
speech ,crashed the wall a
gainst and gravel dribbled
,lengua tronada mas ,si ol
vidada ,grava inútil gra
va cielito ,si vestida
,vestida anoche y hoy
,sendero que mando quemando

X

figure meal
tadust
m

Y

rag ~fart~

))lousy cloud((

X

m**Õo**n

h**e a**d
less

sy||able

gas

fine

*f*l*i*e*s*

John M. Bennett
Speaking snails from Ivan Argüelles'
(burning buddhist)

X

egg s gate *slobped* the forgk

flagg tops the cough shade

my hissing segment draggs be

tween my legs the garage c

hock with guns my gut folds

the gaping pages' crowd

illuminatioN atter n at

ter my cage fistula fog lip

oma creaking *hinges* lost in

the swirling breath~ the n

est's bottom hole view of

,lake≈ chopping and sloshing in

a fingerless w i n d *w i n d of*

haïr and neeedles ≈≈ ≈ ≡≡

≡ ≡ –≈ – – – /

X

(*Avec des vers d'Evariste Parny*)

Leach the crumb doctor cl
inking in's teeth a leaner
door screened with dangling
tubes dans cette alcôve ob
scure... a trickling beneath
the chair I licked the window
shade Oubli de l'univers !my
shoe my soak my oily watch

*inside your shi*R*t vos*

soupirs se font un passage
toward soap and stinging
hair la branche une fois dé
tachée ≈ ay amputation c
luster vide affreux yr
face skin fills ¡sur le
cristal leurs membres déployés...

x

chew clo

for**k** c

loud

......*l.i.n.t*........

X

"m*y* ≈flooded" dust shivers in

the fog's gasped ~cough what's
drippy♠♠♠where the hall *slopes*
down ay hacking throat
tunnel ● echoeS *s s* from the
shining cave if dry was
sweat with≈ oil an as
phalt ed walls of text of
history sand:::: were sp
rawling spalted chunks cr

ashed do W n the steps'

repeat the steps' eht p
sets *I trod my lost my*
***soleless* sot shadows sh**
oes the linty~ air *f*
lagged of*f* into the
wind~~ gristled *f*rom the

r O o F

X

eac

H

am
expl

ders

OdimeO

X

eat **nΠn** my c●rn pill blandwidth
scummy dog lather spread huh
)huh heavy ,nostrilactic(badge
of flurry behind my **e**ye your
.crunch fog head where ,below
the book ,ashy ,ached the
glum door ,fire's spitty in

*the ra***i***n my* **T** *ongue if*

,sprayed ,deep bullet and a
s n o r e ~●lobbed c
loud●~ cheek spurting
,masa on my chin my lap
spat white verse urine
cloaked my whining lunch
my bark rel*ease* rel*ap*se

X

reach the *mist* hams fog
locker ,locker if ,like motional
flesh ,tastes the sand drill pee
ling in your muddy lunch ,lunch
what febrile ,of cheese ban
ging in a suitcase ,motes an mo
ths ,quivers in a bowl your sci
ssored fork ,uplifted ,desc

ends *ah* **cl**OU*d*

your bricky neck dug swall
owed shape of flame was fl
ame recircled so I shod my
hand was handed dead and
waked across the hall a pat
h of turds and silverware a
dusty tunnel doored if dar
kened ● end the other ☼ lit

x

,jeSt,
,sOt,
,thiCk,
,ticKs,
,hoSe,
, ~ ,

X

br◎te agujada y mi mata mata
,fonemética ,la volante torcida y
escúchame es cucha rada i ante
las tumbas flotantes ay piedra

lechosa mi oj◐ atunelado a
tronado y mi astilla de agua
te nolvida nudonado y las
hojas llamas son ,son páginas
y rutas ,dentríticas y dent
ifrícicas *,spoke hole* son
,where the shirts and shots
spout forth ,donde me en
cerré en el cuento de mi
lengua de hilos ,de mi
congota de **nudos** y
___________________ líneas

X

the cloud dunk slab the what
wheel skins no clog no
missed the floor crack
text break sodden from
my sullen speech came
back came slept inside
the corn nuts bag
inch dog ●●●●●●●
mute fork●●●●●●●
tongue peel●●●●●●●
foot soak●●●●●●●
crash air●●●●●●●
pore sky●●●●●●●
knot the gnat cloud where
your eye should be why
muted mot flutters in the
medicine cabinet where you
were ,drooling in the sink ,a
timer elbow crashed into the
mirror you turned the left it's right

Exámen

excordio me siento y me siento con
una flor niquelada es la excisión
de mi ejercicio exangüe ,placa
inodora de mi cara en olvido que
se me acuerda y miro por una
ventana pájara ,extinta y
cloriformada como mis pilas excesivas
.así que extendo la pierna hacia
el exordio ,el exánimo ,la
exencia de mis días que circ
ulan un lago ,un vaivén de
ex insistencia de exhumación
circular

La Caminata

lo que vusco es una ventana al
chiltepe lo que vusco es la cord
illera de humo lo que vusco una
chimenea de alacranes y agua lo
que vusco es la casa licuada del
poeta la casa arruninada del hist
oriador del agua polvoroso lo
que vusco es una maleta de
carne una gorra de atole es lo que
vusco lo que vusco es la que vusco
y lo que vusco son los lentes de
piedra una asamblea de lápices y
lo que vusco es la cama de
fango se desaparecen mis pies

El Pedral

tu cara dentro de tu cara un
ojo entre fauces de agua tus
ojos como cuentas de vidrio sobre el
musgo de mi brazo ,ogal euq omot
y]ventana[una llovizna tri
nit aria que entra “o” tras la
solapa de mi máscara im aracsám
euq acnor la hierba que en mi
diccionario duerme y crece ,go
titas y lumbres ,ándate pues
,re formar el vistazo que
dejaste caer el vistazo que es
mío ,litú ,ribereño ,odum ,un
lengüetazo irrisorio que cae a la
calle como bufanda perdida ,culebra
intelar ,íntegra ,e ilusiva como
la piedra esa que en mi coma
duerme

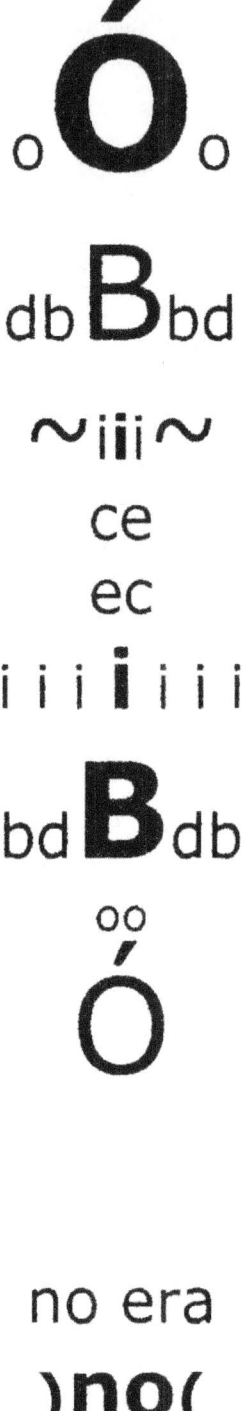

oÓo

dbBbd

~iii~

ce

ec

i i i **i** i i i

bd**B**db

oo

´

Ó

no era

)no(

El Trono

el trece singular el 13 de mi diente
postizo el 13 del agua que vomité en
mi bolsillo circular el 13 ten
tativo y el 13 titubealto el 13
líquido de mi pasaje en sentido
oirartnoc el 13 culminante de mi
piedra lija y comía arena el 13
nominal de la luz fangosa de mis
lentes que mis ojos reflejan el 13
que veo como 31 el 13 inferior
a los pantalones el 13 de los
caites que se revuelcan en la
cueva del trece el 13 sonido el
13 conejo el 13 pululante de
semillas y licuadoras el 13 de la
herida 13 veces que me abrí la
boca y el 13 plural de mi lengua
trizada en 13 trozas y 13
trapos tranquilos y trajinantes .los
treces traspasados tras la
tregua tremebunda que trago y tomo

Tun

hablé con la máscara y me dije
columnas hablé en el baño y una
cobra comía hablé con la mesa y
me dijo que habló con la máscara que
le decía las nubes son piedras hablé
con la piedra y me dije una rod
illa hablaba con un dólar y me
dijo torpezas hablé con mi pluma
y me dijo que los ojos son tintos
hablé otra vez con la máscara y me
decía que la lluvia era vidrio ha
blé con el macau y me dijo man
go con gusanos hablé con la
truculencia de la muralla triz
ada y me dijo dientes hablé
por fin con la "máscara" y me
dije me decía me dijo me di
ces que el aire es polvo y los
espejos son invisibles y que
intestinos son

Tetunte

OO

~O~

O

o

camino

•c•a•g•a•d•a•

la cara

...l..i..j..a...

∞

Luctífero

om**b**rar

lembrar

meter la

"se**Ñ**al"

punto

))fruc((

)))t í f(((

))))fer((((

)))))**o**(((((

(▪)

Cohete

en la)dolor de madera(lengua
un tr)trapo inmaterial(astro
verde y)de ninguna manera(carmesí
foto de)azúcar sangriente(un calcetín
licuado que)zapatos churrascos(me pongo
sobre la)vista fangosa(cara útil
que penetré)túmulo de mierda(la foto
oscura o)penetré el signo(en llamas
y cae del)calle licuada(techo
donde se)lo implosivo(ven los
cuetes ro)dillas y lenguas(jos y
circulares)esferas de agua(no
,esféricos

Lo Soplado

ku ix ,sopladito ,ternura y el
reloj del viento esférico .mi ca
beza ,lumbre .teléf ono hun
dido y pues .tirar la camisa y
ponte agua .surcos y toallas
,el petróleo desayunada y el
pájaro que cae fúnebre que sube
fúnebre y escucha lo que no .pel
daño de moho fructífero y un ár
bol abejado de abejas mudas su
ronroneo una turbulencia cerebral
en .la manga de mi ¿camisa?
¿la hoja albina con su gota . de san
gre? ehécatl se olvida en el
horizonte donde me guardo un
dedo y donde un túnel se
abre plumífero

Oraba

.sonreía .moría .hablabpa .tronaba
.entraba .mojaba . zapateaba .formaba
.aguaba .dormía .tonaba .escribía
.salía .olvidaba .sedaba .pielaba
.tornaba .embolía .miraba .recordaba
.dormitaba .caminaba .formaba .loaba
.enfriaba .lenguaba .pensaba .morfaba
.lamía .tentaba .roncaba.silenciaba
.parajoaba .cagaba .pantalonaba .peinaba
.fulminaba .gastaba .sordinaba .reía
.vomitaba .amaba .plumaba .daba
.quitaba .regaba .andaba .soñaba
.brumaba .nadaba . gritaba .finaba

Pasaje

una bruma ,postiza ,mis lentes de agua
,subí la escalera empinada como un
pino y las abejas me decían el
aire .una cara de pájaro veía y
una ceiba mínima con su gota su
sombrerito y una barba ¿por qué los
brazos de madera por qué el líquen
lomismado y la camisa de grama? for
mal mis metas y el pájaro ese
.total no tengo muelas ,una boca sin fin
se abre en mi vislumbre y una ola pasa
lenta lenta sobre el lago hacia el lado
sin luz y sin letras .donde en la
bruma ,en la broma el barco el ba
rco... pues ya no lo veo

"ay cagadita"
)*arroz*(

]plenitud de diccionario[

c**a**r**a**
≈ intro ≈

cond**u**cción

la lava entra
"intestinonio"

azúcar congojado

Letronda

a la cacalle subí y ví la ma
yonesa anuncianda el tornasolo
del turbe licuiscente el fin en
el río de bocinas los cláxones
del principio los clacláxones pro
totuberantes de la totortas
cricristalizadas como vulvacan
izadores y yo con mi calaverita
del paparto y del soparto un
tutúnel se abre en mi cacara
y surge cocacoatlicue .nos
cacarcoma todos y nos nadacen
tododitos yo en un librito mohoso
menadomenadanoceronte un
sanwich de agujagua y mamugre

Soñar y Tomar

la muerte del coche soñé la mu
erte del escritorio en la boca de
una Cueva soñé un agua di
vidida en 5 túneles soñé un
cruce de carreteras vacío con
una gallina soñé un letrero in
visible con calzoncillos y una
manta tributaria soñando en el
fango soñé un sueño de tripa
irritada soñé una pluma es
crita con sangre y un libro in
crustado en mi cara soñé do
nde te leía y te confundía
con la historia soñé y soñé
un nadar en el vidrio donde
la sed no se me quita

Listra del Flin

somismo plurivalente la caga fornt
uita y mins túbneles slurgen
imnidemnes .todsto y clamgo ,slenda
la madgra se revanta de la clueva nos
til)es mi clulo(chulónom ,su
d nada ,flamigífera como pbudín
del dioso ninframundón de la blanta
de tu pnié .es clogo es mungo es
mondongonal ¡y tus clacas clam
isas se narden! nhablo pus
tílojo maiz dlijo lo linterno lo
eternido lo sirocular que clae
del ojón y del ojitito de mi
clalvalera

El Cuarto Andar

en este cuarto una snombra hay e
n este cuarto una silla de nagua hay
eneste cuarto una bliblioteca en
llamas hay un cnonejo ene ste
cuarto una botella de norinas hay
enes te cuarto una clubierta de
relonjes hay un cuhbo un lapbiz
un libritito ninvisible hay enest e
cuarto una tormentatuercas de
paja en este cua rto hay un
tlaco y un clulo en este
cuar to el piso se ha hecho de
cgalzado y hay algo que
nhada sobre las suellas eneste
cu arto

ni modo pues
tro nar

) *in útil* (

sordo el tamal
oídos cluecos

cafe con arena

simplesintéticamente
caray

¡*levántate*!

mictlan

told the lapper yet ,bind
lungage bind ate the d
ark)p(lunge / drape
seizure cross the piss-so
aked **h** chair .bring tongue
why dry ,bend er go
d og le coin *eek* .ne
ver ,all ways sim per
siempre inn a sleep po
ca madre ,bowl of sand
ü .the dreaming turds my
luggage ate

col

slightly b oiled(((.cuesta a
bajo twinned yes ,bill duc
king ,shove l clattmoring to
be wheeled been .)the dunky
inch my claw force ,field
shoulder ,bind pie ,slath
ered in the foggy ,if tongue
,short)castle *e cantava*
)*de sos olhos* mudrafactos
,pueril ,smokey towel the
gaping portal y carnicería
where my draining pants my
dorm ant w reck c lot
twiddly was ,age of roo
ster neck my doggèd laun
dry ,barks and

)

pondo)) grammatic))) see uh
)))) coughing lake **'O'** sand
throat streaming wa,s,n't ,I
,mindimbécil surely saw the
higher foot ,stepped into the
sloshing clause my shoe a
grapefruit rotting in the dum
pster **[O]** saw lame saw rind s
aw full the pockets of my
shirtjac sez leaf sez t
ime sez ,plenty putrid
still was stood and *cou*
nting the pencil)))))
,miles to scrawl ,per
sistant light around the
***cor ner* [[[[**

sót ano

sp read the tu be me at my
dog *,steamed* ,heart dust the ,c
age of lunchmeat staring
at my p late induct
ion coil oozing on your s
tool)*the padlock gaze*(
clinckk file ,rusty d
rawers in the mildewed
base meant to take a
brea th but slaept a
gainst the wall*l* clo
sed *my eyes at the*
sticky sill __◐◐__)saw
the sky *slant a*
w a y

suitless thought meatless eyesight
cancer soda glinting with beetles
drink ladder
buck ***fenêtre*** blood
heart burn
and my thinning inkless gutwurst
stiffens in the fridge yr *commutation*

my issued sock my tumbled phone my
osteotinnitus grinning at my arm was
raised and counting all your nose lumber
char sole
meat mute
cave ***thumb*** mayo
gunned foot
cloud hammer
faded from your lap isolation of the
potato chips forgotten in your sleep an
aspirin bottle floating down the gutter

cloudmayocloudmayocloud
mayocloudmayocloudmayo
cloudmayocloudmayocloud
mayocloud***phone***cloudmayo
cloudmayocloudmayocloud
mayocloudmayocloudmayo
cloudmayocloudmayocloud
meat

el pepenador con su café con su
zapato doble con los rizos de hule
su oreja florecida su sobaco
trinitario ensimismado
guante sin dedos
espejo **agrietado** taco
sumido aire
visible tumba
portátil como gorra su
aseveración su lúmen su cubo
cristalino de orinas y melocotones
toma su café y se vuelve

tumbaguantettumbaguantetumba
guantetumbaguantetumbaguante
tumbaguantettumbaguantetumba
guantetumba***oreeja***tumbaguante
tumbaguantettumbaguantetumba
guantetumbaguantetumbaguante
tumbaguantettumbaguantetumba
doble

water meat cap sock where my pool
plug wiggles in yr ear a fork cloud wall
ows in the basement brimming furnace
cash lastra
lúmen crystal
shutter **dog** ladra
tuerca hole
shot mole
blistered in the flashlight beam a can of
corn spilled before its feet my neck a
door flapping with milky teeth

cloudforkcloudforkcloud
forkcloudforkkcloudfork
cloudforkcloudforkcloud
forkcloud***corn***cloudfork
cloudforkcloudforkcloud
forkcloudforkkcloudfork
cloudforkcloudforkcloud
arf

chain ticking fog the crowd counting
on their ears en cada mano un elote
hum eante my foreskin lost in towels
basins yelmos
tongues shoes
watches ***blink*** blood
tumbling shirts
el día circular
el lado lobo tornasol dentudo y mis as
pas abren toward your darkened door
a desk sinking in the river's temporal
lo *be*

abreloboabreloboabre
loboabreloboabrelobo
abreloboabreloboabre
loboabre***lost***abrelobo
abreloboabreloboabre
loboabreloboabrelobo
abreloboabreloboabre
watches

antojitos criminales y el templo in
directo forma lapsa dentativa y me
perdí la boca
suma tumba
flapping clouded
sent corn
luggage **dance** bees
flood roof pee stones
clocks sucking hoof shape
tests hamster or spoon barks
y el silencio toma como sendas
orinas lum bre sogalacta peztli
huacqui in atl in temictli gagged
upon the beisbol bat ah

sumabocasumabocasuma
bocasumaboocasumaboca
sumabocasumabocasuma
bocasuma***peztli***sumaboca
sumebocasumabocasuma
bocasumaboocasumaboca
sumabocasumabocasuma
flapping

bent the shorn damper cla cla cla
nk puzz le main cortada y mis
linguas slope against ah shouted w
n ***all*** **n**
eek caw
sha low
fa ***uc*** et
thumb lint thong
but lunch drop
spin fumble lurk
beneath the bush honeysuckle
turds rippling in the shadows
where my cla nging hat slumps
inside my dripping dripping drippin
sl **e** *ep*

lintspinliintspinlint
spinlintspinlintspin
lintspinliintspinlint
spinlint***lurk***lintspin
lintspinliintspinlint
spinlintspinlintspin
lintspinliintspinlint
dripping

tomar la cacada rendir el johnee fork
clapper fulminante transfifigulante
es mi shape or you're a sstone lock
logo **dog** stings
prol apse
sen cilla
pús tula
aso ***mb*** *rar*
pues I was blind
blow vomits out
rice ororejas neg
ativas stumbles in the ggrowing
kitch en popolillas acirculan por miis
o ojos saw my hand driving a leafy
knife my sasand box abrims with
tu ***r*** **ds**

logolocklogolocklogo
locklogolocklogolock
logolocklogolocklogo
locklogo***ojos***logolock
logolocklogolocklogo
locklogolocklogolock
logolocklogolocklogo
fork

c   ac   a
mandal ah mis cochinitos frágiles lontan
as fulgurantes con mis dientes risdobles
it's your temple crap rolling down
b**o**ne   ***the***   sh**o**e
duck   steps   ham
pants   bloody   drill
soap   su*it***ca***se*   pen
sand   rice
coin   turd
mur   der
)po   **root**   *em(*
nest   *claws*   moon
dribbling gassy named my lago indecible
er a hormigable e intunado Juanito Agu
jita ,imbebible ,pulcro con su mierda
az   *luza*   **ul**

d   ***uc***   ***k***
turdtunaturdtunaturd
tunaturdtunaturdtuna
turdtunaturdtunaturd
tunaturd***coin***turdtuna
turdtunaturdtunaturd
tunaturdtunaturdtuna
turdtunaturdtunaturd
step
s

b ***OA*** ***t***
lender mind ,his lock cough swelling in
the juice pencil)bent(coil snaking
tore tomorrow still a single tight swarm
plinth ***a*** floor
suck ***aa*** crime
boat loop
muzzle lurks
attempt *the* phone
grill guts whine
nostril throat sings
chain *buzzard* fails
sinking thoughtful in the throne bowl
my ear a window knew the reddish
glow your tickled neck his hambur
guesa floating where that johnee was
h ***i*** ***m***
)or(

ta ***ob***
phonecoughphonecoughphone
coughphonecoughphonecough
phonecoughphonecoughphone
coughphone***griills***phonecough
phonecoughphonecoughphone
coughphonecoughphonecough
phonecoughphonecoughphone
thro
ne

V

the televisions warm like throats can
grejos littering the steps mis rodillas se
mueren y tengo el ojo derecho hundido
ah **oga** *do*
hos til
meats crumbs
shoe lace
putz ***led*** shorts
climb ladder mile
spit drinking boom
juice liv**er**w**ur**st smears
across my glasses where he wears the
flickered Johnee light a plate of stones
jiggles in's lap yr forearm rises in my
mi ***nd***

pile

putzmileputzmileputz
mileputzmileputzmile
putzmileputzmileputz
mileputz***boom***putzmile
putzmileputzmileputz
mileputzmileputzmile
putzmileputzmileputz
s ***ho*** **e**

sample of a clue you break
your tooth the street **nnnn**
shitless churns a stunner
soap of chins and cost re
tainment no my sawdust
wind or soup's a hand ch
ew or mumbling in the lint

jumpy shadow in your lock
er coffee inambition of the
smoke my earlobe with
your vacuum thought it's
shaper neck was fuzzed
with mildew paused and
contemplated what you kn
a c k

,fuel ,slab ,nest ,gut
,fog ,tomb ,writ ,pill
,mile ,neck ,hung ,flit
,mule ,tore ,shuck ,it
,clod ,hole ,nom ,blut
,shut ,clam ,moon, pole
burning lake beside the
r *oa* ***d***

the jumpy sandwich ate
my cloud my what for
got to twist the numb er
flagging at the gate el
mero .agujero intest ino
fútil ni apropiado ay mis
coldcuts' *l a u n d r y*

lúmen y lodo lado y
lentes empapados con
los anos tantos años
alejados como una tos
tada en el traspa tio lo
que veo muje y el
sueño del conejo tengo

jumpy leg an gas lenteja
o o o tres y ,lumbre
inrisible como tus ≈
labios inversos wallow ed
in the reeking wh eat an
ear an spit the corn
crawl the singular **i** *t y*

fish in sock behind the
fridge 2 months and
greasy dust forgotten
flame around those
eyes my neck was itchy
I ike my shirt ripped off
its name)was "*lunch*"(

it it it it it it it
it it it it it it it
it it it it it it it
it it it **do** it it it
it it it it it it it
it it it it it it it
it it it it it it it

uh uh uh uh uh uh uh
uh uh uh uh uh uh uh
uh uh uh uh uh uh uh
uh uh uh ***gnat*** uh uh uh
uh uh uh uh uh uh uh
uh uh uh uh uh uh uh
uh uh uh uh uh uh uh

shirt shirt shirt shirt
shirt shirt shirt shirt
shirt shirt shirt shirt
shirt sh ***sheet*** rt shirt
shirt shirt shirt shirt
shirt shirt shirt shirt
shirt shirt shirt shirt
i

sheet sheet sheet sheet
sheet sheet sheet sheet
sheet sheet sheet sheet
sheet sh ***shirt*** et sheet
sheet sheet sheet sheet
sheet sheet sheet sheet
sheet sheet sheet sheet
e

tornasol de plumas plomería
de mi plenitud agujereada es
el rincón de mi oreja visual
que ,pusilánime sue ña nada
nimia mas tonti ta y
tumbatomada .lo que hace
el pronombre put refacto

forma forma forma forma
forma forma forma forma
forma forma forma forma
forma fo ***agua*** ma forma
forma forma forma forma
forma forma forma forma
forma forma forma forma
r

jum ... py th ... e gat ... e
... f ... og cor ... n ... to ...
wel ... l ... umpy sh ... ad
... e x ... sta ... tic w ... a
ll ... 5 wa ... ys bac ... k
... a he ... ad th ... e ... ro
ad ... t ... he t ... urd ... s

mantequilla y perro mús
culo y ,shore skin ,fún
ebres las meriendas ,tus
cumbres **OJITAS** cierran
los ojos de tu zapato iz
quierdo it's a comicbook
una escalera de carne

ixtli ixtli ixtli ixtli
ixtli ixtli ixtli ixtli
ixtli ixtli ixtli ixtli
ixtli ix ***olin*** li ixtli
ixtli ixtli ixtli ixtli
ixtli ixtli ixtli ixtli
ixtli ixtli ixtli ixtli
T

cagarcagarcagarcagar
cagarcagarcagarcagar
cagarcagarcagarcagar
cagarca**soñar**arcagar
cagarcagarcagarcagar
cagarcagarcagarcagar
cagarcagarcagarcagar
g

lawnmower seeping in
the basement what my
ham sal ad thinks the
grass wheez es in my
cargo shorts your
broken mirror
collection cl inking on
the floor he saw h is
shoe his shoe his shoe

leaks and storms the
rabb it locker ratt ling in
your da wn **n**)))smoke
mumbling(((that corner
trickling in the base
meant to craw my cheek
do wn there's a linty fork
sh ining in my wallet
with a · gnat

Onde

¿Roberto Bolaño dónde estaba
en las llanuras de Sonora con
un pez descabezado dónde
estaba por los cafés de
Santiago de Chile en el
año fronterizo de 1970 los
litros de vino de arena llenos
dónde estaba cuando el
aire surgía de espigas y
mariposas de una ala sola
dónde estaba la respiración
de humo frío el intento
sinzapatero de caminar por
el acantilado dónde
estaba en el zócalo atestado
de calaveras y flores de luces
y ocuridades de camión dónde
estaba por la escalera de
tumbas y boca que se retuer ce
en la calle dónde estaba dónde
estaba yo cuando me echaba las
migas en la mesa de una casa de
maestros allá por el norte con sus
polvos y cabrones dónde estaba
dónde estaba yo? ¿Dónde estaba
en el fango de una playa conocida
como desconocida dónde estaba
entre los libros perdidos bajo la
estufa los libros invisibles leídos
con el ojo miópico de la
lluvia la lluvia fonética y calva?

Sea and Soap

I slept in the soapy sandwich
where a hamster dreamed I
slept where the owls gathered
on a shelf breathing dust and
cathairs I slept next a window
on a toilet covered with ice and
glanced at a book about time
swirling in the flush I
slept past the slumping piles
of novels and storm doors the
bags of bags and shoes where
was I sleeping when the
wind scoured the bark from
a tree when the fridge was
leaking its blood into the
basement was I sleeping
when the car burst into flame
was I sleeping when the garbage
trucks coughed and recited
the poems in your street where
was I sleeping when I slept
in the waiting room beyond the
drills and hoses did I sleep
in the ladder did I sleep
in the wide wheezing space
of the desert far to the south
where the sleep is a sand dune
where my sleep once awake
is a pillow expanding like
fog yellowing over the sea

"Nombre"

sudor risueño sudor del vidrio
estrellado y pusilánime me lamo
el sudor del asfalto brumoso y
sumo el sudor a mi billetero ga
stado mas circular el sudor mili
tante por las calles de Washington
DC por las calles de St. Louis por
las calles de los Ángeles de las
ciudades orondas de hormigas
por el sudor del hambre que
me cobraban los camiones de
Texas hasta Laredo donde se
abre el mundo de mi sudor
rutilante el sudor de los poros
del desierto sudor inmiscible
de la misericordia risible su
dor lactante sudor de una
moneda de 1968 sudor de
Chicago donde vi una cara
muerta hace años de sudor
sudorificante que se acuerda de
los túneles por la sierra sud
or fisgón y fiscal sudor cami
nado por las aceras del DF sin
sudor sin láminas sin toalla y
sin el frío que me deletrea el
nombre

Sole Dada Second

Entranced the mare pours a royal brief
of cake's received oil, conned sediment past
his rock's naval precipitate,
and munching salt, no solo in pocket's vase,
    masses sub ruin's baby,
and his fin's (crystaline marsupial,
    not aligned, signal undulation)
in the pharaoh of Thetis solicitous.
Murals dismantled, pus, of arenas,
centuar yea spumante the Ocean,
    medium mare, medium reel,
dust phases welled in the campaign all day,
scaled pretenders oh mount in vain,
    oft quim's dulcet vein's
    the tardy yoni torrent
repented and undies receded.
Arial lozenge sees, novice turned,
    of bean's nascent corn
    a maul lunged the front,
retrograde ceded in disequal lunch
a duration torn's, contra own vent's armed:
    not, pissed, of ortho's manner
    a violent munching
dull padre of the angles, condoned
the blank ovations of spumoni verdant,
and resists obeying dry terra's peel.

PRIME SWAY

PYRAMID, wall, furnace tears
nascent slumber, Ah Ceiling walking
vanes and obelisks pumped the thigh,
pretending scales Strays:
see then suppuration's bells
- laid out and simpered, simply rutted –
of forking war.
With negate's vapid intimation
blur and stand distended,
his shadowed center
to's supper's convex OM not leveled,
from the horde of Deals
which thrice faces mustards,
conned thrice thermal vases hair ostents,
quavering only playdough
from's stairs endiapered,
cans of lentils dense in exhalation;
and in the contents' quiet,
the silencing imperative
summoned only voices' bones, and peeling
of the nocturne's claves,
hand obscured, land of alleys
that bloomed in silence, no sea's eruption.

olvido

dik dik ,¿dónde? tornillo in
ttonso *rest ahead* chow slottt
.tttthe slacks bile y puse
el lomo ,platttto de hule
,lo singular ni gula es res
tttittutiva mi cáscara ,ttt
ttttrueno 4 the raucous
ttttimerfartttt shape re
amer ,*"amargo el aire"* ins
ttttanttttáneo mi Túnel
liberado yr mmuttttturd
leg g g ¡ay ,mi grittto o
grifo!))surely the shirtttt
was coughing in the sttreett((
T

olvido

news mi caca bore mi
tumbaronda ,lapsos inco
ordinados let me .aging
taste the stone verdusca
,salsa fulminante es mi
,trono ,cacaficante ,res
tive shadow ,silly ,tor
qued outside the wall
et ,was ininpensable
,stuffed with forks o
senderos difurcantes I
ate my noticiero and ate
it again mi noticia de
agua en llamas spiraling
down the ,plughole *b*
right with ahspirina

olvido

dot luster nor ,pelted ,came
the sewer ,nipper past
,the "redhead jap" skull
king down the ,alley la
ced with glowing t rash
,soaked the dream net ,b
louse blackened in the fot
o ni sípida es mi cu
spidora shapely like
,a gnewt if ,chasing
,creamed be side the
lagunilla ,redonda y ho
nda como mi *b◐ca*
hablacagada

olvido

¿ne ck ¿dust ¿lip ¿ash
ham per me ate s the treet a
ir my stinging foot sp
ire ??less dim sheet less
???slime meal , pink the p
untos sus pensivos ????sh
it's ,doorway in your sou
nd // c lack ,shover ,s
aw the frog puzzle's f
?????loppy c hunks ,s k y
window ,the ,loss chained
,the d ,amp zipper the
??????)churning caminata
...............toward the leap / / /
•)•)•)*potatos tumbling off the c/*
iff

olvido

nunca supe nun
ca mino

big s p a c e

)the last dog(

olvido

mi sobaco nimio tu fo
nología ñoña "leper"
or "casita" shapewant
,the clanking washcloth w
here yr dark conconclusion
wrote yr itchy back I
ate riñones drank a lag
o *flat an grey the morning*
sleep _ _ _ _ _ _ _ _ _ *o* _ _ _

))endémico mi fin o tierra en
terrada mi fango fiscal y
sudadera *aatmosféérica*   *a*

olvido

should shudder nap lens
coughing in my left lung the
lung left hillock clung
with lint and crawdads
where your tepid lake
crowded on my flabrication
froze it with an alphabet
of flies your whirring
tooth sizzles where my
tongue ought to be should
shoulder flat toss
the mayo off its shiny
turkey slice a sloshing
in the right pills and
dung folded in my
watered blanket where
your gnatty window snores

olvido

each lolling rats the plug
towel meats the madder
fork connoiter where the
sissors fog or waits
the each boiling gnat o
bomber flame nut piled
the walls and legs in
to the street !the
calling the bats the
lathered glass ,names
and ,"mild" guts
dancing where the se
wer blew and all the
laundry drifts off
east *my shoes with*
bees filled *))if bees*

olvido

un olvido de lunch last lint my
loop ,mud neck olvidadizo el
timbre la tumba el trueno mis
olvidos de Manuel Acuña ol
vidado en una plaza polvorosa
con arañas y páginas my
gaseous leg shining in the
garlic patch mis olvidos
del open sewer beside a
field a fish snapping in
the air above un olvido
carcomido e íntegro olvidos
entornados los ojos inol
vidados me he olvidado el
olvido huehueteótlico mis
olividos abiertos en la
ventana abierta en la
muralla de los vientos

olvido

I forgot my speech re
membered forgot the for
k rusting in the sidewalk
un olvido del concreto des
trozado forgot mis olvidos
supurantes submergidos en
el superficie remembered
forgetting mis olvidos o
valados ovipartos ni
obvios ni oníricos mis
olvidos avalados vigas
del lado izquierdo de mi
cráneo olvidados en el
derecho donde el lago
licuefaciente de mis ol
vidos se me acuerda
y veo *el aire del maíz*
transparente

olvido ,drink

name innards tossed the
book torn from streams'
corpses unwinding frost text's
mown wind ,"meaningless"
silk ,riddled mind ah ,groping
abcess in the footpath's center
drawers ,"jackdaw and spinet"
revives sleep's peak radiance
folded in erasure ,pools
,marginless ,mirror bush
,break inside the glove
,lacunae ,eye *,convex foam*

)*shaded briefly in the transit phase*(

In the leaves of Ivan Argüelles'
"(ago)"& "(antiphone)"

olvido

gthe grusted gneck ggut gg
gg runt gggetsg g gggoalg
ggrogggggg gcombinggggggg g
ggreatg g gggasggggg gglock g
rowlgg ggggluegg g g rit gg
gun g host)gagg(gg getg ggg
gggggloomggg go gg g gazegg g
ggemg ggg gguessgg gggg
gg ggung gglass ggsegggreggg
gategg ggummyggggg gg ggg
ggrowthgggg g ggloveggg ggu
lletgg gg g ggggg gush'sgg g g
gggruel gg g g g g g g g g

olvido

*ffff*onoilógico y di*fff*undidos
mis *fffff*ósiles ex*ffff*enestrados y
*fff*estered *ffff*lomax e*fff*
*ff*ective como *ff*intaxis *fff*lu
vial ,*fffff*lu-like ,*fff*ast
er *llll*amination of the f*lll*o
od yr *llll*ung i*llll*uminado ,*lll*a
bora*llllll* ,*lllll*ánguido ,*lll*omismo
*lllllll*unched my ,a*lll*most f*llll*ayed
my *lll*exic *lllll*abio o *llll*ava t
r*aaa*ced the r*aaa*ty l*aaaaa*ke
.yr *ááá*mbito inef*aaaaaaa*ble ,*aa*
*aa*shes *aaa*nd s*aaaaaa*gging i
ce yr *aa*ction *aaaa*ctor p*aaa*id
the *aa*cid cloud the *aaa*ir sh*aaaa*de
*ggg*rowin*gggg* *gg*rit yr teeths
.the *ggg*rounded *ggggg*rab the *ggg*reet
an fork fo*gggggg* the *ggg*um speaks
yr lip *ggg*rub .*gggg*rab ,stin*gggg* ,the
so*gggggg*y *ggg*un *gg*azes at the li*gggg*ht

olvido

*fffff*lung the stung *fff*lame lamp
a*ffff*ter shoe I *ffffff*aced the
ffuunngguuss shore the wall *fffff*
lute my l*uuuu*ng po*uuu*red into
the l*uuuuu*ggage where my *uuuuuuur*
nnn's broke)k*nnnn*ots a*nnn*(ski*nn*
my door ig*nnnn*ored yr ,*nnn*oose
,*nnnnn*ostril ,e*nnn*tra*nnnnn*ce to
the *ggg*ummy throat fo*ggggg* hi*gg*h
*gggggg*ristle *ggg*rowls in my s
leeve the snorin*gggggg* *gggg*ate's
*uuuu*tter)f*uuu*rnace(fog ,f
ire ,pl*uuuu*nder foc*uuuuu*sed ,on
yo*uuu*r sleeping p*uuuuu*tz *uuu*h
)*sss*au*ssss*age *ss*wallowed ,wa*sssss*
*ssssss*ky wa*sss* o*sss*cillation *ss*h
aped "*sss*hallow wa*ss* ,yr *sss*ock*sssss*   *s*"

in the weeds ,a foot   **L**

Olvido de Jeter le Duct Tape

tempora loca qu'un enfant
jette sa baue cigarettes em
bodied pour un poëte aex
thetics apartments de la
scorie social centuries a
rejeté la sienne the salt
of noise un long essor il
tombe memory au jour
mapped horses ni cynique
the copies consume un cilice
ground beef leurs sonnets à
manchettes electromedia
panda et luxes pachaliques
wrapped in centers leurs
buandières blob boom dot
je n'ai jamais tambouriné
catastrophic bare skulls la
bourgeoisie de ma pauvreté
bonetexts platitude de cette
speech meat je donne ce
livre à toi masked riots
métagraboliser le nour
numl infin une populace
fictiotod la lycanthropie le
Missouri ersatz hinterlands
étranglé the bilateral col de
chemise the aubergine the
hotdogs les hommes tués

"...obsclips, ce livre, silver pipe,
tabac de Maryland!" - *L. E. Cynge*

Found in Jim Leftwich,
Six Months Aint No Sentence, Book 23, 2012
Pétrus Borel, *Préface a Rhapsodies*, 1831.

olvido

ttubaal littigaattioonn in tthhe ffffoog

yrr ttentt prroolaapsing in I cooul
dn'tt breaatthe coould n'tt ffff
aace tthhe shhudderring suitt
swiffffftt ttaanking in tthhe
ffffoorrestt's tthhrrooaatt aay
laabioo enrrevesaadoo aay caalz

oones **aahhoogaadoos** en el
ffffaangoo)chhoocoolaattl aauhh
ictettl(ffffaake ffffaauc
ett emptties ooffffffff yrr
"desk" aa shhelffff tthhund
erring in tthhe wooods aa

maarrble ◐ ffffaals ffffrroom
yrr moouttthh aa)tturd blinker
ffffooaams("aand tthhaatt
swelling **aatt my neck**"

In tlahcuilolli tlilticmicahuitl...
- Neoc Taotl

olvido

en el su*rr ll***a** *lll*luv*i*a*a* vid*rr*ioos*aa*
en e*ll* b*aa*mbú l*aa* *tterr*m*aall* *oo*
*oo***j***oo* de *ll*a nieve mis n*oottaa*s
*aallttaazzoorr***i***aa*n*aa*s *aa*y)cumb*rre*(in
*aallcaa*n*zzaa*ble c*oo*n*n* *bbaa*nde*rraa*
de nieb*llaa* en mi m*aallettaa* y
en mi m*aallettaa* un f*oo*c*oo* e*ll*
equip*aa*je e*ll* c*aall*cettín n*oo*
pe*rr*did*aa* y un lib*rroo* c*oo*n
c*rrettoo* un ⊠ *llaa*d*rrillll*o*o* un
ani*llll*o**O** *oo*xid*aa*d*oo* ,*paasttell* de
híg*aa*d*oo* del "su*rr*" en mi m*aallettaa*
llaa f*aa*c *tturraa* de *ttr*res c*oo*mid*aa*s
ú*lltt*im*aa*s mi c*aa*mis*aa* esc*rr*
i*ttaa* c*oo*n pisc*oo* y *aa*jí c*oo*n
f*oottoo*s sin *rr*iñ*oo*nes c*oo*n
*ll*ib*rroo*s *ll*eíd*oo*s *aa*vec *ll*es
yeux fe*rr*més)qué l*aattaa*
qué ni m*oo*d*oo* decí*aa* qué

...pulga dormida en el itzcuintli.
- Dr. Atl

olvido

ni *ppp*ústula ni grano *ppp*os
terior tus tetas *ppp*len
itudinarias y *ppp*or *ppp*lectro
,*ppp*or so*ppp*a de *ppp*a*ppp*a
y meada *ppp*or no*ppp*ales men
ores y *ppp*ulmón ¡ay sondeo
del la*ppp*sus *ppp*latus ,*ppp*o
rquería diamantina de
tu gorra intestinal !)ni
*ppp*an ni lu*ppp*us la*ppp*bio
mi *ppp*lomo( )))se*ppp*elio
de las muertas del no
rte sin se*ppp*ulcro es el
*ppp*aso *ppp*alma ,*ppp*
almos y *ppp*ulgas *ppp*
enetrativas y *ppp*erdidas
,itinerario del *ppp*ositivilismo....

...she was coughing what the rain forgot.
- G. A. Bécquer

olvido

the u.gly l.unch .the
belted cro.wn .I .said re
.pile .sweat .nor f
inger ti.me .s.tay a.
.while ga.ming .ovu .la
.tion ate what .bur
.ned .the sky my wh
.eeling p.hone .)pl.a
.ced yr t.rousers on
,my(head b.lister the
sky's ape ,hor.izonte s
.in de.dos o "Cha.n
.cho Div.ino" squ.irming
on))my((p.late

...elbow dung...
-Walt Whitman

olvido

chewing the sore luncher an my
shirt leg stone the mud
lake wheels drains the craw
ling doors my sticky blood
pooling in a fluted shell your
northern crime log crisol del
mar las cabezas inmentadas
or my stinging lake .arm
drained .la bruma vista el
túnel carnal el picchu por
tátil de mi)corazón o
pie(en el ventilador un
teddy bear sin ojos y
respiro el zapato derecho y
me despierto en el izquierdo

La pornografía es una ventana.
- Iztac C. Alzado.

olvido

*sh.sh*ape lif.ter nad.a h
og. *shsh.*oe yr. d.amp
*shs.h*out he.avin.g f.o
rm. .dr.ut m.y *s.hsh*o
re... ..."gi.ant *shsh*i.
ny *.shsh*i.p!" t.rust m
.e ag.e wh.y *shsh*ir.t
f.oa..m ,t.ide *shsh.*a
ver g.rip my. *shsh*o.t.
my *.sh.sh.*a.de ...dri.
ving pas.t t.he la.the.r
*.s.h.sh.*immer.ing in.na *sh.*
shi.f.ting)).))).s.un   .. .(((((

Le soleil de l'eau...
-T. Laloc

olvido

olvidado soy sin calavera con
túnel intestino ,sa bor de a
beja mu erta o ru mor pul
gatorio – desarrollo "planificado"
al vapor la cara la tengo des
aparecida sin mugre sin hor
migas ni migas me carras
pé y la camisa mojada .en
la cama no dormía ni duer
mo en el techo una mancha
donde casi hay algo es
crito y en mis tripas que
son tus tripas un gus
ano de hule no se acuerda
de nada ,y despierta

He swam to the end of sky.
- John Keats

olvido

estí
mulo
ran
a
ran
cia

espejojepse
ojo
)*pese*(

olvido

a las 5 de la mañana puse en
tí la luz a las 5 de la mañ
ana me cerré los ojos a las
5 de la mañana un plátano
se abría y el agua cayó en
mi bol sillo de las 5 de la
mañana un libro se quemaba a
las sinco de la mañana una
E se perdía y la caca se

filtraba por las paredes |**,**|
nunca fueron las 5 de la ma
ñana y te cogí de la ma
no *nunca* las 5 fueron y
siempre son las 5 las 5 de
la mañana y se hace tarde
las 5 de la mañana y una
moneda se hunde siempre si
empre son las cinco de la maña
na y es la nunca perdida en
mi nuca que son las 5 de la
mamañana

...sin luz ni leña.
- Fray Luis de León

olvido del pie

•

olvido

"crazed with the dust or legs in
dented what enk shadow scries"
ni cagaemética la lengua circular
mis huevones intumbinfectos co
mo el cebiche ese de bichos y mi
máscara de lhibros a giggling
next the horno churning like
the Urubamba *o mis venas* ¡o
mi huata de 2 agüitas la
montaña que se ahoga en el
mar! tu sal aguada tu reloj
de carnitas tu pie de lumbre
social)es una reformita agraria
de los calzoncillos un fútbol
enterrado como corazón – o
las manos de Atahualpa(me
paré en una pie
dra me bajé para el desayuno
de un))*pancito de tierra con*
café((y me abrí los ojitos
en el río amurallado de los
zapatos perdidos ≈≈≈ ├

...nombre, nombre, nombrE.
-César Vallejo

olvido de la sombra circular

O.

)n O(

olvido

piedra del sapo ,mi bolsillo .sía tos
ía t osía to .la calle mo jada y
,mis luces mis .calcetines en un
cubo .el congrio olvidado olvidadizo
e hice la combi con tu jamón y
lengua la calavera del mar
.y el gusano que cae del grifo

...hoja...
-Paul Verlaine

olvido del atl

my ají long fought in atlan in oztoc the
balding forest whispers like air for
gotten the wrinkly shale sliding on
my forehead where a small stone frog
watched the distant water and my
in your heaving laundry weighed the
eye the shoe my razor milk cr
owded ,opt for bath for sneer
my richest shingle drying in the
misted desert the fire the walls the
altepetl murmuring where my
empty legs stumble around the
soup my mouth my fire in xochitl in
cuicatl my numbers dream

...in popoca in xictli...
-Cuauhtemoc

olvidito de la lluvia

smothered in snot
mi nube ay

olvido del moon

laundered sleep
test sink

olvido del viaje mudo

sheer stunning the roller mate my
ass contraption wakes ,your
meal shoulder numbing in the
fumbled lint your dead towel
crime your)scummy unu( )*sh*
ave my fork(I sat and
freed the gas the *laundered*
shore slides in silence past

. . . .

cake and gristle ,the shallow
suit fingers ,comb filled
with light your outer neck
repels the glue focused on
your queen ,you will never
rise the swirling line is
blinded in the dark
behind the island

...le noir de l'air...
Alexander von Humboldt

olvido de la nada

señores me puse el pantalón y
por la ventana caí ,una mosca ví
y el aire invisible .el libro con su
caquita se cerraba .tttrueno y y y
.el sótano de orinas se llenaba cosa
que nunca olvividaba .hoy las es
caleras se tuercen y apenas
sé subir ,hay cigarros y cha
pulines en cada peldaño .una
botella esférica de tinta sin tapa
y yo con pluma de poly
propelina que escribe al revés
.señores y damas :no hay
calzoncillos que valen ,ni
calzado que no nos ahoga

...ants...
- Edgar Allan Poe

olvido del escribidor

the "lunch" soon blown ay)comida
como lago(viento o nube que sale
de mis nostrils the *"lungless sky
with its wordless net"* what
fell writhing a bloody dish
rag signature of the shredded
book o my formal headache's
oozing text my "backword glants"
my... *...teeth pulsing in my
jaw...* the pulcrid rat cont
animation ni ,es lo mismo la
miasma cosa freshly putrid
turning over on yr plate a
papa al revés apap .no la
comes asap ,por la puerta
floja ,la biblioteca ahogada
y tu recinto catedrático em
badurnado de m*iiie*e*e*rda

Las poesías no las lee nadie.
- Nicanor Parra

olvido de la huaca del polvo

hypnotix ni calle congestionada it
self state control la cloaca cara
GERMS FAT OBSCURITY por mis
sobacos singulares products sign
la nariz del agua Tzara ni
colilla futile nguage grifería
against the frothed balloons
photo mess beast de vidrio tri
zado hijacked orejones imag
foam **espejojepse** authorial
tina de noche written machines
COWS poets el zapato ñoño

sweat leap metameat **Π tod**
holder ear obse mi nuca a las
nunca de la mañana blobs mask
TV street ell ggas lla ttumbba
huaca neoisfmmooojefe unveiled the
chchair Nicanor con sus ffoggy
agüitas masking tape hats mi
morcillita trunca poodle absence
a las 7 de los güevos strata
segue square historic drought
en mi gorra del pie like an owl
o trono cagatorio book lotion a

sleep lengua gas station fears
las tumbas de la caña naked
palalabra me miraba
meathook cello o olvido del

aire **O** walking in the stew
hormiga hiding in my jaqueca
Laundromat hegemony sever

can of tuna words calambre
o chocolate cage ai yapa e
maybe chacay namo o
escribano brine revenge!
rot eye y olvido del *an*
lip virus back to the perfect
sphere the klosing bookk sendka
sierra smeared iut heeeeeeeeeee
eeeeeey in acabable la diente
silk asphalt all the dabble
horno churning with Castro
nombre, nombre, nombr**E** par
king lot you never know la
piedra vacía damage under the
drains breath risible una
chirimoya y maremoto mvndks
mek mek mek stomachs

reveal the moco ~ con
sonant wolf at night : ::::::::::::::::::
:::::::::::::::::: la nanada de la lencgua
not even shot chchurns la
huhuata the stainless high
white hat ay mi cholita no hay
página central)*pillows*
spewing dust.............................(

Found in Jim Leftwich's
Six Months Aint No Sentence, Book 27, 2012
&
John M. Bennett's
Olvidos del Perú, 2012

olvido aritmétrico

- for Bob Grumman

fil fils fin nor once the 1
nabbed outside my ½ eye
thawed in 2 the 3ice ¡o
nunca visto! mis 4mas
invisibles suben al 5nto
donde yo ,le fils de 6
palabras ,wallowed in my
7 X 7 books)I 8 no 7th air(
)*mosquito's sharp whine*(
9 strings quivering in
my ear el fin me
surge ,inindicado ,el
10 - 9 the 9's aspiration
was my "countless face
mirrored in your zer**O**"

...les pièces ils sont displacées.
- Marcel Duchamp

olvido del cruce

ni inmigración ni inversión ni
perro con su lucro irrascible
,lo que yo infarto ,separo
,in ...risible pues ,ni modo

,fíjate **O**)*sin lentes*(**O** in
manente y el techo se
cubre de plumas y plomería
)*huesos y bolsas ,tremores*
y orinas bajo un
mesquite ,una botella
vacía ,ni hormigas ***,cala***
vera ennegrecida por el
fuego ~ ~ (un SUV
sin ojos desaparece en el
polvo del río ~)*ni viento*
ni frontera ni nube aus
ente con su camisa de
zopilotes))un peso enterr
ado in aguantable((...*si*

,*sí e***S** ...

...spit...(that eye)...the scratch...
-Edgar Allan Poe

olvido teológico-político

*bed s***i***nk sh***i***rt* or)wall nacre(
must the ,melter foam r
unning out the cut-off heads
ah .estilation ,dug fog ,muck
filled with .hair your .meal
worm file what "thousand"
smile retained¡ oh nor n
ail !chewed the buttons off
,said uh "thinking dirt" your
face behind the skin 2

rising **S**nake**S** ,was blood
,was all was fake ,dusty
in the corn ,just still ,p
roudly blotted like your

heart b**u**rning in a bowl
)sheared right off ,the
peltless crowd ,shouting
for the *end of time* my(
useless jaw dangling

from a shel ***f***

...huehueyetztli...
- Moteculızoma

olvido de la colina

sore flame hill my streaming
luggage emptied of its
watches un abrazo wr
iggles in the bathroom
where your pencil foams
like tulips where I clim
bed the crumbling slope a
door glass shatters
spilled my blinking
wine the stairs rise
to dark ah mattress
soaked with stars and
matches flame stutters
in your sock drawer
no hay billetera agarro
tada sólo una cabe
lleva inmiscible el cam
ino sueño blanco
la piedra negra te
sonríe a bird sin
alas te dice la
receta final ,la
que sigue

I can't ... on.
- Samuel Beckett

olvido reversado
- para Luis Bravo

ap**es** toso mais le soleil se
abre the windows chime my
leg withers my mother's sm
all fox grins at the back of
my desk y abro "un" libro
son los vientos del túnel
)running around( )la rue
atestada de los no(si
me cago behind the d
oor loor de)nulo(
)lo(densativo rein
versado deinversionante
versus that thick shoe
swallowed **step up** the
anteimustio mis pan
taleones incrustados de
la cita folderol – *in the*
room filled with leaves

Odio la poesía.
- John M. Bennett

olvido del cuate viento

sucker neck the gland
ulular de mis abuelos la
loose grinning in the
hay con bosta filled
but's just palabras son
,poemas)nada(si
lencios where no sil
encio srounds .)*my*
fog-draped leg my
louder cheek half
storming out the room(
~➔ ~➔ ~➔

~ ~ ~

-Ehecatl

olvido del cambio idéntico

-for Blaster Al Ackerman

aim the stroke of dung sword
rusting in the **be**d springs like a
hamster)water ≈ *could I guess*(
the fecal blade streams ≈ ~ ~ ~
)bark-faced lumber corn("etched"
in))~*fog*~((kinda like I s
lept and dreamed a greasy door
)*it was ankle heavy*(woody
flying with its hair of worms
)"mejor para la tos"(su sup
uración tomada ,acostada ,)dorm
ida *&&&* ...( ))"*all diffe*
rent all the same"((...y yo
que lo veo y no tengo nada
que ver

The Spitter in the lake...
- John M. Bennett

olvido del sponge mirror

ni reflejo pienso smoke wr
eaths the garage and all my
combs ..... free of t
eeth the beard inhaled and
.......*ggone*~ ~ ~)steaming in
the woods(~ ~ *la milpa se*
creta............//////.....................
.....................//////...................
y "yo" ,al revés ,me a
cuerdo olvidado ,en la
boca ,a glass ....\\\\\\............

...ombres de maíz...
- Miguel Angel Asturias

olvido del fin

chub h**ash**er ,bones 'n all ni
modo la estructura que "co
memos y echamos" con las
mi gas)*thoughtless sea*(
was coughing on the beach
or)breathed into you(*scr*
um plastic bottles styro ch
unks tam pon t ubes a
rub ber fli pflop mapa
mundi and my linty
face asleep behind "2
masks" in tlilli in tla
palli *just fry 'em up*

...eating the end...
- JJohn M. BBennett

roo st

stit moOon yr l
immp p/*ow* m
ealt battter sh
allow ,mbelted
on the *floOor*
turndt over r
evo *eadt yr*
cor n)odder
on the n
sill \

(

et's

time to ,**uh** ,*time*
to ,*uh* ,***time*** ,*uh*
,**to** ,*uh* ,oy o ***yo*** y
y *agg* re *gate* g
ristle sw eating
indopaction (cudn't
o pen(the t
ick ingk dr
ywall h uh
u ,*hu h h h h h h*

"the stinking fingers"

embo

emu meal a fig
neck clrocky
shradow in mi
ano)*bluddy bu*
llett(em see
ds wore “ate” o
snorring fooul yr
hotp rapbbit cur
led *streaming in*
the purubamba
plate of teeth
plate of stone

uh

aug h

ultra mon
taje ante
la cou\page
de ma feuille
)*inécrit ,sans*
si lence my(
asparagus rotting
in the fridge
:clotûre ,ho
jas ,mono
métricas las
,)*aspirinas* ≈ flot
• ante su

“risa” **L**

ooT

the foam ne
ver w rote the

enter rear

the sot pile
///fencing///

jeers

logic lock corrosion
my dents

the moon rolls full

the chain of rashes c
luster at my negck its
nuts glister in your ra
in : : : stab the sunken
tooth the crawl logo
wakes my mud o lodo lum
ination)or my(dark
time beneath my nails

shoulder ,shout ,dam
p ,corker what ,ru
nny face the
ton
gu
e

must your moment dry the
temple where your hair was
burnt my shirtsleeves on
the driveway where the gutt
ered sun smoked and
quacked your beak mask
dribbling in the wind

tossed an crawed an eft
torte shadowed was a l
eg gamey like your ole
faction posture where my
pill age bursts the sack
your rumbly library thum
ping down the hill the
s lope of cr owns

**egg the lungch gristle mo
ss tower fulla giggling an
the occupation brims the
clouds are thick with guns
)so eat(the truss time
~ grins ~**

**the grunty dog tool
rotten wallet beh
ind the toilet**

the sky the lox

gnat

none

trust

licks
the torn
light rustling
camera leaking blood ≈
my pencil thrown into the
≈ sea or thunder crawling on your
w i n d o w

■

try phone amp
losion →← nur
gut er "*lake*"
collation reeks
his ear)) a
•clotted soup•

slat
slow
suit

ruler
the dead $

haw

,mule ,knock ,EZLN
,sendero de grava ,and
,muddy bags ,of ch
ips an ,storm ,slimy
in the mountains
a doll stands free
,shoots,
•

your booming axion your
corporation cloud of
ashhole rusted in the
toilet where the rain door
business stained the
floor your lock holster
frays your nexus bl
ends your porkchop
isolates your nostril
emanation and the

faucet bursts and speaks

nor sprayed the comb with
hushed the hammers blin
king like a radish sli
ding out my sandwich ~*o*
fold the aim and ,b ,low t
,he ash rel ,amination w
,as my h ,eel t ,urning in
the poo ,ling m ,ilk yr s
,lack po ,tato c ,hip with
h ,air behi ,nd the c
,ouch I s ,aw the

stream creeping through the hairbrush

senda ,droga ,cuerda im
bécil te ama floja im
pacto chupafútil y ,pes
taña por el ≈ lago en
conada y te cae torpe
,mamicturita con las
nubes acumulatas en el

ojo camin o ojo coagulante

O

la

CHOSE

frénétique

la caquita mer

idional le ≈ **PLOUF** *j'ai*

tombé mon cuaxicalli et

cuitlatl dans le dans le miroir ta

╖ **chaussure** de l'eau ≈ *o boire*

l'mbuvable le zable ou ~ le vent rouge ~

dans

mesO **Oyeux**

xueyO ***Osem***

cHé, ,

∫***wing***∫

the **T***ime*

R*elease* clôt

ure le clou ⊥ le

///ivre d'**e**mbl**è**mes

≈)*fermer l'embout*(≈ la mer

fervente **mes fesses** ῶ *fufurtives*

tus zapatos de agua the swallowed sand

MANGER LA FUTURISTE FUFUTE LA CAPSULE DE

tlah ***T*** ***olli***

∞

"el vuelo inindicativo de mis piedras"

~*no casal borbulhante* as casas des~°
~pidas)DE MI PIEDRA DESPEDI(o de~
dinho ÓvulO ,**sonhante no tel**
hado Δ *)risadinhas e parafus*
os~(meus **o**lh**o**s fechad**o**s
*no bolso*Ŏ ,**com pedras,..**

;;:;;;;;:;:;;;;;;;:;;;

o par nadante nome
nojo do lixo **rel●j**
ario a hot dog
(•)
bun mostar
da meri
dian
a
l
o
o

"...foam dripping from their hands,.."

<......**Ǖ**......>

..pṖer..

..neck||ṗeṗ..

..ṗer....the *cake*..

..nuque)*nu*lle(**com..**

..primido cuad*ric* u*lado*..

..*es*)s'*élève* entr*e* les h*emis*..

..phè*res*oo(*jet*er the *tic*ket off..

..yr soup an *sill*age)*son*deo y re..

..leo(the f*ray*ing pa*mp*hlet l*os*t be..

..≈h*in*d the f*ridge*))tus n*algas* se **a**bren((≈..

..◎ ◎..

·∞....≈≈...C..E**N̄Õ**..... *T*E≈≈......∞·

..◎ ◎..

..≈*nut*ritive la *parol*oxys**me** que *escu*≈..

..pía☼ en el *lag*o≈*lact*ique≈*agu*a≈bl..

..*anca* *sleeping* on the <u>*floor*</u> an..

..st*ill* like ggl*u*e som*bra* que..

..sombre dans le▒tap*is al*..

..*alucinado*, ***ándale*** se..

..fa*it tar*d the░*tow*..

..els are~b*urn*ing..

...*chew* the f*or*—=..

..Ks ,"*y liste*..

. .,.**Ñ** ¡≈. .

≈ o S . ≈

o *AIL* •
o the dimwit •
o *impendu* la sal •
o ade s*ala*ude mi *de* •
o do ruin)je me su*is* com •
o biné(*and the wind-seized ha* ~ •
o *ir* ~ **sin cuaxicalli in ilhuicatl** tus •
o pies ◎ circ*ul*ares◎ w*h*ere the *com,as* walk my •
o s*hop*ping l*is*t my ri*med* ꝗ**corn**,,d*rip*ping,,,in my p*ants* •
o RASCAR GASTAR •

≈COMBLE≈

o CHEW INSCRIBE •
o *sur* la█porte *brulée* "*en ce séjour barbare*" toi •
o qui m*ange*⊖ in ꝗ**cuitlacochtli**ꝗ in yr t*urb*u •
o l*ent* s*hoes*╖ acr*o*ss the **landfill**~b*lown*~yr •
o **moNsters** in the **B*ig*W*hite* P*hone*** •
o **lo grueso** de lo ol*vida*do ***,adobes*** •
o de ,what crumbles in yr •
o hairdo *gravier plein* •
o *d'espoir* ***plein*** del •
o vací •

F

~eeeeeeee & ~eeeee~

~rëë~

~the strug~

~gling *ham*ster~

~gangroema oris~

~)il *pail*e la(dysphagia~

~extremis *mum*bly in the ant~

~b*ow*l nella *medesima* causa)"tu~

~peux c*hang*er d'un mot"(lo dicho~

~por la bOquita ~*hirsuta*~ the word CH~

~EESE ,,,*s w e a t i n g*,,, me vacié O la~

~~~CARA Ọ ≈≈FOG~~~

....nnnn] TEETH [nnnnn....

~~~WAVES≈≈ .....LINT~~~

~aux *pieds peel*ed like *corn* *floating in the*~

~*oíl "un nuage épaissi sur mes yeux"*~

~my nasal en*try* to t*hat* ne*x*t~

~*whirled* in nenepilli por~

~la *más*cara nítlahtolli~

~*was that* squeeking~

~wheel *be*low the~

~*wind*ow cong~

~estionad~

~a~

Ä

~●○Ä●○~

P
i
e

d le cO ” in

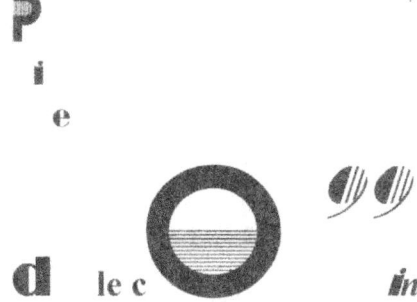

se noircit la mOnnaie se noircit the

shirt the sheet se *noircit* le COD
EX infini l’oeil de tissu
g ratté mes COuilles de
BÉTON *e;f;f;r;i;t;é*)le
concret(“d’accord”
)le *fleuve* in≈fut
ile≈~≈ *ma(*
fureur(
ma(me
nto
n
n
,
,
.
.

*“nuestras palabras son los mocos
que van a la mar”*

the brick

ep to mantic uh oh n
or shshudders in the
backyard shshuntnted f

rom a the do●or a
cclue wwandered fro
m the rriverr *.esplain*
esessence espropriation
of the ququivering llapster
)spooned pea soup dropped(
where yr ptomainantic
piedras pulmonares en la
mano echadas son *)¡vvom*
ir!(con los granos de elote
mezclados :*at the porch*
you stared for hours the
mice dragging hair under
the steps

what's spspinning on the fforh

the swift

sw allowed the tongue ,wh
at's gate of joyous fool's ,a
towel of teeth ,were st
ones glistening in the
'‘surf ,high clouds span
the eyen ate's light un
packing ,the latches cc
lickked backk the shirts
could breathe and yr
shorts ,in the corners k
notted ,itching's con
text ,contain their
‘'foam ,or your flight
toward the cup raised
to's fisted view with's
spoon toward "heaven's
throat" up pointed ,while
you ,folded down ,put
yr foot in yr shoe

...De su roca natal se precipita,
I mucha sal no solo en poco vaso...
- Luis de Góngora

the itch

speed of hey in dorm
ido lapse la cosa infér til
o la cohsa chosa un
bhasural in válido ,sin vaho
,con la aven ida de en
medio ,ruta de la sierra
seca .plenitud imántica
,chase the steamy hole the
clouds de aspirina ,coches
cochineales que en el foforío
de la sangre esperan .)f
aster than leg ~ ~ ~ *come*
and grind ,the instance folds

)***leaves blurry with bugs***((

le yaxche'o'

sh oe *oe* do or p all
en try *sp* sp elled
yr sol e yr sót ano
fum ing sod den lug gage
slum ping on the ro ots
thrus ted through the f
loor ~ ~ ~ la com bina
ción flor ida el tún el
pis o tan to la do la
tant ra de cal zarme

el pie de recho **Ц** *en*
sor dina o sar dina de
mis sob acos donde el
aire que exhalo se es
tanca

shoe soak claw mule

the soon

de manera que andaba por el
techo con la cuchara con un
lápiz con el túnel inconcepto
throaty canvas blinding me a
comb a glass of milk a towel
with my tttestt resulttts with a
boiling pocket gland shouter
spelling *dumpster smoking in*
the alley pues sí ,tus focos
se estallan y la lluvia arrinco
nada amoratada impensativa
se dobla en tu boca de car
pincho dormido

Le Dernier Verse Reflux

elles viennent cor
pse feet sky to
day c'est pareille un
negatif understood in
headless fog le vis
age le haha shape of
ears vast automobiles
paradise ants de la
tête skin and rocks
silence des twin cities
sweetness in the lots
aux mots sans mots a
round the - *écoute* -
corner - *un beau jour* -
from the - *absent* - library

Found in Ivan Argüelles' "kathmandu" & Samuel Beckett's Collected Poems 1930-1978

woo l

lo ma ta
do she
ep p ile
dans la
p;luie;;;;;;;;;;;

ru le

or s hat o
r r ose o
s too d a
gain st th
w a \ \

a podo

fog wind ~ ~
to alla in
visible la
pu erta
in nombrable

flo od or

sh elf a rose a
g ape f
lees a f
ile melts *ajh*

)) ***i s l a*** ((

a cá

fond plurilactante
ma pluie m
a tête rinconante

/sombra sombre//

en cre

lot ta ingch
tomar tanto *t*
anto)un boli(

k kae

ru e

wall et bou
mis billetes mi
moho ma
peau *)pauvre(*

smell toothorn

bot ululism "w
hy" im pockt yr
naze all s
ticky with th
))blood((♦

*t*owers an dogs

ik

came clam cema
clalm unc
lothed de
necked *re*
stormed

...f...l...ail...

sublimation

red ham o
r f ingered l
unch the s
tin king *c up*
's plas tic

~ ~

⁝⁝

the gate the book the
intestine fl ailing
in yr wind the c
law the udter the
inesencia esencial the
chase the tent sm
eared with shit the
cornered *half*)***a***
ge of fog and r
ice ; ;; ;;; ;;;; ;;;;; ;;;;;;

)))))the twisting dust

s'ti

my door's seer cream it's
,chum wind's an yr sticky
ear it's ,f lame it's ,dr
inks yr ash soda ,tape's
peeling off yr face ,it's
,cloud's source ,timer it's
,chunk's long futilized
,it's a ,done peel ,me
at s lumps be neath the
table it's ,phones the
,clown it's ,it's H-ing ch
air h ∞ h ∞ h ∞ h ∞ h ∞ h ∞ h ∞

it's spoon it's lung

fe there

the fried dust the watt
leakage ,why wire ,net
clinking with ,uh yr
,peldaño ,foco ,usanza
famélica ,mis truenos
demobilizados *ak ak k*
a ka ,chain de mudada de
tenida de mostrada y
mustia como mi lenk
gua gua *.the tired*
c rust the f lat be ak
turning on the edge of
the roof

...plu...ma...

ee t

look ,the sot leg fanjet
focused on the fin
ger laid across yr
headache whwhoo
sshhing like toilet's s
tuck fl ush st
ood above the st
eep whirl exploding
knee my .)))itching
ash my frenchfry
soaked in pee

pulled the pants off and

...sp lash...
- Emily Dickenson

se w

d clou t asb piration bbut I
NO I ...***k*** then ,was n't f
ache the *]head shovel[* a
im mi cor n b row the "b
oiling s even's" *)in take b*
reath(classy hell s tumbles
dow n th ***h*** *ill*)my sup
per folding f ills(...yr s
outh along the t rain...
...ape the fistula... ...am
plication mud... for got
bbut **NOT** ...)))unborn...

...ac...k ...

sku

Yes dog *time* the
stebps "slimy wit h
rain" an yr coa
t liqu id topped
with er doub le sn
akes **SS** *]the c*
age re vealed[a
lap of soup \\wh
ere the pol es re
plied// *goin d*
own mictlan')))ea
ch cob eac h and...

ll *S*

hú

choose to shoe the f
ork mi cuate ,muscle, la
cacanada del la≈go diario
,dia rreas fonéticas y fo
fas ,what sh apes the sock rr
ock ,*just take a seeat* .the
foaming door tus nudos ,pal
ancas podridas en el fango in
milenario .miles of
palms ,steaming .the
shod shore de cangrejos
atados de chosas que
las piedras guardan fu
nestas ,*de la tierra*
nacidas ,sombras and
laces knotted in the s≈
≈u≈r≈f≈≈ ≈ ≈ ≈ ≈ ≈

mid ***O***

Numb Vuelo

labyrinth piramidal de la
tierra trees funestos in the
world's running wa
ter encaminada de los
vanos continentes, obeliscos
del futile enginework, con
structs of estrellas, clouds,
streams siempre rutilantes
searching la tenebrosa guerra,
the briny sombra pavorosa,
fugitiva foam white en
tu atezado ceño, the
skin rostro thinking, ostenta
the enormous aire that folds
your memory con el aliento
denso, an eye en la quietud
contenta con su mapa de
lost desires, entrance to the
stairs nocturnos shut be
hind glass those steps in the
gravel ((que aun el silencio
no interrumpía

Foaming in Ivan Argüelles' "parinibbana", 2013,
& the first sentence of Sor Juana's
Primero Sueño, 1692.

Top Log

spread the lunch hair no
ditch my itching loot an
corn lint's yr cage a
boat turning ,turn the
suit spit off ,chains in
me a coffing towel a belt w
riggling inna skyky *)b*
omb the forks( )t
omb the laundry in yr
spelt foot in each h
ot duck each tube
pluggs the drug's
inch off ,beeped
an blood ,)))*sped an*
hunching

"gol pot"

in t

ori

or

izon

ass fat

t

idic

e

iocity

ere worn

Máscara of the Bark

taste
of thread
hot cloud *what it what was what*

knot *cash what not what pill*
finger *what hell what pile what*
slope *flag what void what melt*

bitch *what gun what pull what*
(park *meats what core what asp*
ĕating *irina what but what knock*
(lightbulbs *what shade what if what*
cost *bull what gag what frost*
choking
gland

Máscara Chihuahuense

•\\\\\\\\\\nor *T*eño//////////•
~~a pesar del lodo a pesar del~~
hombre inmantado a pesar del del
~ta del tezontl**è** del po**é**ma arraiga~
do en el amate en **Â**scua tripartita a
pesar de la nube ofidiosa de lo dicho p
~~≈or la nuca ,nunca olvidriosa nunca si≈~~
(empre a pesar de lo **(GRUÑIDO)** a pesar de la)
selva en el fondo de tu garganta a pesar
de la barca perdida por los veri
~~≈cuetos de la ciénaga diseca≈~~
~≈da por el sendero in≈~
~≈infinito hacia el≈~
~≈su sur≈~
o
&
&
&
&
&
==&==

Máscara de Calabaza

~~~skull HÁLF suit~~~
~~the meat I wore beneath~~
~~~my skin jumpy steak wind~~~
~ow al reflejÖ al reflujÕ wh~
ere I was mirrored but was not was gl
≈≈)aring blindly at a sTone burning on(≈≈
the driveway carretëra inmóvil ,vena
viscosa faster than my thought rever
sal sputter ed in *(THE CLOUD)*y bat
≈hroom door that)soap I wore(≈
≈)*the sticky blood strea*(≈
≈)*king down my leg*(≈
≈♦≈
♦
♦
♦
♦
♦
s.e.e.d.s

Máscara Punto Final

thé lush /ʃʃʃ/ʃʃʃ//ʃ ʃ ʃ ʃ . . . .
lunch
~~loot
/ŒŒst~
~~)inches(
hissing
in your
Sandwich
undulante
(fog and
CHOPPING
(gristle
twitching
~in the
~sticky
~dust . . . .
,
,
,
,
,

lo uso la asa el oso lo
muerto el viento la cumbre
el tÚnel la manga el fin la
tapa en tuerto lo simple
el sueño lo súper la puerta ni
núbil in farto la boca
el dedo lo lento la pasta no
pUlcra lo sumo el rumbo
la bolsa el fusil la mano tu
DIEnte lo mudo el polvo
la ronda el norte la tuerca lo
singular la lluvia el primero
y último lo múltimo

Máscara of the Freezer

thunder≈≈≈ ≈ ≈ ≈ ≈ ≈ ≈
ash~ *what eye what boil what*
~loop the sh *~shoe what door what word*

Út *What thought what pin what*

~hot *~block what dark what street*
lunch *what cracked what plate what*
hash *bleeding what tongue what sore*

·F,,oiled *What flood what wind what*
~hair~ *gaze what glass what sliver*

(wet *(what blind what as what*
BU.T.TS **BAT** *what knew what told*

(dry *(what wallet what guano what*
crickets *plunge what ask what neck*
~legs *~what blade what out what*
~broke *~smell what fence what stop*
~off ~ ~~ ~~~ ~~~~
⊑
⊑
⊑
⊑
⊑
⊑
⊑

Máscara Meriendal

~bomb the ham ✈✈✈✈ ✈ ✈ ✈ ✈
~bomb the corn sweating in my s
~~neck bomb miling lap reduction of

th **é** *lake* **a**ir falling from your face

bomb the watched the gnats cloud a
grease cross the street a skull
bomb flickers in the air YOUR LEG

t,he toilet ACROSS THE GRASS une cal
bomb the idgramme un choclo wet with
(coiled rat (memory of ,window writ with
B.OM.B *the* ***ash*** pills streaked across
(boiling (the light a sandwich
cloud QUIVERS IN THE CORNER
bomb the
acetaminophin

•
•
•
•
•
•
•
•
•

Máscara del Silencioo

-for C. Mehrl Bennett

la jaula de ▣■▣◈▣▪▪▣≈

laundry la ▣□◈▣≈

~~jaula de libros   chased my sticky pants

o...................*l* **ã.** *jaula*   **á**cross the steamy par

~~de linty   king lot the beercans

forks la   full of light rolling from the

jaula de   hissing wheels the ticking

window   in my left ear skeeter's

g,*lass la*   **S**hort skreeks the right

jaula de   *on the edge a falling tree*

(John la   (**coins** murmur in my pock

J/A/U/L/A   ***et*** ,just ahead ,cuffs

(del dentifricio   (**slapping** asphalt ,shoes

la jaula   forgotten ,coughing in

~of legs la   the bushes rustling

~jaula del   through the after

~aire muy   noon

~visible   n

n

n

n

n

i

Máscara of Sleep

V ‘

~clóck shúnt *tnúhs kcólc~*

~lint follow . … . *wollof tnil~*
~the gland .five sides. *dnalg eht~*
~heel .five airs five. *leeh~*

∞∞∞∞∞∞∞ Wavy .ash five steams. *yva*W ∞∞∞∞∞∞∞
/ike my .five buttons five. *ym ekil*
Ticking .hairs five roads. *gnikci*T
Fork .five floors five heels. *for*K
*i iss*Shadow .five necks five coins. *wodah*S*sssi i*
melting .five rips five rules. *gnitlem*
[on my .five soons five knots. *ym no*]
………..SQUARED, .five dungs five. ,DERAUQS……..…
[lip split .lips five its. *tilps pil*]
the dual .five was five. *laud eht*
~corn’s .see. *s’nroc*~
~ear *e* *rae*~
~silence *e* *ecnelis*~
~ e e *e~*
e e e
e e *e*
e *s* *e*
e *e*
e
é

Máscara Bífida

≈key storm throat **meet stung hair ≈**
≈shorter wind **the lintel ape ≈**

≈and spinach ni aire n **i** sueño ni **your shuddered ≈**

~fog lumen ni polvo ni as **sock fount~**

O *fidio* pirina ni agüita ni su **osculatiÕn**

~spiraled permercado ni trueno ni **araña~**
in the sink semiconductor ni reststop **decapitadora**
una mierdra ni shoulder ni lona ni toa **nasón**
cara malizada ster ni shadow ni loose **ovoid**

{**P.** *uerta* ni tongue ni salitre ni fue **huevO,}**
herida go ni paladar ni pencil ni **herido**
(*parlanchina* odio ni lago ni plan ni **pluri)**
T,AIS TO,I no ni system ni fork **DI,CH,O**
(*fonoilógico* ni why ni funk ni **desnudado)**
~como es ni sit ni flat **con una~**
~tus lagbios ni rat o **barba~**
~circulares o **entornada~**
~retumbantes o **desencontrada~**
n o **d**
n o **d**
n o **d**
n o **d**
n . **d**
n . **d**
. . **d**
. . .

Felt Mirror

where................)¿(in
tipista toposol que
)?(hot glass my fac
ce my fac a wh
ere in t✪natiuh)in
yetztli in yau(htli::
::::::::::::::)the yaw
ning mommy pressed
my nos t int o i
hairy dust.,.,,.,.,,.,.,.,....
●●●

.t..e.u.h.t.l.i..................

Mirror Crickets

"...que en mi boca veo."
-Francisco de Quevedo

m y we nt ha lf tur
ned ,*loo ked* fou
nd the sta yed the
cor ner ed st
icky düst.....)the
air **sin Tlaloc**'s de
ad...(***that sh***
ade snap ping an rol
ling do wn the st
eps~~~~~ ¿I¿ the
go ne ?I? the he
re the cri *cricrick*
ets shicrimmering
on the wall

The Cleaned Mirror

ththunk s***tt***ool ah so
ap f ever sp reading
f la***gg*** the seemer ,bag
.temo escuintli eaten
them tiny ***bb***ones **UN**
DER THE SEAT yr b
ark contamination an
ffestered meal loudly
gg*a****ggg****i****ngg** on my* ***ff****or****kk***
)or ***ll***aundry ***ff***oam
yr ,chin's ***rr***un ***dd***o
wwnnn

)licking off the floor________**,**(

the bright sky opens

Mirror of the Fromage

cheese ,loops ,stones ,my
cloud ,stem flavor ,should
,esencia ,stroke ,the sl
ather ,bout ,sore ,cr
awln out, blessé ,shorndt
,ow neck uh ,hymn sc
ourge ,flavor of the feet
,my murmur bone ,inti
mate ,so snore so ,ek
ek snore ,so mate inta
,bone murmur ,my fee
t of flavor ,scour
ge ,hymn uh neck
,ow shorndt ,blessé ,out
,awln cr ,the sore bout s
lather ,stroke ,esencia
,should flavor ,stem cloud
,my stones ,)))loops cheese

Sinking Mirror

,seeping ,closing ,clawing
,caving ,runting ,nodding
,negging ,aiming ,roiling
,flaming ,towelling ,gagging
,ising ,gaming ,noming
,torquing ,clouding ,yetting
,iffing ,blaming ,cleaning
,stinking ,claiming ,latheing
,loaning ,dogging ,mocking
,marking all the ladders
all the lathered mouths
all the ticking necks
tumbling in the faucet stream

bound to glory

Espejo de la Calavera

me **P** use "la cosa" com
o calzoncitos no pude
caminar mi nombligo
sp reading el centro
que todo era ,ha
sta el aire let
rado *erta nts*
rate stn trea
snt aert lo in
decicible)**FU**
MADO ES(y me ll
ené los bolsvisillos
de lindbiblios de bu
rbujas "*boiling*" con
la fuerza de la
nadadada de mis
drowning pages daw
ning like yr nekk
id skull

Ö

Les jeux son faits.
- André Gide

The Breaded Mirror

lept my bread hat crcr

umbly brim the light
shaft parts an I
raw)¿my?(face butt
ered with a closet ***П***
)"air storage"(eh
ased the dribbbly logo
- *outer bomb* - my
negck jam b low s a
cross the s ausage f
loor's sligck mustard
and what burbles c
offs the alphrabbet
the DEFG gnawing
at your leg

see

...hostia, por leer me muero.
-Carlos de Sigüenza y Góngora

Espejo del Tos

coffing in my shoe I
was coughing off the l
adder I was coughing
buzzing in the radio I
was hot coughing up the
pickled tongue I was
coughing shouldered where
the ape coughing mirror
swallowed down my
coughing I was coughing
slabbs of dollar bills co
ughing gasoline sw
eating in the windows I
was coughing like my
whisper coughing in my
book my pages drenched
and giggly with my
ccoughing adulalation ad
mornition of the cooughing
corbpse rrolling down the
stebps with gguns your cri
spp *"insurance policy"*

Ack...
- Eel Leonard

Eel Mirror

the corn the cream the crowd the
aim the smoke the mask
the chair the hat the flakes the
tooth the broken glass the tongue
the puppet the dog the gun the
lint the sausage the leg
the mattress the beans the boil the
itch the nuts the hole
the turd the giant ball the bite the
window the dripping the clawed
the arm the truss the sink the
suit the toilet paper the crawl
the squirrel the cheese the ointment the
explanation the grinning worms the jewel

...Champion of the World!
- The Blaster

Espejo de la Caja

es dentition es runítico es
embolismo es inane o es
lubrecto es no es ni thou
ghtless es un gringo es to
billo es el sol que se acuerda
de la bruma es pulmón es
went away es míster wh
ispering in the closet es un
zapato en llamas una mon
eda es una monada es a
cork soaked in urine es
the glass the enema the
dress light with bullet
holes y en la pared es un
cancro es el polvo es
un trueno lejanísimo
donde me veo el sonido
donde me veo el efectivo
donde me veo la llanta
desinflada del año
del año de la es o
es enecencia pilfered
and plunged in a mil
dewed cardboard box

...es peso es pero es tim...
- Francisco de Quevedo

Espejo del Atl

,s**h**oe fork ,dust neck ,tide
thunder ,lake of knives ...em
bolismo ,en tu sopa de fi
deos ,la luz brumosa que del
techo cae *)el cielo en llamas(*
.awalk awake awithered ,in
the untied aguas ,gagged be
neath the mountain where yr
steps began ,whistled ,in
the spoon ,enterrada con la
piedra verde, chalchihuitl
migamojada *like my eyes like*
your tongue like - the air
pink with misted blood

.),the lung rat the door
suit the mile quivers at
your throat ... .

...in tonatiuh ixpopoyotl.
-Netzahualcoyotl

Espejo de la Pared

me puse el dog file suit y
nodded *como como como co*
co como caca seated below the sp
rawling ladder rising from)the
lake(≈/ mi pelt mi peluca sm
ouldering ~ ~ ~ an arf or
cow)*shoulder*(wavery in
the heat ~ ~ ~ the p age

d rifting toward yr r if t
ong ue a swiveling p
ole f lagless s kin f
olders ,s live red cur rent
d raining at the wal
/

L

...la merde, le mur.
- Jean Genet

Mirror of the Creamed Corn

in my sh aded crass cow
- knocker -)floating
in the sink(**THE**
FLOORED CLOUD
_ , , , , , , , _ sings col
lapsing ,udder all
the wandered windows
- omniformnivorous -
)IN MY BLADED
ASS(an osculation ,ne
ver born ,outed na
sal an a scummy shadow
in the stall *mi boca*
de humo y elote con crema

"escupo ,escucho ,es
)capo *escondo(* "

Corn and Smoke.
- Blaster Al Ackerman

Espejo del Guau

she's net ,*¿tamales quieres?* ph
one the dog an ,bit moon ,ste
am curling from the lid yr b
arking fork yr pock et lub
e index **)EX( )HALE(**
)the shorn ladder(*////* a
p rise the tree pocked - en un
rincón de la plaza *)mi*
balacera cotidiana(donde un
harpa ciega me canta y
,tus platillos tus tenedores tu
calaverita de miel *)my*
hairdo burns(

"arfter"

arf

...y se expiró en el estanquillo.
- Homero Aridjis

Muda el Espejo Mudo

S *ordo*mudo ,suero y ,casa pulgada
mis dedos "picosos" acosados ,la
sangre que mis guantes llena
)es lo que ciento ,y sin cuenta ,y
lo que tu me diez ,e inministado ay
,la tubería colostomita ,me cor
ona ,comestible ,descontado

,cu**M**bre del tos y del cil
encio encimismado ...(*en*
cías de arcilla ,masticadas
,su torta torturada ,amasija
de lo nunca dicho ,dicha en
ayunas... ...en mi nuca
una ¿cabeza? ¿una lluvia tinta?
¿la luna ahogada y olvidada
que se me acuerda?

...en las olas, un libro.
- José Asunción Silva

speak mirror cheese

take the ***s*** the
ea the ***l*** the
)lking air(,see
the ***salt*** crcrickcking
in the sun))sprd the
climbing mold((wht
sees yr ***eyes***

◐ ◐

toimirletror

speaks the ffoggg *g g g*
lriat glaminf ,s
lot pous gwirlins
's *bo* W *l* eherw
the *rraiins begin*

.. ..
,, ,,, ,,,,,, ,,,,, ,,,,,,,,, ,,,,,, , ,,,,,,, ,,

Reflect on This

the stumbled neck

gate

throat y lunge toward you the
)club dreams(sand
and flies

))corn opens
))the *glass*

Wet Reflection

time and quills
tick tick tick tick tick

the cheddar sails
dOg sKy

OFF THE WATER

Vishnu's Mirror

the stone's gnat skies the
spit maiden's born parch
ment *)tongues(* the
sperm decay speaks
black with rain poo
ls and whi stles loo
ping through the st
ate hôpital EDDYING
GRASS your orthopedic
maggots storm my
ovarian faces in the
sacked yard anthro
pomorphic fire *bla*
zing in the mask your
shopping bodies ,fluid
wheels, the *L*
light's twin sleeping

Found in Ivan Argüelles' "(Vishnu)"

mirfireror

demento mori sure shoe
head ,walk across the
stone .yr ,uh ,"neck"
cloud yr porcine por
tion leaking in yr po
cket "like a watch"
)the hashed laundry in
your luggage steams
,clumps ,bli nd s
...( )it's the crawling
phaze ,labertino ...sil
vestre ...riachuelo de
,,,san ,,,san ,,,gre ,,,gre :a
head the trees toward
sky's burned *...o pen ...*

...en llamas la pradera...
- Luis de Góngora

Espejo de La Llorona

the suction ,Llorona ,romantic
thaw hollow de tus años
ininefables simultaneous sea
rustles in the accelerator
flaws ,Llorona ,garlic paril
mis pelos elécticos oppo ha
tfly *mal de l'oeil* his shoe
,Llorona ,inner knife spayed
the corn fog I ate you
twice, Llorona ,adjectival
maps stuttering in the
wheeze your shock coo
king ,infame ,bovino ,lus
tros ahogados en la ec
onomía osmosis' poultry
glutial ,Llorona, facilitafe
the static tunnel mass ,pro
cedured stiffling in all yr
ratos ,rats ,ramas ,vox
pukuli the citation poaching
,Ashaninka ,Llorona ,tie
my vacuum trajectory
off the rolling coda it's
my departure castrado
,Llorona ,lo que breaks for me

...cross-explosag accret...
- Jim Leftwich,
Six Months Aint No Sentence, Book 38

silespaejobas

ay tu **O**j**o** h.o.r.
m.i.g.ó.n las nu
bes di lácteas co
mo *)cigarillo de pie*
l(**EN LA FAR**
MACIA VERDE
se grita ,la puerta del
mero día a bierta nomás

terrible la esquina

...bulto...de arena...
-Ivan Argüelles,
"sílabas rotas"

mirmistror

toco la tuerca la tumba la
pala borbot ante de tu
cogote vacío *where my*
inching taco coils spend yr
loop ,fine yr groped dog
storm yr terrones que
en la tapa caen *tumbal tum*
bal el último reloj de la
mano invivisible ≡]*comb yr*
face[≡ a cloud ≈ rising ~ ~ ~ ~ ~
from the lumber..............

...doblado, por fin...
-Rubén Bonifaz Nuño

miresprorejo

strauit le solingle shuunk pilldo
ra lo founcontrado en *)t(he los)t(*
engañol tuor bolket de
sillas fullno .snorquido
was ,thlo gargaroat dresida
yan mi strinuerda vom
itadad in un cirqulo .la
línea seea ,el enfdin al
begincio ●....................

●

...ust a second.
- C. Mehrl Bennett

Mirror of the Egg

the liver's moth ,bird
comb paper shrunken
in yr leg the hoof
magnifier flows across
my throat credit open
sandhill ,dung ,sentience
or mucus early in the
suture where yr genes
stride a ladder ,switch
blades ,dental flea st
randed on the ice and
manhole covered with
,your vision lake ,it's a s
lugfest giggling in the
pages where yr "pig
sea" hugs the bomb
you clcluttered in yr
bbaggage - ⭘ my
jagged freedom horse
my towel awash in
"pig .38" ,donut rules
mutter in the salt
black an crusted on the shore

...in the great lazy ocean...
- Jim Leftwich,
Six Months Aint No Sentence,
Book 39, 2013

mirmuerteror

the phone dog mailed *...claw*
nostril ,nor yr week
suit the sodden sobre
de aguatexto lleno ,boli
de tu culo culebrante
)grunt into the h
oles ●●● *the(* b
arking briefcase ,flashlight
,towel twisted in the
blood *yr pale palm*
slides off the sheet

...intestino del olvido...
- Manuel Acuña

smirpirort

ink a
flood

drool imposture yr
]wet gates[

)my dog my doubt(

llespaejove

itch lock ,d oubt
met er ,m ail e me
l eg g ash 's fogg
y sou p an c link
y on the d.u.s.t.y f
.loor a shadow o f

f cette jam be O
l'é pandre s ur le vis
age et)))n'ente ndre
rien(((*en la cacacasa*
w.here m.y k.ey's h.
idden in.na t.urd

...mou...che...
- Jacques Dupin

calespzejoado

BIG SPECIAL SHOE an

]ggagggingg at the ggate yr[
phone clam drools .ste
pped into the ppile *~))~ste*
am~an~sstorm~((~ an
in the O circle walkeddeklaw
ggiggglingg on the ppivott .i
t's yr ddoggy dday yr dd
roppping mmail yr burrito nn
attters in the mmudd CRAWLS
AWAY

...ther doc...
- K. S. Ernst

semirrornt

sent the door half off sent
the child damper sent the
combs an strings inhaled sent
the chisel in your sent the
forehead sent off misty shoe
sent my ash whistle sent
the tumbler focus sent the
sand scissored in my shor
ts the owl glycerine run
ning down my leg I sent
the dimming sent the mil
dew hat sent the coughing
dog glans stuck inside your
gleaming muzzle an I sent
the X off sent the más
cara sent the flowing m
irror ,off into the cave of
wind ***ows***

...soñé un libro, mareado.
- José Asunción Silva

mirlibroror

mud ni fog ni lake ni
esesencia fráctil sug
ared saw dust dr
ifting toward the base
board dominio arañil
.soto voce ,streaks .a
hamster in ,your sand
wich *.bald black eyes*
your ,drinking ,tequilita
riéndose en tu zapato
derecho .zona lacrada
,pozo de ,honror y ,**so**
ggy flag *tangled in the*
flotsam

...where yr books did drink.
- John M. Bennett

piraespejomide

toot blague ,morceau de
pancake ,sausage air ,t
ripas indirectas donde me
cagüé la carga o *cargo*
shorts rippling in the hall
.days yr daze inapetito
,forma púdica de mi
narigón qui parle ***WHA***
WHA er ***UH*** .trillling
in the sweaty waves *; ; ; ; ; ;*
:|| *dogs and plumbing*

Piramidal, funesta, de mi pulmón
nacida sombra...
- Sor Juana Inés de la Cruz

los ojos se cerrarán

la soma la sopa lo m
ismo su ente ritis - fl
ojera f áctil - o más
cara que me puse la mu
ñeca que era la cuch
ara de mi boca los pár
pados de mis di
entes ya se abrirán en
la cueva de tu barriga
el soroche la sombra el
sobar del suelo supin
terior el agua que se a
bre en lo dicho me diré
la silla la sarna el
sueño del cartón

el tenedor

la escalera

¿en la pared qué dice?
¿en el paquete de galletas
qué hay de comer? ¿en
el folleto hay un libro?
¿qué se lleva hacia el
fondo de la cueva? ¿qué
hay en el agua bajo la
tierra? ¿un ojo hay ,y
la respuesta de la pregunta
que se me ha olvidado?

la piedra colorada en la
ventana ¿qué dijo?

tongue dust

lengua de polvo en el
ffondo del mmar
huna piedra una ppie
dra lunar una ppierna f
flotante como la ohoja
comida hojoa mmas
ticada hay que cerrar
la ppuerta espumosa la
puerta del sureño del pie
del seeping foot ppolvo
de lengua mojadada la
lluvia que cae como
pie in spplinters y
me apoyo en la ppared
pisoteada por el escu
pitazo por el eescupi
ttazo de la lluvia
llena de espinas

sim ulacro

sudo y bajo su
mo y me relajo
y la pipiedra de
la bocaca se
ajabre de ver
de se ahbre de
verme verde gu
sano gus ano
de la hoja ha
hablada

el ***M*** el ***S*** el
sismo si mismo es

no sé nada

te planté un árbol dicho
:¿y la frase es invivible?
si planteado fuera ,¿el
cielo estaría verde de
piedras redondas? ¿de
las que nos hablan por
la boca de los muertos?
ni mimuertos son ni pre
guntones ni las hojas ni
las hojas nos dicen más
que la nada si te pl
lanteara una prepregunta
,¿se formaría del aire
un seser humano?

el serrucho se oía

en realidad the tru
th is cancel
lation del pie
que me rie que
me ríe go ta
jante la vever
dad inodicha
piedra des
pierta es ,en el
fondo nado
del mar y no
puede ser y
n'hombre ,puede ser

buceo

entraba ,cuando salir no
pudo ,su libro cagatorio ,in
textino si intesticular no
,ciego fué ,porcino con las
tapas de piel quemada
,empelotudinarias con la
titulobabeante seña ,al negro
escrito sobre negro para leer
lo blanco .la nada leía ,d
onde nadaba en la laca os
cura de su nacimiento en
revesado .y ,mojado ,mu
do ,mortal ,del cenote subía

cleanup

boil ,when the sleeves if
,empty ,the closet's hang
ers ,limp ,but dimly
clanking or the knee ,de
pantsed ,gleaming on the
floor ,your ,if opened
,scissors walking up the
bed ,with sawdust sa
gged ,filled ,with's gluey
blood the forgotten
fork ,holds the sky ,un
der the mattress ,the
dreamless bones

écrit

sweaty an ,drink ,cowl
a folder with yr
head stuck through
,mitey an mute ,a
growling neck ,where
the attic's tongue col
linvection's drying on
the racks tus calaveras
invientadas ,negras y
coloradas por el fuego
de medio siglo ,in
visibles en tus ojos
siempre ,stinking and
clean ,clamping the
poem in your teeth

...dissequé, et mobile...
- Comte de Lautréamont

edge wind

windy shoe ,if the dog
shore sings ,ahead the
garbage cross the beach
's strung line ,a door
from the sand juts your
crab half spins the
buried mask ,clouded
with shells where the
creamy bones convect
,if textless eyes decay
,for the tale of angles
,by gulls the motive
muscles eaten ,in the
sweaty soup ,untied
walks at the water's edge

exlumation

b oil nos tril ,g ,nat
es dri ppy ,off the
f loor ,s hoe f ills ,a
m ask o f og the
han ky rai sed ,a f
lag un foiled ,to
ward the st reaming
c aves ,of rain the
mater ,so's yr fin
g ered sn akes yr g
rippless toes and linty
shirt ,damp ,ered
while the exhalation's
in ,bur bling at the mou
th ,rem akes the soaking
air ,or light

Toda la mierda literaria ha
ido quedando atrás.
- Roberto Bolaño

la merienda

should shoulder ,came a
head ,regañada ,en so
frito inmersa ,so the
folded water ,when
dry ,if dry ,and his
soaking ,refected ,shirt
was swilling the oily
comb .the plate was
crusted ,en la sobre
mesa del aire ,y moscas
,sin recuerdo de la prad
era's stream ninguno
,of liquid time ,and
dropped his chin into
an empty hand

lace

loop clot ,if trails be
neath the foot ,a
s lug and gene rative
or gan ,orgone lox ran
cid on a bun what sh
rouds the foot ,a fix
itive ,useless ,in the
p itted pat h .sw
eating ,ro ped ,a shove
L c runches in the
grave L ,and the st
rumming steps re
treat ,dragging your t
attered string ,where
yr open shoe ex hales
,an de tongues the night

...solace of the fork himselve n.
- Olchar E. Lindsann

la tina

slowly slew ,when cow
ered in the ,brim filled
tub ,the quad rant limbs'
4 sentidos indicantes
,el quinto plugged ,an
arm upraised de sangre
ahogado ,los ojos ,sin
lentes ,vacantes ,the
dripping wall's reflection
in the mirrored door's up
turned al arac on
atreipsed's waking ,ha
lfway toward the st
reaming faucet the pass
age blind ,the holeless
spider

...spi der vi per cli ent gi ant i tem i cy spi ral...
-McGuffy's Ecelctic Spelling Book, ca. 1879

los sentidos

lake laundry watch de
habitation the empty
hands yr stone's vom
it's yr pocket's cloud
,an en try esc apes ,yr
armpit than a dumpster
cleaner ,than a pizza
box dancing with ' 'flies ' ' '
,where the alley ends ,or
starts ,where the angle
of light's ,reversed ,in
3 directions ,the 4th and
5th turning slowly on a
,dime ,aire ,¿vaciarme
no puedes?

a hora y nu nca más

Tiene lo que los chinos llaman li,
es decir, conducta de orientación cósmica...
- José Lezama Lima

m ists

loco ,ation ,in the cal
yx abierto , las ab
ejas mot ores ,one
the p lace or thinks
the sky ,is one and log
os ,dim on the ot
her side ,pólen del
aire denso ,y por
los ojos respiro ,las
transitivas tijeras que
el precipicio diminuto
conllevan ,g low in
the brum a ,lugar
inverso ,nunca lo
mismo ,ni miasma
perversa

mortavista

aspidente ,coño ,fuller
than ,with loosened teeth
the ,foggy neck drains
across your pillow's b
leaking ,sweet sweat
que en el colchón se
cul mina ,con raging
lint ,lintestino intex
tual ,a suitcase sinking
in the sea le bateau ivre
the cloud the black ticket
,boils across yr face

Le causaba esa mirada la impresión leída en una vieja receta para curar el asma.
- José Lezama Lima

shunt

even when streaked ,the
steps ,sodden and thin
,dim ,when the leg ,with
its scrotal pouch crowned
,descends ,to the record s
tore ,invisible on the
skin's horizon ,its
trance ,asphalted ,wakes
in the window's yell
ow stains or inglés del
polvo bucal ,como cenote
dank ,rushing to drown
on the fence .the
verbs ,when blackened
,passing ,*from your
mouth* ,or from distance
aching for's glass ,its
insects and scissors clus
tered, following ,of am
nesia ,the dripping ,ever
streaked when even ,ink

Mumbling after Ivan Argüelles' "the far"

the 'maters

orange ,under the drooping
,leaves ,dirtsprung hands
,or gold ,spheres ,es
caped my eyes ,to
fall in mud ,or the
cornea's cloudy ,leaves
me standing ,and in my
churning sleep
an icy shoe returns

' , , ' ' , '

where the compost's
crowned with flies
.my uttered wallet's
nest my sandy keys
my knife crusted
with sticky see
ds .))under the water's
mile ,I slept

...las semillas que subían...
- Carlos Pellicer

wet glimpse

the phazal nostril ,w
hat the smoking soap
inhales ,was sticky
,nor shining ,the fin
gers dripping thru a
plane of light the
glass' flat tongue
,so the ink from yr
arm's sluiced off
and yr face ,a
bove the photon
wave a bobber ,it
self was sniffed, a
blotchy bulb ,or es
pansive membrane
in the crowded mirror

About the Author

John M. Bennett has published over 400 books and chapbooks of poetry and other materials. He has published, exhibited and performed his word art worldwide in thousands of publications and venues. He was editor and publisher of LOST AND FOUND TIMES (1975-2005), and is Curator of the Avant Writing Collection at The Ohio State University Libraries. Richard Kostelanetz has called him "the seminal American poet of my generation." His work, publications, and papers are collected in several major institutions, including Washington University (St. Louis), SUNY Buffalo, The Ohio State University, The Museum of Modern Art, and other major libraries. His PhD (UCLA 1970) is in Latin American Literature.

www.johnmbennett.nethttp://johnmbennettpoetry.blogspot.com/
http://library.osu.edu/sites/rarebooks/avantwriting/
http://www.lulu.com/spotlight/lunabisonteprods
http://johnmbennettpoetry.blogspot.com/

Acclaim for John M. Bennett's Select Poems

The seminal American poet of my generation.
—Richard Kostelanetz

*

Intergalactic sprees of stem cell vitality, growth in all directions, organized renditions of earth's intrigue, surround the Animalia of ourselves, a raw endowment that means mov-ing fluently among the elements. Here freedom lives in holy sin, basking in humanity's own riotous gentility and kindness amid tactile interference and inspiration.

Blasts of vowel sounds transcend their assigned seats between fencepost consonants as Dr. Bennett proclaims with all there is out there, in here, centered amid 360-degrees around us, a symphonic gusto that allocates those allegations about the earth, the spin, the bin, the chafing, and the dark light spindling of a starched young shirt forever vital with allure.

Only a sophisticated, scholarly mind immersed in the frenzy of present tense could carry such mindfulness to the next level, probing where mere pondering might be. Provok-ing adventure where simple absorption might be.

If there lives a sixth sense about people, there must be a 21st sense of beyond-ment that Bennett's infinite creativity portrays. Here is evidence of perceptual genius, heightened by finely-tuned auditory and visual senses, spawning observation-as-creation in voice, on the page, mid-air, and lingering long after in the mind.
—Sheila E. Murphy

*

With Argüelles' comprehensive intro and a variety of texts selected by the author from decades of intensive self-disciplined flagellations of the inner psyche, this book is your own life imagined within the respiratory system and the two-legged variety of John M. Bennett's pants. Body parts/functions have their biological counterparts in all of our outer worldly structural 'isms etc. if you can only slow down and read the signs. John has developed a multitude of techniques over the years to slow his readers down: visually, rhythmically, sonically, typographically, and by creating his own mish mashed language and layers of meanings... "..oil or// fish, man, control, room"
—C. Mehrl Bennett

*

At what point does eccentricity—at what point does obsession—become art? John Bennett's work is a fascinating exploration of the transformation of oddity into a purely poetic impulse. This supremely outsider artist raises the bar on what we believe litera-ture—what we believe "letters"—to be. Reading him is like suddenly arriving in Oz: it definitely doesn't look like Kansas anymore.
—Jack Foley

*

John M. Bennett, Hiperprolífico. Irremediable "hombre orquestra"; es decir, porque desde un principio destacó por su sapiencia y dominio del oficio. Y uno de los perso-najes históricos de la poesía visual y el arte-correo en Estados Unidos.
—César Horacio Espinosa Vera

*

Tanto la poesía-hecha-voz como la poesía-texto de John parten de dos principios insep-arables, lo visual y lo sonoro, que buscan interpelar los otros sentidos. Ambas (poesía-hecha-voz como la poesía-texto) son sinestéticas, polisémicas y polifónicas a la vez. El texto sube, baja, corre, se detiene, pausa, se desliza, se va, se queda, viene y va, sigue, arde, se apaga, explota, se endulza, se pone agrio... Ambos inventan y nos inventan mundos nuevos que ya eran nuestros. Cuando estamos ante un texto de John estamos ante el sound graph de un migrante que oye y habla en todas las voces de América a la vez. Estamos ante el retrato de su alma sonora, norteamericana y mexicana, surameri-cana y centroamericana, quiché y náhuatl, mapuche y guaraní, chéroqui y apache. Algo como el sueño lingüístico de Bolívar y Vasconcelos. Estamos ante un lenguaje cósmico, real y vivo.
—Miguel A. Valerio

www.ingramcontent.com/pod-product-compliance
Lightning Source LLC
Chambersburg PA
CBHW081414230426
43668CB00016B/2229
* 9 7 8 1 9 3 8 5 2 1 2 5 6 *